Over My Shoulder
3

Over My Shoulder 3

A Collection of
"Over My Shoulder" and "Passed Times" Columns
published in *The Post-Star* from 1994-2003
Volume 3: 2001-2003

by

Joseph Cutshall-King

Over My Shoulder 3
A Collection of "Over My Shoulder" and "Passed Times" Columns published in
The Post-Star from 1994-2003; Volume 3: 2001-2003

Editor: Julia C. Cutshall-King

Cover design & all artwork © 2020 by Michael George King, Black Swan Image
Works, Frederick, MD

ISBN: 979-8-5680-7347-5

First Edition

Printed in the United States of America

A Matchless Books® production – https://pipingrock.wordpress.com/

Dedication

Over My Shoulder, Volume 3, is once again dedicated with love to my wife, Sara, who for decades now has supported me in, and suffered through, my mania for history, and to my daughter, Julia, who has inherited that mania.

Acknowledgments

My sincerest thanks go to my editor and daughter, Julia C. Cutshall-King, who throughout helped me to assemble and review the columns in Volume1-3. She weeded out the boring and dated columns, and, ever the Good Editor, she encouraged, prodded, and poked me to keep me on track. Without her, Volumes 1 through 3 would not have materialized. She is my joy!

Thank you to my brother Michael George King of Black Swan Image Works, for his beautiful design for this cover. This is the fourth cover my artist brother has designed for me, his first for my historical mystery novel *The Burning of The Piping Rock* and the next three for Volumes 1-3 of these columns. Michael has now fully turned his attention to creating beautiful artistic works, which he continues to bring to the public via Black Swan Image Works. To view them, go to: https://blackswanimageworks.com/.

As with Volumes 1-2, for Volume 3, I give thanks to the publishers of *The Post-Star* and to recently retired Managing Editor Ken Tingley for the courtesy shown in allowing the reprint of these columns. And to my various editors who suffered through my work over the nine years I wrote my columns, thank you—especially City Editor Bob Condon.

To author and friend Gail Terp, thank you again for your professional proofing. Gail is a retired teacher who now writes nonfiction for children. Many of her books can be found at Crandall Public Library, Glens Falls, NY.

This passage that appeared in Volumes 1-2 still holds true: Spouses always thank their spouses, but mine is a sincere one. Thank you, Sara, for your support and encouragement. As with my other books, this one could not have happened without you. I love you for your "nudges."

Lastly, "Thank you, my readers!" You remembered me and held true to your word that, if I collected the columns in a book, you would buy the book. During the nine years I wrote these columns, you faithfully read my work, helped me to create more of it with your ideas, corrected me when I was wrong in facts, sometimes railed at me when you disagreed with a position I took, but always kept coming back for more. What a pleasure for me to be back this last time. Trust me, this will not be my last book on local history. See you soon!

Joseph Cutshall-King

Other works by Cutshall-King

Fiction
2011: *The Burning of The Piping Rock*; a historical mystery novel; Matchless Books®.

Histories
2020: *Over My Shoulder 3; A Collection of "Over My Shoulder" and "Passed Times" Columns published in The Post-Star from 1994-2003; Volume 3: 2001-2003.* Matchless Books®.

2019: *Over My Shoulder 2; A Collection of "Over My Shoulder" and "Passed Times" Columns published in The Post-Star from 1994-2003; Volume 2: 1998-2000.* Matchless Books®, publisher.

2018: *Over My Shoulder; A Collection of "Over My Shoulder" and "Passed Times" Columns published in The Post-Star from 1994-2003; Volume 1: 1994-1997.* Matchless Books®, publisher.

2017: *WATER & LIGHT: S. R. Stoddard's Lake George.* Chapman Historical Museum, Glens Falls, NY, publisher.

2008: *Cornerstone of the Future*; history of First Presbyterian Church of Glens Falls, NY. First Presbyterian Church of Glens Falls, NY, publisher.

2001: *Con Amore – The Italian History of Fort Edward*; with Italian Heritage Committee of Fort Edward Historical Association, Inc., publisher.

1987: *Hospital by the Falls*; History of the Glens Falls Hospital, publisher.

Newspaper columns
1994-2003: "Over My Shoulder" – Weekly column of history and commentary in *The Post-Star*, Glens Falls, NY.

1994-1995: "*Passed Times*" – Seasonal column of history and commentary in "The Time of Our Lives" tabloid of *The Post-Star*, Glens Falls, NY.

1975-1985: "*Chapman Museum*"– Weekly column of history and commentary in *The Post-Star*, Glens Falls, NY.

As co-editor
1996 - *Sherlock Holmes: Victorian Sleuth to Modern Hero.* Scarecrow Press, University Press. Co-editor with Charles R. Putney and Sally Sugarman; collation of presentations from conference "Sherlock Holmes: Victorian Sleuth to Modern Hero."

Radio
1978-1988: Author, producer of *LEGACY*, weekly program of history and commentary broadcast on WWSC AM, WCKM FM, Glens Falls, NY.

Table of Contents

Foreword 1

Introduction: Welcome and Farewell! 2

SECTION 1: Glens Falls History 3

Hyde played major role in city's architecture 3
Women's club helped shape city 4
Bathhouse was joint effort 6
Governors familiar with area 7
Hughes rose to eminent position 9
Hughes, from Glens Falls, rode reform to governor's mansion 10
Hotel was conceived by local bigwigs 12
Hotel saw famous guests 14
Queensbury Hotel has memories 15
Glens Falls problems are cyclical 16
Class recalls neat stuff of '61 18
Community had money, but no place to put it 20
Watch out for that cliff 21
And how does your garden grow? 23
'Winging it' 25
Debate centers on log drive 26
Gutless Wonders 28
Orson Richards 29
Take a trip back in time 31
Common names, uncommon origins 32
All things are possible 34
Charting history of Glens Falls' buildings 35
History buffs get chance to raise grade 37
Looking back — and ahead 38

SECTION 2: Area History 41

Book was 4-year labor of love 41
Slavery, Confederacy cannot be separated 42
Speaking up about the painful past 44
Washington County should honor Douglass 45
1816: the year of no spring 47
Mettawee or Mettowee 48
Jane McCrea death still a mystery 50
Spellings varied long ago 51
Revolution through a minister's eyes 53

Schools should keep America first 54
Our beloved "ogas" make news 56
Revolution took a turn in Whitehall 57
Agricultural history at the fair 59
Burleigh was a self-made man 60
Burleigh was big in politics 62
Ignoring our closest neighbor? 63
More Canadian patriots 65
U.S. and Canada more than neighbors 66
Infamous dates are forever joined 68
Children last hope for saving history 69
County court dispute goes way back 71
Region's Black history needs exploring 72
Blacks' unsung Revolutionary heroes 74
Black patriot soldiers were unsung heroes of Revolution 75
Lost items of days gone by 77
Readers miss more than beta 78
Let's go, Rangers 80
Past comes alive 81
Imagining local life during the Revolution 83
A hero without honor 84
Reflecting on the eagle, enlistment center 86
Heirloom finds its way home 87
Look to history for answers 89
Fall of fort could have ended celebrations 90
Battle of Hubbardton to come alive 92
Burgoyne campaign moves into Fort Anne 93
A fresh look at Jane McCrea 95
Fortunes – or misfortunes – of war 96
More data needed on minorities 98
Working to provide a little dignity 100
When America left its childhood 101
Burgoyne's troubles started in Ti 103
Arnold emerges as hero of Saratoga 104
Capitalize on Saratoga's history 106
Pies symbol of an end of an era in Corinth 108
Son of the USA 109
Helping piece together a puzzle 111
A birthday worth noting 112
Time to rename Broad Street? 114
Collective memories go way back 115
Let's play `remember this'? 116
A wrap on collective memories 118

Time to talk of many things 119

SECTION 3: Personal and Family Memories 121

Young bill collector gets the last word 121
Bag was father's link to peace 122
Split over store's demise 124
Daughter not alone in Saratoga 125
A Dickens of a verse 126
Oh, the power of Santa 130
By 83, she should have been flying 131
Relative shows possibilities are endless 133
Childhood memories of Saratoga 134
Song versions may reveal your age 135
Childhood memories of Decora 137
A magical day at the track 138
Summer memories with Kinks and Frank 140
Death brings back schoolboy memories 141
Memories of holidays gone by, via the back porch 142
Beefing about food history 144
Thoughts of a Christmas couch 145
Christmas unveils thoughts of two lives 147
Bidding adieu to 2002 148
So many columns, too little time 151
Raining cats and dogs, but mostly cats 153
Whispering memories come calling 154

Afterward 157

Index 159

Endnotes 177

FOREWORD

The gift of a good storyteller is to take you outside of yourself and then subtly draw you back again, unfolding bits of the tale that remind you of yourself, and make the characters in the story relatable—no matter how long ago, nor fantastical the tale may seem.

I grew up having my father read to me at night. The Grimm Brothers and Mother Goose come to mind, but so do the tales he created from his memory and imagination. Once, out of desperation, he read to me from the biography of Elizabeth I; hundreds of pages long, it was dull reading bound to lull a child to sleep. I was hooked; I wanted to know what she did next, and why—as my father (I imagine) equally hoped to know the same about my sleep patterns, and when they would kick in.

That is the gift (and in that case, curse) of the true storyteller in action; I was in a time and place I'd never be able to conceive of, but I felt that I could. A story connects us, no matter who we are or what we've experienced. We understand because we're reminded that we are human, and that time and space separate little when it comes down to it.

My father's columns—whether you're familiar with them or not—foster that connection. I'm honored to have been able to edit them and know that you, dear reader, will enjoy them as much as I have.

Julia C. Cutshall-King, Editor

INTRODUCTION: WELCOME AND FAREWELL!

This is the last of three volumes of my "Over My Shoulder" and "Passed Times" columns I wrote for *The Post-Star* from 1994 to 2003. I am grateful that readers have welcomed their reprint. Over a quarter century has passed since City Editor Bob Condon[i] and I first discussed my returning to write for *The Post-Star*. Whether Bob was a little trepidatious I can't say, but I was! It was nine years since I had written my last column. However, Bob said that Managing Editor Ken Tingley[ii] had approved my starting out with a column called "Passed Times" in a quarterly tabloid section, "The Time of Our Lives."

That tabloid was discontinued in 1995. By then the column had gained enough readers' interest for *The Post-Star* to offer me a bi-weekly column, "Over My Shoulder," combining local history and commentary. In 1996 it went weekly and stayed as such until March 2003. I ended it when I took a job out of the region.

In all, I wrote 402 columns, all but eight "Over My Shoulder." This book is a selection from "Over My Shoulder" columns from January 2001 to March 2003. As *The Post-Star* covers Warren, Washington, and Saratoga Counties, I wrote columns on local history covering from Ticonderoga (Essex County) in the north to Saratoga in the south, east into Vermont and west into the Adirondacks. I also wrote commentary on events of the day (often rants). Thanks to Editor Julia C. Cutshall-King, columns too dated, too topical, or too dull were eliminated.

Bob Condon was not my only editor back then. Others included Will Doolittle,[iii] Dave Blow,[iv] Fred Daley,[v] Mike Mender[vi], and Mark Mahoney.[vii] Bob comes to mind most often, as he was also my editor when I was a correspondent from 1995 to 1997, reporting on southern Washington and eastern Saratoga Counties. I learned from all my editors and am grateful to them.

This is not a scholarly book. I have always written knowing history can be deadly but hoping I could make it enjoyable enough for all to read. However, I always used primary and secondary sources. Primary included newspapers, public records, booklets, pamphlets, diaries, journals, correspondence, audio, and video recordings, many of them mine. Secondary included every published history I could buy or borrow. Some have been cited, others not. Our house groans under the weight of paper collected in the days before the internet had become the trove it is today. Since then, to my wife Sara's distress, I have added more paper to my own library, not to mention hundreds upon hundreds of gigabytes of scanned and downloaded documents, maps, photographs and the like. My mania.

One last word. In this volume Editor's/Author's Notes, Postscripts, and endnotes, I dispensed with the formality of referring to myself as "the author." I have also taken the liberty to be a little more personal in those.

Finally, let me thank you for reading these columns. I truly hope you will enjoy them as much as I enjoyed writing them.

Joseph Cutshall-King

SECTION 1: GLENS FALLS HISTORY

NOTE: Since 1892, the Crandall Public Library has been physically and culturally central to Glens Falls history. The story of the decade-long struggle to expand the library, referred to below, is epic. It would be another seven years after this column before an $18.8 million addition was dedicated in 2008. Its existence owes so much to the vision of Christine McDonald, Crandall Public Library's Director from 1979 to 2012, and to Dick Merrill, then the Library Board Chair. McDonald described Dick as "a partner in leading the $18.8 million expansion project," saying they "worked together as a team...[nearly] every single day."[viii]

"OVER MY SHOULDER" COLUMN FOR JANUARY 6, 2001
Hyde played major role in city's architecture

The recent defeat of Crandall Library's efforts to expand its home must have brought a tear to the spirits of its first benefactor, Henry Crandall, and to Louis Fiske Hyde.

Although less recognized by name than Crandall, Louis F. Hyde was vital in shaping the institutional architecture of Glens Falls and some of America's more influential architects came to Glens Falls because of him.

Yet Hyde did not come here until nearly 40, an established, successful attorney in the Boston region. You may have recognized his name as associated with the Hyde Collection. He and his wife, Charlotte Pruyn Hyde, assembled the fine arts collection that, together with their home, would become the basis of this renowned museum.

You may also associate Hyde with his book, *History of Glens Falls, New York*. A biography of him in the book states that Hyde was born in Warren, Massachusetts in 1866. He took several degrees from Harvard including an LL.B. from Harvard Law School in 1890. From 1892 to about 1902, he was an attorney with several Boston railway companies. It was in Boston that he met and married Charlotte Pruyn, who was studying there.

Hyde joined his brother-in-law Maurice Hoopes on the board of Finch Pruyn and Company, owned by their father-in-law, Samuel Pruyn. By 1906, Louis and Charlotte would establish a home in Glens Falls.

As the family papermaking firm expanded, Hyde made his first architectural contribution to Glens Falls at Finch Pruyn. In 1905, Finch Pruyn made the transition to being a major papermaking plant[ix] with the addition of an enormous mill that forms the core of today's plant. This profitable move was marked by building a new corporate headquarters of gray fieldstone. The architect chosen for the job was Bostonian Henry Forbes Bigelow, an acquaintance of Louis and Charlotte Hyde, still living at that time in Boston.

Bigelow's influence continued for, in 1910, he designed the first true hospital structure for the Glens Falls Hospital. Maurice Hoopes was president of the hospital's Board of Directors. Until then, the hospital had been operating in the former home of Solomon Parks.

Almost immediately after, Bigelow designed the homes of the three Pruyn sisters, Mary Pruyn Hoopes, Charlotte Pruyn Hyde, and Nell Pruyn Cunningham.

Bringing the architect Bigelow to Glens Falls was only the first of Hyde's many architectural coups. Let me add here that, while I am presenting here mostly oral history crediting Hyde with the achievements, some published accounts exist. However, I have never heard any challenges to Hyde's contribution to Glens Falls' architecture.

In 1925 Hyde was on the architectural committee of the First Presbyterian Church of Glens Falls when it was decided to build the present church. Hyde's influence was double. Its architect was Ralph Adams Cram, dean of American architecture's Gothic Revival Movement. Moreover, the world-famous Samuel Yellin of Philadelphia made the wrought iron fixtures for the new church, completed in 1926.

Hyde's influence continued. In 1931, he was President of the Crandall Library when the present building was completed, having been designed by the renowned American architect Charles Adams Platt.

The next year, 1932, St. Mary's Academy opened, its design also by Ralph Adams Cram, who based it upon Westminster Hall in Great Britain's Houses of Parliament. It is my understanding that Hyde also played an important role in securing Cram to design the new academy.

Most of Louis F. Hyde's architectural legacy survives today. The Hyde and Cunningham homes are a part of the Hyde Collection and the adjacent Unitarian Fellowship [*Unitarian Universalist Church*] occupies the Hoopes house. Finch Pruyn's corporate headquarters stands at 1 Glen Street.[x] The First Presbyterian Church and Crandall Library grace Glen Street and St. Mary's-St. Alphonsus School is a key Warren Street structure. [xi]

May the spirit of Louis F. Hyde hover over the Crandall, the city and the general population as decisions are made regarding the future of an architectural treasure that deserves expansion, not abandonment.

"OVER MY SHOULDER" COLUMN FOR MARCH 10, 2001
Women's club helped shape city

You're known by the company you keep.

In which case, the company kept among the women who gathered in 1924 under the banner of the "Zonta Club of Glens Falls" provides us with a lesson in civics and women's history.

The Post-Star recently reported on the Glens Falls Recreation Commission's plans to create a third bathhouse at Haviland's Cove Park. While the existing structure to be replaced dates to the 1950s, the first bathhouse was built in 1926.

Creating that bathhouse in 1926 was the Zonta Club's first project.

The founding meeting of the Glens Falls Zonta Club was held February 1924 at the Rockwell House, the hotel that stood where today (Mayor Regan please note) Hudson Avenue intersects with Glen Street. Glens Falls' Zonta was formed as part of Zonta International, an international women's service organization, founded in 1919 in Buffalo.

Both local and national women's organizations were flourishing in our region when the Glens Falls Zonta Club began. But Zonta was novel for its focus upon women executives in business and the professions, a concept that barely existed a generation before that. Looking through the Glens Falls Zonta Club's founding members and early history, for which I am indebted to Betsy E. Lucci, I realized that its local origins presented a larger picture of women's history in the region.

Here are Zonta's first officers and Directors, and their professions or place of business:

President: Burke, Maude D., Superintendent, Glens Falls Hospital
First Vice President: Miss Annetta E. Barber, M.D.
Second Vice President: Miss Inez M. Bissell, Librarian, Crandall Library
Third Vice President: Miss Angela M. Hackett, in the retail music business
Treasurer: Kathleen Kelleher, Glens Falls City Chamberlain
Secretary: Florence T. Bromley, Director, Adirondack Girl Scouts
Director: Ruth H. Sherman, ran a Travel Bureau
H. Bertha Larkin, Tri-County Blind Assoc.

Space prohibits listing every charter member, but let's look at all of the professions of the original 1924 members. It's eye opening to see the Zonta Club's varied professions, because their work tells us that contrary to stereotypes, women then were not just textile mill workers, shop clerks or secretaries. This was a time of social revolution.

Here are the 1924 Zonta members' professions, or line of business, or place of business, as taken from Zonta minutes: hospital superintendent; two physicians [one a General Practitioner and one an Osteopath]; librarian; music retail; Glens Falls City Chamberlain; Girl Scouts; travel bureau; Tri-County Blind Assoc.; attorney; dean of girls; Miller Automobile; Caterer; *The Post-Star*; Warren County Court and Probation System; Exec. Sec., Red Cross; coffee shop; dress shop; bridge instructor; photographer; Washington County Charities Aid; antiques dealer; treasurer, manager, Empire Gasoline; Washington County government worker; and gift shop owner.

Membership, incidentally, embraced the Tri-Counties: Glens Falls, Bolton Landing, Hudson Falls, Fort Edward and Saratoga. Of the women in the club, almost a third were married, thus breaking another stereotype that only single women had professions.

A prime example was Katherine B. Sears. Sears was the Dean of Girls of the Glens Falls Academy, of which she and her husband essentially shared the administration. In addition to her duties there, she served as Zonta president in Glens Falls, then became head of the state Zonta and finally, in 1928 went on to become national President of Zonta. She co-founded the Little Theater Group of the Glens Falls Operetta Club (today's Glens Falls Community Theatre) making it one of many civic organizations she affected.

Next week we discuss in depth a few more early Zonta members and talk about Zonta's first project 75 years ago, the creation of the Haviland's Cove — and some surprise information about Zonta's role there.

"OVER MY SHOULDER" COLUMN FOR MARCH 17, 2001
Bathhouse was joint effort

What a difference a week makes.

Last week I wrote that the Zonta Club of Glens Falls, chartered in 1924, played the key role in Haviland's Cove Park's first bathhouse being built in 1926.

Actually, thanks to Zontian Betsy Lucci, the fact has come to light that the first bathhouse was built in 1924.

To appreciate the work Zonta did, allow me to talk just a bit more about Zonta's founders. I came to know Zonta well through one of its members, Edna Cutshall, my mother-in-law. And knowing her, it made sense that Zonta's founders were bright, talented and "can-do" people.

A perfect example was Zonta's first president, Maude D. Burke, Superintendent of the Glens Falls Hospital. Burke had trained at St. Luke's Hospital in Manhattan and at Johns Hopkins, and had worked in the office of the US Surgeon General.

Another example was Rose Minnick, who worked in the Warren County Court and Probation System. She was a champion for underprivileged children and a key figure in starting a camp for those children on Gurney Lane in Queensbury. Others exemplary members were Josephine Demarest, Red Cross co-founder; Florence T. Bromley, Founder and first director of the Adirondack Girl Scouts; and Else Bronne, head of Bronne Shirt Co. in Fort Edward.

Zonta brought its members considerable power to bear in 1924 for the new Glens Falls City Recreation Commission, which wanted a beach at Haviland's Cove. Spearheading the Zonta project was Katherine B. Sears, who launched into full negotiations with Mayor Orville C. Smith and about half the world to get things off the ground.

Things clicked! For the first bathhouse, which was wood, Finch Pruyn sold lumber at wholesale and donated the services of Harry B. Kendall to draw the plans. Volunteers in the building trades helped: Alexander Duplex Construction, Clayton Woodbury of Woodbury Lumber, Clarence and Leonard Kingsley; J. B. Hartman; and the firms of Jerry West, Joseph Fredella; and Robert Rheinlander.

Walter Robinson[xii], head of the high school manual training classes, brought his students to work. The Rotary club and Hugh McNair and his boys from the YMCA came. Construction was completed in 3 weeks. Kendrick and Brown furnished brown stain and Zonta members put the stain on.

International Paper gave 88 yards of canvas for the dressing booths. Merkel and Gelman gave 3 dozen bath towels. To keep the logs in the river away, Finch Pruyn donated a huge boom, and city engineer Ernest Meyer and his department supervised its placing. Zonta paid its bill.

While the bathhouse was constructed, trees and brush were cleared using Call Hardware[xiii] hatchets. George Bayle of Glens Falls Portland Cement contributed dynamite and men to blast stumps from the beach.

Ralph Holman, the "phys. ed." director in the public schools, was hired as "Recreation Supervisor," as was Mrs. Elizabeth Waters, as "Matron." A caretaker, also in charge of concessions, lived in the rear of the bathhouse. There was no charge for kids, but adults paid 5 cents to check clothing.

But all was not complete and here is some little-known history about that. The road to the beach crossed D&H Railroad tracks and needed planking to make a safe crossing. D&H didn't mind but didn't want to do it. Adirondack Power and Light Corporation's Elmer J. West was a prime mover in getting his company to provide land for Haviland's Cove.[xiv] Katherine Sears got West to negotiate a right of way with the D&H and to get the South Glens Falls International Paper plant to furnish and place the planks. Wow!

Sadly, the bathhouse burned, either in 1926 or `28 and the city replaced it with a concrete block bathhouse. However, Zonta's role continued and its initial effort lives on today.

Here's a proposal. Name the new bathhouse to be created this year in honor of the Glens Falls Zonta Club and the unsung role of women in our history.

I think it's a swimmingly good idea.

"OVER MY SHOULDER" COLUMN FOR MARCH 31, 2001
Governors familiar with area

When Governor Pataki speaks at the Queensbury Hotel Tuesday, we should remind him that three governors came from this area.

And there was a time when New York State Governors spent more time in Glens Falls – and they didn't even have to be originally from the area to do so.

First, let's discuss those Governors originally from here, with some brief biographies. In future columns, we'll do full-length histories.

Nathaniel Pitcher, Jr., of Hudson Falls was the region's first Governor. He was born in Litchfield, Connecticut in the fall of 1777. According to Kingsbury Town Historian Paul Loding, Pitcher's parents fled Burgoyne's invading army in 1777, while Pitcher's mother was pregnant. As Paul says, Pitcher was conceived in Kingsbury, therefore he was technically a native son. Good enough reasoning for me, Paul.

Pitcher started his political career as Kingsbury Town Clerk in 1813. He served as the eighth Governor from 1828 to 1829, the term of office being only two years. He also was a member of Congress in the late teens and early twenties and then after he was governor.

Loding notes that Pitcher's portrait is one of two missing from the hallway outside the governor's office in the capital building. Pitcher died in Sandy Hill May 25,1836

The next two Governors from our region were, in order of service, Charles Evans Hughes, 36th Governor, and John Alden Dix, 38th Governor, although Dix was born first in 1860. Both were born in Glens Falls, at that time a Queensbury village.

Hughes was born in a house that, in 1862, was on Maple Street about two blocks from the hotel. It is on Center Street today and a marker in City Park commemorates him. The son the David and Mary C. Connelly Hughes began his career as a lawyer. He served from 1907 to 1910 as a reform Governor, who sponsored this nation's first workmen's compensation law. In 1908, he signed the charter for Glens Falls to become a city. He left office in October 1910 before the end of term to be justice on the US Supreme Court, of which he would later be Chief Justice. He unsuccessfully ran for President in 1916. He died in 1948.

Dix is claimed by Warren and Washington Counties. The son of James Lawton and Laura Stevens Dix was born on Canal Street, now Oakland Avenue, Glens Falls. His family moved to what is today the Hibbard home between Lawton and Dix Avenues in Glens Falls. However, at the time of his election, he lived in Thompson, Town of Greenwich, where his home still stands.

The Democrat Dix was actually the next elected governor after the Republican Hughes. However, Horace White served as interim Governor from October 6 to December 31, 1910. Dix served from 1911 to 1913. He also began as a reformer but was undermined by fighting between the legislature and his office, and a split in his own party—in other words, politics as usual. He died in Santa Barbara, California in 1928.

Now, aside from birth, Governors actually liked to come to Glens Falls to visit. Even after moving away, Hughes returned frequently. Governor Alfred E. Smith would often visit his friend, publisher A.B. Colvin. On his way to the Adirondacks, Franklin D. Roosevelt would always stop at Fitzgerald's Restaurant on the Glen Street hill.

The celebration of Governor's Day, September 23, 1933, perhaps offered the most governors assembled at one time in Glens Falls. Established in 1894, that year's event was held in City Park and at the Glens Falls Country Club. Invited guests included incumbent Herbert H. Lehman, and past Governors Hughes and Smith—even a gubernatorial candidate, Charles H. Tuttle, who had been Republican nominee.

So, Governor Pataki, a warm welcome back to this "governor-rich" region from us—and the spirits of your predecessors.

"OVER MY SHOULDER" COLUMN FOR APRIL 7, 2001
Hughes rose to eminent position

L ast week I mentioned that in future columns I'd offer some full-length histories of our locally born New York State Governors.
As this coming Wednesday is Charles Evans Hughes' birthday, how about today?

Here's an expanded history of Hughes. I am still assembling information on Governor John A. Dix and would appreciate anything you could send me here, care of the paper.

By the way, many of these columns come from information sent by readers. I welcome suggestions and, of course, any information that you can send along. Please bear in mind some suggestions I've received have not proven useful for a column, especially those telling me "where to go."

Charles Evans Hughes, the 36th Governor of New York State, was born in the Village of Glens Falls, Town of Queensbury, on April 11, 1862.

Hughes was the son of David and Mary C. Connelly Hughes. The Rev. David Hughes was pastor of the First Baptist Church on Maple Street. At that time, the family lived across the street in a house that was later moved around the corner to Center Street. We'll talk a bit more about that later.

I haven't proof, but logic dictates that Hughes attended the Glens Falls Academy, then on Warren Street. It was the best school in town, and years later Hughes' daughter attended it.

Upon graduation, Hughes attended Brown University, graduating class of 1881. Brown's website history of Hughes claims that he "grew his famous beard in 1890 in the interest of efficiency - to save trips to the barber." Whether or not that's true, Brown's statement that by 1890 Hughes "had a busy commercial law practice in New York, with a side interest in Republican reform politics" is true.

In 1905 the state legislature appointed Hughes to investigate corruption in the city's gas industry. According to "A Short History of New York State," he was so successful, he was asked to investigate insurance company fraud. Hughes found abuses in insurance company executives' diverting company funds, cooking company books, making bribes through campaign contributions to the Republican Party, and bribes to Democrat and Republican legislators, and bribes to the press. I think the only person they missed bribing was the guy cleaning the men's room in the Capitol Building.

The problem here was that Hughes was a Republican. Understandably, a lot of his party hated him, but being political realists, knew that he was the only person who could beat the notorious publisher William Randolph Hearst in the upcoming 1906 gubernatorial campaign. They nominated Hughes and he, indeed, beat Hearst.

During his two terms, Hughes continued his reformist ways. He established public commissions for utilities and mass transit in New York City, taking potential illegal gain away from both parties. He refused to appoint his party's hacks to office, offending Republican bosses by suggesting that the appointees should actually be qualified to hold the office. The party was stunned. Its notion was, "Hey! The appointee's breathing, isn't he?"

Hughes pushed through a bill limiting campaign expenditures – talk about ahead of his time! – and set up commissions to investigate fraud in district apportionment, the insurance industry, and other areas. Both parties hated him, but the people loved him.

He strained that relationship with the people in 1907, and spoiled all the fun in Saratoga Springs, by getting the legislature to outlaw bookmaking at racetracks, because gambling was not allowed by the state constitution.

Nonetheless, the people reelected him to a second term, very probably because he enacted 56 laws to protect the working person.

Next week, we'll see how Hughes remembered his hometown in some special ways, look at his quest for the Presidency, and watch his rise to Chief Justice of the United States Supreme Court.

"OVER MY SHOULDER" COLUMN FOR APRIL 14, 2001
Hughes, from Glens Falls, rode reform to governor's mansion

We complete the story of Charles Evans Hughes, born in Glens Falls in 1862.

Hughes stayed connected with the place of his birth. After graduating from Brown University in 1881, he moved to New York City to practice law. During the decades following, from the 1880s through to the 1920s, we find his presence in Glens Falls.

Hughes had a summer home in Bolton, on Lake George, but he did more than pass through Glens Falls on the train. He joined "The Glens Falls Club," a men's social club that had its headquarters on the second floor of what is today the M. C. Scoville Building on the corner of Glen and Ridge Streets. Later, it was the Elks Club[xv], and in more recent times, the home to LARAC.

Hughes socialized with "those who were" in the village. Many in that club were behind a movement to make the Village of Glens Falls a separate municipality and after Hughes was elected governor in 1906, he made it a reality. On March 13, 1908, native son Charles Evans Hughes signed the law making his native village of Glens Falls the 46th city in the state.

As we saw last week, Governor Hughes was a reformer. His activities attracted the attention of President William Howard Taft, who named him as Associate Justice of the United States Supreme Court in 1910. During his nomination hearings, opponents grilled Hughes, charging he was too anti-business because of his reforms of the utilities and his establishing the nation's first workers' compensation law.

Hughes had entered the national scene. In 1915, he left the court when chosen to run as Republican presidential candidate against Democrat incumbent Woodrow Wilson. Perhaps a mistake in Hughes' campaigning was honestly telling the American people that he would go to war if necessary. Wilson promised to keep America neutral and won the November election. Five months later, the US entered the war.

Around this time, Hughes daughter, Elizabeth, fell ill at the family summer home in Bolton. The Hughes family took a home on Warren Street in Glens Falls for a year or so during the war, while Elizabeth recovered. She attended the Glens Falls Academy, just down the street and befriended a young girl named Polly Hoopes, who also lived on Warren and attended the Academy. They remained friends for life. In the 1970s, Elizabeth would return to Glens Falls to dedicate her father's birthplace on Center Street as she also launched the Supreme Court Historical Society. She stayed with her friend Polly Hoopes Beeman.

Hughes returned to corporate law, but was recalled to public life from 1921-25 as Secretary of State under Warren G. Harding, then Calvin Coolidge. He became a judge on the first World Court in 1928. In 1930, President Hoover named him Chief Justice of the Supreme Court. With authority, he steered the court through the harsh new realities of the Depression. The conservative court often didn't do what President Roosevelt wanted and Roosevelt tried to "pack" the court by expanding it to twelve, and adding justices who would vote his way. Hughes outmaneuvered FDR's attempt.

Hughes championed civil liberties and free speech. Though labeled a conservative, Chief Justice Hughes kept his progressive label by supporting the

Wagner Act of 1937. That act created the National Labor Relations Board, which gave unions a chance to become established in the late 1930s.

Hughes retired in 1940 and died in 1948 at age 86. Today in Glens Falls a marker on his birthplace and a monument in City Park commemorate one of the legends of the American judicial system.

May the history of Hughes be kept alive by the three local governments that rightfully claim his birthplace, Glens Falls, Queensbury and Warren County, so that his example may inspire our children – our governors and Chief Justices of tomorrow.

NOTE: Now nearing its 100th anniversary, The Queensbury Hotel is a wonderful example of the downtown renewal taking place in Glens Falls. The next three columns were written as the hotel was being purchased by the Connecticut-based Queensbury Hotel LLC. Fifteen years later, on March 28, 2016, it was purchased by Queensbury businessman Ed Moore. The hotel is being managed by Spruce Hospitality LLC, owned by Ed Moore's son Zack Moore and by Tyler Herrick. Herrick is the General Manager. Since 2016, The Queensbury Hotel's historical architecture has been restored and 21st century amenities created. It is a joy to be at The Queensbury.[xvi]

"OVER MY SHOULDER" COLUMN FOR MAY 19, 2001
Hotel was conceived by local bigwigs

She is 75 and looks and acts a third her age.

She is the Queensbury Hotel, and this year marking the 75th anniversary of her 1926 opening.

The Queensbury came into being in the early decades of the 20th century, an age when concrete and steel united with a Colonial Revival style to create hotels such as the Queensbury or the Gideon Putnam in Saratoga Springs, which is a few years younger.

The Queensbury Hotel started as the dream project of the Glens Falls Chamber of Commerce, parent organization of today's Glens Falls Chamber of Commerce and the Adirondack Regional Chambers of Commerce.

The original chamber of commerce began in September 1914 and among its board's initial aspirations was creation of a new hotel, totally in sync with the tenor of the times. The City of Glens Falls was only six years old and many of the names on the new chamber's board reflected the corporate power of the city. Egbert W. West, the chamber's president, was head of the Glens Falls Insurance Company. Martin Luther Wilmarth headed a long time furniture company. Elmer C. West was president of Adirondack Power and Light. George Tait was the founder and head of Imperial Wallpaper and Chemical.

There were hotels in Glens Falls, most smaller, that could accommodate a good number of guests. The largest, the Rockwell Hotel, was built in 1872. It was Victorian in appearance, decidedly passé, and with its interior wood framing antiquated in terms of safety.

Nonetheless, a plan for a new hotel would take ten years to accomplish. In March 1924, chamber leaders met with a hundred area business people in the offices of the Glens Falls Insurance Company. They formed the Glens Falls Hotel Corporation, a stock-holding company. Among its board of directors were the same chamber directors mentioned above, plus others: George F. Bayle, James McPhillips, Benjamin McCreery, Louis M. Brown, Egbert W. West, Frank M. Smalley, Fred W. Wiley, Maurice Hoopes, Daniel H. Cowles, and George Tait. All were prominent business people whose presence meant that all the region's largest banks and businesses were represented, such as Finch Pruyn & Co. of which Hoopes was the president.

Most symbolic was George F. Bayle, the hotel corporation's president. Like E. W. West, Bayle was a self-made man. This far-sighted president of the Glens Falls Portland Cement Company had been on the City Charter Committee, was co-founder of the Community Chest, today's Tri-County United Way, and an unparalleled civic leader. Under Bayle, the hotel corporation raised nearly $500,000 in about a month. Today, that would be the equivalent of at least $10 million.

The hotel's foundation was poured in the winter of 1924-25 on the former site of the Wallace T. Marsh home. Originally this had been the site of the home of James C. Clark, son of the Rev. Billy J. Clark, founder of America's first temperance society.

The original 125-room plan was scrapped and by spring of 1926, a 151-room, 5-story hotel was completed at a cost of $750,000. Its concrete and steel frame was state of the art. So, too, was its Colonial Revival design reflected in its exterior of brick and interior of handcrafted woodwork, with pilasters, dentals and other flourishes. In keeping with that Colonial motif, the renowned Griffith Bailey Cowles was commissioned to paint the exquisite mural of a scene from "The Last of the Mohicans."

All was now ready. In next week's column, we'll look at the grand opening on May 14, 1926, and follow the hotel's history to the 1980s.

Remember to pencil in the Queensbury Hotel's open house this May 29-30, during which there will be a large display of historical memorabilia and the chance for you to tour the hotel.

See you next week.

"OVER MY SHOULDER" COLUMN FOR MAY 26, 2001
Hotel saw famous guests

In our second column on the Queensbury Hotel's 75th anniversary, we've come up to the hotel's opening in 1926.

The hotel corporation held a stockholders' banquet on May 7, with President Bayle as toastmaster. Music was supplied by the famed Ben Bernie Orchestra, with a young unknown named Bennie Goodman, who'd headline there later.

When the doors formally opened May 14, 1926, the public was ecstatic. Newspapers couldn't write enough.

Under the management of the American Hotel Corporation, the Queensbury had every accommodation of a four star hotel in Manhattan. It was so successful it added another 56 rooms in 1929.

The stock market crashed that year as well, and for the better part of the next 11 years, the Queensbury ran in the red. Then in 1940 under hotel director Robert Collamer, a new promotional campaign began to attract conventions, a new cocktail lounge was created and the Queensbury began taking "permanent guests," people who lived full-time at the hotel.

In 1941, the hotel had its first net profit in years, "$2,636.93," according to *The Post-Star* of January 1942. Unfortunately, the attack on Pearl Harbor a month before left the board of directors reporting it, "impossible to forecast what…1942 will produce for our hotel." Wartime travel restrictions forced the hotel into the red again in 1943, but it was profitable from 1944 on.

With war's end in 1945, the hotel aimed at skiing, a new industry, which had blossomed here in the 1930s. A 1948 promotional hotel booklet shows happy skiers quaffing drinks in the lobby beneath the mural.

But 1945 brought another innovation. The first "motel" appeared in Los Angeles and soon Adirondack roadside and lakeside cabins were giving way to the cheaper and highly competitive motels.

When the mortgage was retired in 1953 the hotel made costly renovations. Yet by 1955, revenues were down, although still in the black. President Mark Peet reported two hotel chains, the Sheraton and Schine, had expressed interest in buying the hotel. In 1956 Schine bought the Queensbury for $850,000 and the stockholders dissolved the corporation on its 30th anniversary.

The Schine firm also owned the Rialto in Glens Falls, and numerous other hotels, theaters and radio stations. In a nod to motels, Schine built a drive-in motor entrance, and created the old Lantern Inn, since removed. Live acts played there, such as Woody Herman whom I recall seeing at the hotel in 1962.

A 1976 *Post-Star* article noted that, in 1968 the Queensbury was purchased by Kamyr, a fairly new firm in town, and Continental Insurance, which had just bought the Glens Falls Insurance Company.[xvii] Interestingly, of all the hotel's founding corporations, only Finch Pruyn survives.[xviii]

The article noted that tradition lived on in two long time hotel employees, Leo Lemery, who began in 1932 and Hilma McIlvaine, who started in 1945. And speaking of tradition, who among you recalls Sidney Ridley, the last doorman at the Queensbury?

The article mentioned famous guests such as Eleanor Roosevelt, Duke Ellington, Marion Anderson, Guy Lombardo, and Perry Como, to name but a few.

I recall Bob Hope visiting in 1980, the same year Garden on the Park was created. Hotel Manager Leo Turley hired a designer Kendall McKernon to put his stamp on that addition. Ken would return in 1985 when the hotel did major remodeling on the north side, including adding a swimming pool.

Two weeks from now, I'll return with the last installment on the Queensbury, with some history of the last decade, some personal memories, and some dreams for its future.

Because of the timing of the Queensbury Hotel's open house May 29-30, this second part of a three-part series on the hotel coincided with a Memorial Day column, which will run next week.

Meanwhile, help celebrate the Queensbury Hotel's 75th anniversary by visiting its open house.

"OVER MY SHOULDER" COLUMN FOR JUNE 9, 2001
Queensbury Hotel has memories

For two columns now, we've run through some of the incredibly rich history of the Queensbury Hotel, which turned 75 this May 14.

We had arrived at the 1990s. Paulette Ricotta became General Manager in 1990 and like her predecessors, she instituted changes. In 1993, the Lantern Inn was "retired" after three decades of watering the citizens of our region. The hotel management created a new bar, The Fenimore, in the area that had held, since 1926, a flower shop and barbershop. The barbershop moved within the hotel. The florist departed completely.

Ms. Ricotta was succeeded in 1999 by Heinz Sheffold, who has been with the hotel since the 1970s. Under him, the hotel has entered 21st century with its own website and seems well-poised for the future. I wish him well, for the Queensbury is a vessel that holds personal memories for thousands of people, including your family and mine. My wife and I have a multitude of memories that could be yours as well.

Sara has memories from her teenage years of receiving formal dance lessons there from a Mr. DeWitt. I recall, as a teen, giving a speech there as part of a service club's efforts to develop public speaking in teens. The only thing it developed in me at that moment was an intense desire to be ill in the men's room because of my fear of public speaking.

She and I share the memory of a Beaux Arts Ball in 1979, just after we'd met. And at it, we met a lifelong friend Jack Wiberg. In another column I wrote of a time, 20 years ago this month, when my parents came down to stay at the Queensbury to help celebrate the birth of my daughter, Julia. I can still see Chrissie[xix] behind the bar, serving our celebratory drink, while the circus performers, in town then at the Civic Center, poured into the Lantern Inn after the show.

How my parents loved staying there. It was their getaway place, and they befriended many people there. Our family shared its joys with the Queensbury. Its sorrows, too. Three years later, when Dad was bringing Mom down to Glens Falls for chemotherapy for her cancer, they'd stay at the Queensbury. The hotel staff treated them as family.

Whether the people who have walked through the Queensbury lobby have been Eleanor Roosevelt or my in-laws, Edna and Harland Cutshall, the hotel embraces them all in a community history. It has made history, as well, and should continue to do so.

And to do that, its neighbors and the City of Glens Falls should work to use it for the purpose its creators intended. They should reflect upon the dream that spurred creation of the Queensbury Hotel.

For when we dream, we create. Let me share a historian's dreams for the Queensbury. I'd like Evergreen Bank[xx] to take that blank parking lot next door and, in concert with the city and the Crandall Library, create a multi-story parking garage to serve all four entities.

I would like to see that foursome coax Mr. Charles R. Wood to invest in building a convention center attached to the Queensbury in much the way the convention center, hotel complex works in Saratoga Springs.

I would like to see a multi-story shopping mall be a part of that complex and to spur the City of Glens Falls to once again think like a city and begin to build up and to build underground and to use the resources it has for its good and the good of the region.

For the good of the region was what spurred creation of the hotel. This 75th anniversary is the perfect time to revisit the dream that brought the Queensbury into being in 1926 and see what it can inspire in 2001.

After all, that's what history is for.

"OVER MY SHOULDER" COLUMN FOR JUNE 30, 2001
Glens Falls problems are cyclical

Th his column falls in the category of "yesterday's issues are today's issues." Among the papers of James A. Holden at the Crandall Library is a wonderful address on civic improvement he gave before the Glens Falls

Lyceum in December 1895. Judging from the notes on it, he probably gave it again in 1897.

His lengthy address indicates Victorians' willingness to sit for hours, listening to lectures. Imagine that today, what with the majority of people, myself included, having developed a three-minute attention span geared to commercials?

This man of many hats—state historian, banker, Glens Falls Village Trustee—was intensely involved in the civic improvement of Glens Falls. He addressed a list of issues very much alive today.

Water, if you'll forgive the mixed metaphor, was a burning issue. Holden said the village needed to meter residential users of the water system. Commercial enterprises had been metered, but residential customers' careless use and leaky faucets were wasting water. Also, the new sewer system had increased water use.

Now, 106 years later, metering is being done.

He commented, "Whenever water works are controlled by private corporations . . . meters are used with good results. Why should not a public corporation be as careful of its interests as a private one?"

While honoring the efficiency of private ownership, Holden opposed it, writing, "that the private stockholders would have the benefit of fat dividends from their investments," while, I assume, the village would only enjoy efficient service.

Still, he complained that the system needed a commission to get rid of the stink of politics and needed a filtering system to get rid of the stink of the water.

The whole issue of water brought up the street conditions. Holden said that after creating the sewer system in 1893-94, the torn-up streets had been repaved incorrectly, creating great ruts on Glen Street.

Politics again was at issue: "It is time to stop the prostitution of the village economy by interested people securing appointments in any village department so that pecuniary or moral debts can be paid."

Holden also complained that although the "Sidewalk Department" was created in 1893, property owners weren't cooperating. No change there.

Oh, and straight out of today's news, here's Holden on municipal street lighting. He wondered if "it would not be more economical for the village to own its own electrical plant and supply its own light" for its 85 arc and 1,400 incandescent streetlamps.

The police department? Holden's criticism was aimed at the village politicians: "The present village police are policemen by courtesy only" and had "no proper powers," because the department was "made the sport and plaything of politicians." Holden said an independent commission was needed to protect the police department.

Holden criticized the volunteer fire department, claiming the only reason it was able to do such good work was because "for the first time in its history it was properly equipped [by the village] with the necessary apparatus and supplies." Saying Glens Falls was the only village its size without a paid department, he called for paid employees to augment the volunteer fire fighters.

Today, this issue is rising again in rural communities, fueled because volunteers are becoming increasingly scarce.

Holden's last topic, cemeteries, is one I shall return to: "I approach this topic in shame and sorrow. With full knowledge of what I say, I pronounce the condition of our Cemetery a disgrace." This could be said today regarding many cemeteries in New York State. Our state does nothing to enforce its cemetery laws, thereby carelessly allowing cemeteries to be abandoned and vandalized. It is a scandal no one wants to touch and one waiting for an investigative reporter.

Thank you, James Holden, for reminding us that the price of civilization is vigilance.

Or to put another way: "If it ain't broke, you ain't lookin' hard enough."

"OVER MY SHOULDER" COLUMN FOR JULY 21, 2001
Class recalls neat stuff of '61

While the Glens Falls High School Class of 1961 is celebrating its 40th anniversary this weekend, they'll have a hard time deciding what was the most important event of their four years.

Because, from 1957 to 1961 there was lot of "neat stuff," to use a phrase popular then.

Maybe you're thinking of the Soviets launching Sputnik or Little Rock, Arkansas desegregating its public schools in 1957. Or 1958, when the first atomic submarine, the Nautilus traveled under the North Pole. Or 1959. Alaska and Hawaii became states. Castro became premier of Cuba.

Eisenhower was President for most of those four years, offering politics as exciting as warm milk. But, by their graduation in 1961, Kennedy was in office, promising to go to the moon and asking the class to join the Peace Corps.

But here's reality. Politics and current events didn't matter as much as music, funny fads, movies and TV in creating the Class of 1961's memories. The Berlin Wall was built in 1961, but "Kookie" combing his hair on "77 Sunset Strip" had a greater impact.

The class was drenched in a new music, rock'n'roll. Chuck Berry, Elvis and the Everly Brothers were standards. Some knew the words to "Stand by Me" better than the national anthem.

The 45-RPM record allowed girls to carry their music to a friend's house and sob along with a Connie Francis song, as they tried on short shorts and chemise dresses, while trimming their hair in poodle cuts.

After that haircut, Connie's song "Who's Sorry Now" had far more meaning. Guys haircuts were flattops or, for the rebels, DAs the initials being interpreted as Duck's A__. You get it.

The class danced to Chubby Checkers' Twist. Here, for the first time, was a fast dance where you didn't hold your partner!

For the class that teethed on the Mickey Mouse Club and the Howdy Doody Show, major TV shows now included American Bandstand, The Fugitive and Ozzie and Harriet.

Everybody was spinning a hula hoop, probably pink as everything in the world was colored pink in the late `50s, including entire kitchens, T-birds and Corvettes, and Ford Motor's big "Whoops!" – the Edsel.

Speaking of big, this class lived through 1959—cars with BIG tail fins, the introduction of the big-breasted doll named Barbie, and the big death of Buddy Holly. Bye Bye Miss American Pie, indeed.

This class was one of the last to regard downtown Glens Falls as the "hub" for every need, from places to hang out, such as Madden's drugstore, the Palace Lunch, or the Ideal Restaurant. Downtown, boys shopped C.V. Peters, girls shopped Merkel and Gelman's.

They watched "Psycho" debut in the Paramount and Rialto theaters downtown. No Cinema 1-50. The only movies in Queensbury were drive-ins and this class didn't attend drive-ins to watch the film. They were there for the submarine races, to the background music of Johnnie Mathis.

No, Queensbury was country. Quaker Road, then called the by-pass, was just being built, as was the Northway. In 1961, although McDonald's existed, there was none yet on Upper Glen.

The Class of 1961 graduated to the strains of the alma mater, played by the school band. Then, to the tune "Hit the Road Jack," they plunged into the sixties, many probably reflecting Roy Orbison's hit, "Runnin' Scared."

Now, 40 years later, the alums return. Tonight, the music of their age will fill the air. While many will sing the alma mater or perhaps "Stand by Me," all voices will again lift in unison to the words of this one classic song:

"Who put the bomp, in the bomp she-bomp she-bomp?
Who put the ram in the rama lama ding dong?
Who was that man? I'd like to shake his hand.
He made my baby fall in love with me."[xxi]

Oh heavens, they just don't make songs like that anymore.

Happy reunion, Class of 1961.

"OVER MY SHOULDER" COLUMN FOR AUGUST 5, 2001

Post-Star Editor's note: *Today's Post-star is running extensive coverage of the 150th anniversary of The Glens Falls National Bank and Trust Company. In his column, Joe Cutshall-King starts with the bank's beginnings and earliest years.*

Community had money, but no place to put it

The Glens Falls National Bank and Trust Company is celebrating its 150th anniversary – and it might just be national news.

Why celebrate a bank's anniversary? Because Glens Falls National is a homegrown business with a history so personal, it's often referred to as a "who." It is the last locally created bank still headquartered in Glens Falls. Of America's thousands of banks, it is one of the few locally grown banks still locally run. That's history.

The bank's heritage is intimately interwoven with that of Glens Falls and Queensbury, where it began August 1, 1851. In 1851, Glens Falls was a booming village with over half of Queensbury's 7,146 citizens. Since the feeder canal's widening in 1832, canal boats had been carrying Glens Falls' commodities south to Albany and New York and bringing back money, lots of money.

Lumber was king. Lumber baron Abraham Wing III, grandson of the town's founder, was credited with perfecting the means for floating Adirondack timber downriver to Glens Falls, where its lumber mills cut millions of board feet of lumber. In that year of 1851, an enormous log catcher, the Big Boom, was erected on the Hudson to help pen the floating logs. More logs were received. More lumber cut. More money made.

Other products were shipped. Keyes P. Cool first produced local lime for shipment south in 1832. Albany and Manhattan were built with it. Raw hides were tanned at Colonel Benjamin P. Burhans' tanning mills in Warrensburg and other tanneries, then sent to Glens Falls to be shipped out. More money was shipped in.

Glens Falls grew like Topsy. Incorporated as a village in 1839, its population tripled by 1851, by which time it had, to paraphrase Seneca Ray Stoddard, dozens of lumber mills, grist mills and gin mills. It had two newspapers, four hotels, six churches, private and public schools, innumerable dry goods, hardware stores, foundries, furniture and carriage manufactories, and the like.

In short, it had money. But it had no bank.

In 1849, thirteen businesspeople, most tremendously wealthy, had formed the Glens Falls Insurance Company to provide local coverage for this boom town. Now two years later, a group of its subscribers decided to remedy the village's being "bankingly challenged" – that is, not having a bank.

Again thirteen people joined hands: Benjamin P. Burhans, James Buell, Dr. Billy J. Clark, Keyes P. Cool, Daniel H. Cowles, Benjamin Ferris, Walter Geer,

Bethuel Peck, Byron Rice, Peletiah Richards, David G. Roberts, Halsey Rogers, and Abram Wing. Richards was the insurance company's vice president, and Clark, Cowles, Peck and Wing were among its co-founders.

They met in the insurance company's offices in the Daniel H. Cowles building on the corner of Warren and Ridge Streets on August 1, 1851. The Glens Falls Bank was established. It opened for business in that same building in December 1851 and immediately issued its own currency. How's that for confidence?

It needs a book to describe the founders and their impact on local history. Take for example, Benjamin P. Burhans, who served as the bank's first president until his death in 1875. Interestingly, both he and Peletiah Richards had served as state assemblymen from Warrensburg and both were co-founders of the Warrensburg Masonic lodge.

"Lime baron" Keyes P. Cool had a grandson who would be the first Mayor of the City of Glens Falls. Daniel H. Cowles, a successful merchant, had a grandson Daniel H. Cowles who would serve as bank president from 1931 to the mid-1940s. Some founders would affect national history. Physician Billy J. Clark founded America's first temperance society in Moreau. All 13, however, left one major legacy: today's Glens Falls National Bank and Trust Company.

The young bank accrued enough wealth to build its first building, on Glen, just below today's Hudson Avenue. It burned in the fire of 1864, but symbolically, the only remaining thing from it was the vault. The money was safe.

A second bank building was erected in 1865, the year the bank became nationally chartered as The Glens Falls National Bank.

It was the end of the Civil War. The Glens Falls region was about to explode even more with development and Glens Falls National was in the forefront of it, being a part of our community's history, as it has remained to this day.

Now turn to Maury Thompson's[xxii] feature story and follow the rest of story of the Glens Falls National Bank and Trust Company, up to this moment – and into the future.

Happy 150th!

"OVER MY SHOULDER" COLUMN FOR AUGUST 11, 2001
Watch out for that cliff

Just call me the Roadrunner.

In a recent editorial, *The Post-Star*'s Don Coyote referred obliquely to a request by certain people in Washington County, myself included, for the county supervisors to investigate the reuse of the old Washington County Courthouse after the new jail is constructed.

The editorial cartoon stated, in full: "Let me get this straight: The old Washington County Courthouse isn't sound enough to be a jail, but with a little work it should be fine for office space. What's wrong with this picture?"

Amazing. A few deft phrases and the entire issue is summed up and disposed of.

I don't think so.

It's not my intent to rehash history. The decision has been made and within a year a new jail complex will sit in Fort Edward. The lovely 1869 Washington County Courthouse with its homely 1918 jailhouse addition, plus a separate frame building and several acres of land, will all cease to function in a jail capacity.

I do not know the ins and outs of the state laws and regulations governing the kind of structure deemed adequate for prisoners, except to say that, like those rules governing hospitals, mental facilities and other buildings with highly specialized functions, the rules for prisons are infinitely complex.

Since what's done is done, then two things hold true. One, the jail is going to be somewhere else. Two, the old jail is on the verge of standing empty.

Like many, I have asked the county to support appropriate studies to see if the building can be recycled.

I wonder, where did the notion come into the Beloved Coyote's head that if a building can't be usable for one purpose, it is unusable for all purposes? For that's the essence of the editorial.

Part of Don's problem is wording. The phrase, "isn't sound enough to be a jail" makes it appear as if the building is about to collapse onto Route 153 killing everyone in it. For all the reportage done, I don't believe it was ever reported that the building itself was about to be condemned. All the state said was that in its present condition it just wasn't functioning according to state rules. The resulting consensus was to build anew, rather than attempt another renovation for the purpose of upgrading the present building as a jail.

Also, the phrase, "isn't sound enough to be a jail" implies the building has had only one function—patently not true, as the Don himself refers to "the old Washington County Courthouse" and not the " old Washington County jailhouse."

Don's other phrase is a lulu: "with a little work it should be fine for office space." Who said, "a little work"? Is that true? Nobody knows. I don't. About the only thing I know for certain are death, taxes and dental floss that shreds upon impact.

That is why many people in Salem and in the county are asking for a study to see if there are possible uses for the building.

The first principle of historic preservation and reuse is getting information. We know we have an outstanding piece of architecture for which there might be other uses for government, nonprofits, private business, or all three. Experience has shown a second life for buildings very similar to the courthouse.

But how will anyone know unless those with experience in this realm are asked to study it, to say whether reuse is an option? We need full information for intelligent decisions.

Many of you have seen the Warner Brothers' cartoon where Wile E. Coyote attacks the Roadrunner by using some harebrained scheme, but ends up falling forlornly into a deep canyon, while the Roadrunner runs off saying, "Beep Beep."

The problem was, Wile didn't get the full information before attacking.

All coyotes need the full information.

Beep beep, Don.

[EDITOR'S POSTSCRIPT: Fortunately, the Town of Salem took ownership and, in 2002, the citizens of Salem, NY, created the Historic Salem Courthouse Preservation Association Inc. The HSCPA beautifully preserves the building and provides excellent programming for the region.]

"OVER MY SHOULDER" COLUMN FOR AUGUST 19, 2001
And how does your garden grow?

[AUTHOR'S NOTE: In this article on the restoration and opening to the public of the King's Garden, I mentioned that my brother, William F. King, worked there summers under the supervision of Teddy Teriele. As Bill wrote me recently, he was there five summers.]

This summer Fort Ticonderoga reopened the King's Garden to the public after eight years of restoration. According to information sent to me by Fort Ti, it was first created in 1912 by Stephen and Sarah Pell for their family estate, the Pavilion.

The Pells owned adjacent Fort Ticonderoga, the restoration of which they began in 1909. They called their walled flower garden "the King's Garden," the name the British army gave the garrison's garden in the 1700s.

In 1920 the Pells commissioned a formal garden plan by landscape architect Marian Cruger Coffin. This restoration uses her original design plan, right down to the same plants.

A few years ago, I had walked through the King's Garden while it was under restoration. Although I worked at Fort Ti as a teen over thirty years ago, I'd never seen that garden. In fact, few were allowed to see the gardens then. They were, essentially, private. So, I'm glad they're available to the public now.

It occurred to me as I walked through then, and now as I prepared to write this column, that Coffin's design never would have survived as long as it did without the work of the gardeners who maintained it for decades.

Gardeners such as Teddy Teriele, in Ticonderoga. I called Teddy, who was the gardener for both the King's Garden and the orchards from 1961 to 1981.

Teddy said he had succeeded Mort Porter, who had worked for Stephen and Sarah Pell. Teddy had worked for and Mr. and Mrs. John Pell, the next generation. So, Mort Porter and Teddy Teriele covered the majority of the garden's existence before it ceased to be, a few years after Teddy left.

Teddy was there when I had worked for Karl LaPointe, along with his sons George and Cy, in the Log House Restaurant. Later Teddy hired my brother Bill to work for him in the gardens.

So, just as it was for the Pells, being at the Fort was a family affair for many people, including Washington County Attorney Roger Wickes and his wife, Carolyn. Both had worked there. From 1979 to 1884, Roger played in the fife and drum corps, gave tours and worked on the gun crew.

Though he didn't do garden work, Roger has a most distinct memory of the King's Garden. One day his gun crew was loading the cannon, from which they fired smooth stones, or plaster of Paris shot cast by Roger Dechame[xxiii]. Their target was a barrel.

Instead they shot a softball, which they'd gleefully discovered would burst into flames upon leaving the cannon. Perhaps they used too much gunpowder on this day, but, whatever, the crowds went wild as the flaming softball soared past the barrel and over the King's Garden wall.

Then, a few moments later, an unhappy Teddy rushed out clutching a smoking object – while offering the crew instructive words, definitely not botanical in nature.

Theirs are among the thousands of unrecorded stories about Fort Ticonderoga, which is approaching the 100th anniversary of its restoration. Those stories might be lost.

Unlike the King's garden, if those memories are not saved, there is no plan for their restoration.

So, Fort Ti, as you cultivate that garden, also cultivate those memories. I'd start with an elder statesman of those who worked there, Karl LaPointe[xxiv], and with Teddy. And keep widening the circle—harvesting memories from families like Wickes, Dechame, Charbonneau, Lawson, Bigelow, Pell, Fitzgerald, Hudson, Leerkes, Walsh, Hibbard and on and on, throughout the US.

And see how your garden grows.

Now, let me tell you about one windy day, when a guide, who was Scottish, was wearing nothing beneath his kilt and . . .

"OVER MY SHOULDER" COLUMN FOR SEPTEMBER 1, 2001
'Winging it'

L et's "Wing it."
By which I mean, let's do a bit of Wing history, and I am not referring to birds or the Wright Brothers.

Perhaps you saw *The Post-Star* article by Martha Pettys on the bequest of Jean Wing Davis to the Old Fort House Museum of Wing family memorabilia and the exhibition about the Wings that opens at the museum on September 7. As the article noted, while everyone always associates the Wing family with the founding of Glens Falls and Queensbury, the truth is that Fort Edward had branches of the family there.

But then, the Kingsbury, Moreau, Northumberland, and Saratoga Springs, among others, can claim Wings, too.

First, a word about Jean Wing Davis, who was a wonderful woman. Through her mother, Calista Wing, who was born in Fort Edward, Jean was the descendant of Abraham Wing, known to most people as the founder of Queensbury and Glens Falls.

I had met Jean when I first went to work at the Chapman Historical Museum, which itself is chockablock with Wing family memorabilia.

I hope her gift will inspire Old Fort House director Paul McCarty and Chapman director Tim Weidner to do a joint exhibition on the Wing family, whose contributing role to this region was substantial. However, contrary to the sanitized histories of later times, written in the later 19th century by Victorians seeking to cast holiness on their forebears past, the family did have its ups and downs, its black sheep and its controversies.

One controversy involved the first Abraham Wing, there being an Abraham II and an Abraham III. Abe the First was a Quaker and as such claimed neutrality in the Revolution. However, Daniel Park, an avowed Patriot who lived across the river in today's Town of Moreau, accused the Quaker founder of being in the pay of the king, along with the Loyalist Jessup brothers.

He could have been. But, certainly in that war, anyone claiming neutrality would have hated by either side — and both sides had no problems in "liberating" Abe's property in the name of their respective causes. It was true that one of Wing's daughters married a Loyalist and fled with him to Montreal. She died there in childbirth shortly after the war's end. Heartbreak was added to a charge of treason.

Regarding Abraham II, we have a bona fide black sheep. This man was, to put it delicately, a crook. He had married a fine woman named Polly who, during the Tory burning raid of 1780, fled with her two babies and hid in the swamp for days. Her story and that of her children are usually offered in place of Abe II's.

A document Paul furnished me states that his fellow Quakers read him out of the Meeting for not marrying a Quaker. He was, also, an "early sports promoter" and offered whole "building lots to the winner of a foot race." These things would not classify him as a villain.

However, he was convicted of assault and battery in 1815 and, shortly after, was convicted of forgery. He died in a Manhattan prison. And here's a fascinating tale that one named Ephraim Crocker related to Dr. Asa Fitch years later. This goes back to the charge of the Wings being Tories. During the Revolution, the Patriot Crocker had been captured by Abraham II and brought to a British jail in Montreal. As he was being imprisoned, Crocker swore to Wing he'd see Wing end up "in as secure a place as this."

Years later, when Wing was imprisoned, Crocker rode on horseback all the way to Manhattan to help Wing recall that time in Montreal. Now, that was a man with a memory!

Aside from Abraham II, aka Mr. Blacksheep, the rest of the family was upright and industrious. However, a claim made for one Wing descendant, Abraham III, is still causing historian's headaches.

More about that next week in part two of "Winging It."

"OVER MY SHOULDER" COLUMN FOR SEPTEMBER 8, 2001
Debate centers on log drive

When I began last week's column by suggesting that we "Wing it," apparently I was winging it in terms of Wing genealogy. So, a correction is in order, thanks to Bob Eddy of Queensbury, himself a Wing descendant.

I mentioned that Jean Wing Davis had bequeathed Wing family memorabilia to the Old Fort House Museum, which already had a significant collection of Wing related artifacts and documents. I incorrectly stated that Jean was the descendant of Abraham Wing.

Wrong. Jean was a descendant of Edward Wing, Abraham's brother. Edward had also settled in Queensbury, where he built a lovely house pictured in the book *Bridging the Years*. Edward's grandson, David, had married Calista McCarg in Fort Edward and their daughter was Jean Davis' mother. In fact the museum has Calista McCarg's wedding dress.

It was because the Old Fort House has so many Wing family artifacts that director Paul McCarty put together a special exhibit of them, now on display at the museum.

Last week I also wrote of Wing family black sheep and white sheep. This week we'll look at a Wing family legend that has many historians squabbling.

Frankly, some squabbles among historian rank with the debate over how many angels can dance on the head of a pin. Others, however, rise to the level where family honor is at stake or where regional and state histories are cast into doubt.

This controversy is about regional and state histories. There is a claim regarding Abraham Wing III, grandson of family white sheep Abraham I and son of family black sheep Abraham II. Numerous Glens Falls historians have credited Abe III with inventing the log drive. That is, to oversimplify the complicated, you cut trees, stock them in dammed rivers or lakes and then float the logs downriver, guiding them to market by a series of booms.

William Brown's 1963 history of Warren County specifically credits Wing, but even before Brown, Wing was being credited by historian Marion Chitty, a very underappreciated historian in her own right.

Stepping into the fray is William Lee Richards. Seeking information on ancestor Orson Richards, Bill has researched law libraries and histories galore, including the 1901 *History of the Lumber Industry in the State of New York*, by William F. Fox.

Regarding log drives, Bill found that the state issued statutes over a 40-year period trying to define the river as a "highway" and how that highway could be used. Orson Richards and partners Frederick J. Barnard, Roswell Weston and General Orville Clark owned hundreds of thousands of acres in the upper Hudson River watershed. They had a particular interest in using the "highway" to sluice their logs to market. In 1846-47 they got statutes enacted to open the tributaries to the upper Hudson River to log drives.

Does this make them the inventors of the log drive or simply the people who got legalized what was already being done?

Others debate the Wing story. Any descendant of Norman or Alanson Fox, of Chestertown, will tell you that the Fox brothers started the log drives around 1820 in Athol. The 1886 history of Warren County[xxv] mentions both Abe III and the Fox brothers in this vein, but credits no one with inventing log drives.

Binding logs into rafts and floating them down the Hudson River was well documented before the Revolution. Conceivably, some anonymous person first thought of cutting the strings on those rafts and floating the logs freely downriver. Adding misery to the debate, talk to anyone from the state of Maine and they will proudly proclaim that log drives began there.

In short, there is no solution in sight to a topic that may be debated for centuries to come.

It may well replace angels dancing on a pinhead.

"OVER MY SHOULDER" COLUMN FOR SEPTEMBER 15, 2001
Gutless Wonders

Gutless.

That was the first word that came to mind as I watched the TV shot of a gaping hole filled with the rubble of the World Trade Center.

I'd seen that building being built in the two years I worked near it. Every day I watched the foundation being poured, the steel rise. Never could I have dreamed it would be destroyed in the way it was.

Never could I have dreamed so many lives would be so wantonly, cruelly and hideously destroyed.

This is an open letter to the Gutless Wonders who did this. Do you think that you have America's measure? You didn't even get our cuff size. What a lesson you need to learn about the history of Americans.

You want to bomb us into submission. You would want us to cringe and cower. Oh, we're fearful, but in a vigilant way now.

You'd want us to be dumbstruck, incapacitated, and incapable of movement, wanting to leave the world, to stay at home, never again to venture out. To turn our backs on neighbors abroad, never again to step into the arena of trying to broker peace between warring parties or even extend a helping hand when nature runs amok and kills as thoughtlessly as you did.

You would want our military to lash out without thinking, reacting with unplanned vengeance and pure blind rage.

And hate? Oh, yes, that above all else. You would want us to hate – hate those who aren't Americans, or those Americans who may look different, or who, perhaps, may pray differently from the majority of those Americans who pray.

Your plan was to make Americans go away. Vanish!

And why? Because America represents, and America practices, and America IS the very thing you detest – liberty. Liberty in all its different faces – freedom of speech and religion, tolerance, dissent, reason, imperfection, hope, and the strength that comes from them all.

You'd want us to strike out into the night and indiscriminately bomb everything in sight so you can say, "See? They are maniacs in America."

And you'd want us to run off like you, cockroaches scurrying in the light, so you could say, "See? They are cowards in America."

You'd want us to hate in the name of religion, just as you do. But you're not religious. You're a disgrace to anything noble that religion brings to the human race and in your afterlife, your milk will be curdled, your honey soured.

To whatever you want, I quote the American general's reply at the Battle of the Bulge when the Nazis demanded surrender: "Nuts!"

You don't tell Americans what the hell to do. Or when the hell to do it. And, Gutless Wonders that you are, you are about to get a history lesson. For when

America brings you to justice – and I know it will happen – it may be in a court of law or it may well be as a bomb drops down your throat.

If do you make it to our courts, and I sincerely hope you do, you will be given due process and representation under the law. For that's the American way.

And if it turns out that the United States drops a bomb on you, rest assured there will be people in the streets that day, some marching in favor of the action, some protesting it.

For that's the American way. And you won't eradicate the American way. Or us.

There was a dictator who tried. Like you, he did not understand Americans. He attempted to brainwash his own people, to obliterate others, and to rule the remainder. He mistook American tolerance for passivity and American love of freedom for wimpiness. As Americans pounded his Reich into the ground, he ended up in a bunker, killing himself, like you . . .

Gutless.

We'll be seeing you.

"OVER MY SHOULDER" COLUMN FOR SEPTEMBER 22, 2001
Orson Richards

It's just like bricks without a mason.

A new local history, *Orson Richards, the "Lumber King of the Hudson*[xxvi], has reminded me that we can collect, catalog and preserve all the documents in the world, but they won't make a history until someone writes it. Bricks aren't a house without a mason.

Written by William Lee Richards of Queensbury, the history is packed with data, much not previously included in formal histories. It's a delight—well written, and a bit quirky as the author, uncharacteristically of him, flaunts historical convention to editorialize.

Like so many, Bill had researched this for years, carrying the information in notes and in his head. Unlike most other researchers, he took the time to write a book.

Bill takes pains to note that while Orson Richards is an ancestor, the book is not "an exercise in ancestral aggrandizement. Let the man's actions be his judge."

Regarding the phrase "local history," the book actually spans three centuries and several states, as it traces Orson's origins to his great-grandfather who landed in Portsmouth, New Hampshire in 1765. Orson's own life history embraced Clinton, Essex, Warren and Washington Counties, all of which this lumberman deeply affected.

He was born in Plattsburgh in 1801, and learned the lumbering business from his father Joseph. It was not a business for the faint hearted and most went bankrupt in it. Our author quotes the comment about an average Adirondack timberman selling his lumber. "If you walked home, ate nothing and did not drink or smoke after having made the sale, you could keep from going broke on the transaction."

Orson was in the economic free-for-all of the 19th century, which the author calls "an economic minefield." That minefield's largest explosion was actually the Great Depression of the 1930s, an event that shaped the economic life of today.

By the time Orson was 25, he owned "extensive properties" with "over 5,400 acres of timber" in Essex and Warren counties. He was diversifying, buying woolen mills in Plattsburgh, then Sandy Hill (now Hudson Falls), where he would eventually move. He owned a broomstick factory in Moreau. In fact, historians take note. From as far south as the Town of Greenwich in Washington County to as far north as Plattsburgh in Clinton County, from Vermont on the east to Potsdam in the northwest of New York, Orson Richards was a major economic presence.

His timber partners included the legendary lumbermen Jeremiah and Daniel Finch, co-founders of Finch Pruyn & Co. Orson was a co-founder of the Glens Falls Boom Association in 1850. As I mentioned in a previous column, he and three other partners had managed to get the state to legalize free-floating logs downriver to his mills, which Bill took decades to document. It's all there for you to read.

Most intriguing is how this history, for the first time, documents the creation of (and Orson's role in) the very influential Glens Falls Railroad in the 1860s. Connecting at the main line in Fort Edward, it ran to Glens Falls. That line spelled the demise of Fort Edward as the economic power of the region, completing the shift of power to Glens Falls.

The end of Orson Richards' multi-million-dollar empire, already unraveling in a series of lawsuits, was hastened by the Panic of 1873-78. Ironically, he died of a stroke in 1878, right after posting a letter to his best friend, confidant, and life's love, his wife. It took his family until 1941 to pay off his debts.

This must-read very limited-edition history may be found at the Crandall Library.

Congratulations, Bill, on an excellent local history, especially of the 19th century, the period in which the modern age was born. To know our past is to understand the present.

And a note to other researchers: please follow Bill's example.

"OVER MY SHOULDER" COLUMN FOR SEPTEMBER 29, 2001
Take a trip back in time

[EDITOR'S NOTE: This column is intentionally included, despite the dated information regarding the exhibits. It has so many references to puzzling local names. It also leads into the next column.]

Are you and the kids into time travel?

This is a perfect time for it. For example, you can time travel to 1756 and get immersed in French and Indian War history, served "live" by several local reenactment groups.

Today, go to the Rogers Island Visitors Center in Fort Edward. There, Captain Speakman's Company of Rangers and the 55th Regiment of Foot and the 27th Regiment of Foot, will be recreating some important past moments for the public.

Speakman's Company will be marching to Lake George, recreating an actual event that the original Speakman's Company of Rangers did this very day 245 years ago in 1756. They'll begin about 8 am and march to Fort William Henry and the Lake George Battleground Park.

For those who arrive at the Visitors Center, the 55th Regiment of Foot and the 27th Regiment of Foot will be stationed all day at the Visitors Center telling us about… Well, no. Take the kids and find out what they are doing and why. Here's a hint. If you know anywhere in the area with the name Amherst in it – Fort Amherst Road in Glens Falls and Queensbury, or Amherst Street in Lake George Village –this will be a wonderful way to find out why Amherst is used so much today.

For kids this is wonderful, because not even the best software program can come with live human beings demonstrating the past.

Now, that will whet the kids' appetite for time travel and they'll be ready to zoom to Glens Falls for Tuesday's opening of the Chapman Historical Museum's newest exhibit, called "Bloody Pond to Storytown; What's in a Name."

I'm sure you saw the great photo in Thursday's *Post-Star* of Charles R. Wood riding in the Great Escape's pumpkin carriage as he was being honored by Crandall Library. The photo made me hope that Mr. Wood gets to see the new exhibit at the Chapman. First, because he started Storytown in 1955 and second because there will be on display one of the original Storytown storybook figures, "The Cat & the Fiddle."

The theme for the exhibit is so clever in its simplicity, because it explores place names in the Glens Falls – Lake George area, something we all know so little about. For example, the exhibit discusses Storytown, which many people don't realize was the first name of the Great Escape.

And it discusses Bloody Pond on Route 9. If you seriously think about it, the name Bloody Pond is gross, because supposedly the pond gained its name from a French and Indian War massacre, when the dead bodies of soldiers were thrown into the pond.

The exhibit got me to thinking about place names throughout the area. Why does the Town of Johnsburg, for example, have a Sodom, but no Gomorrah? Was it wicked enough with just the one and so it stopped there?

Does having a Hebron in Washington County make it more holy?

We all have figured out that Washington County was named for George Washington, but how many of you know for whom Warren County was named? Elected officials of Warren County hang your heads in shame if you don't.

Why does Queensbury have a Pickle Hill Road? Was someone a gherkin fan? Or driving drunk one night?

It's a mystery. Speaking of which, how many know why Cleverdale on Lake George was named for a murder mystery? (How many even knew that it was named for a murder mystery?)

And who reading this has ever heard the phrase "Hague, Hell and Horicon," which Brian Farrell of Indian Lake always said that his mother said?

Finally, returning to the original name of Bloody Pond, do you think it was really named after a British soldier accidentally fell in and came up screaming, "That bloody pond!"

Only time travel will tell.

"OVER MY SHOULDER" COLUMN FOR OCTOBER 6, 2001
Common names, uncommon origins

An English teacher with one foot too large, a boy orphaned by a dam and a fence without a home.

Those were three immediate images that came to mind when I visited the newest exhibit of the Chapman Historical Museum, "Bloody Pond to Storytown: What's in a Name."

As mentioned last week, its strength is its simplicity. It deals with something you have to know in order to get around – place names – but may not know anything about.

This exhibit conjures up strong mental images, whether you have lived in the region forever, or just a day. Here, working last to first, are explanations of the images it conjured up in me.

A fence without a home was inspired by the name Spier Falls. It refers to the Spier Falls hydroelectric dam started in 1900 on the Hudson River ten miles west of Glens Falls. Started by Elmer West and Eugene Ashley of Glens Falls, it took three years to complete, becoming in 1903 the fourth largest hydro dam in the world.

In the course of construction, unforeseen things waylaid it. An enormous glacial pit was discovered and had to be filled in with masonry, nearly bankrupting West and Ashley. Into the breach stepped wealthy Glens Falls businessman William E. Spier, financially rescuing the project and the two men. In gratitude, Spier's name was given to the dam.

For all Spier's importance and wealth, only the dam and Spier Falls Road keep his name alive, although there exists another piece of masonry connected to him, the fence without a home. On the opposite side of Glen Street from the Chapman sits a fence that stretches between the CNA building on the north and the Church of the Messiah to the south. Built of red sandstone and iron piping, it is all that is left of the once glorious home of William E. Spier.

My second image inspired by Spier Falls is a boy orphaned by a dam. Many accidents occurred during construction. Many workers lost their lives. Among the many workers were Italian immigrants, craftsmen experienced in fashioning stone. One of the Italian laborers who died there left behind an orphaned boy named Dominick. Eugene Ashley and his wife adopted that boy and Dominick Ashley's story brings a very personal note to that immense project.

The section of the exhibit on Lake Sunnyside inspired my first image, of an English teacher with one foot too large. Lake Sunnyside was first named Round Pond. How it was renamed you'll discover when you visit the Chapman.

The photos in the exhibit of the pavilion at Lake Sunnyside brought back my memories of 8th grade. Our English teacher, Mr. Robert Clark, gave us a bon voyage party at the Lake Sunnyside pavilion. We'd never seen Mr. Clark out of formal attire and suddenly here was this large man with a huge shock of blond hair, standing in swim trunks at the water's edge with us, laughing and joking.

As we looked down at our bare feet, we all screamed out, as kids will, that one of his feet was huge! Yes, he said, at least three sizes bigger than the other, and he laughed. And we laughed with him.

But it's not his feet for which I'll always remember Bob Clark.[xxvii] No, I shall always remember him for bringing me to a love of reading. In spite of my parents' efforts, by the time I hit 7th grade, comic books were my heaviest reading exercise.

Bob Clark changed me. He had his students buy paperbacks through some club and asked me what I wanted. Randomly, I picked Ernie Pyle. Fine, he said, but you have to read it. I did and the love of reading entered my life.

Bob Clark died this year, mourned by family and friends. And by students whose lives he changed. He will be remembered with every book I read.

Thanks for the memories, Chapman Historical Museum.

"OVER MY SHOULDER" COLUMN FOR NOVEMBER 3, 2001
All things are possible

The news tells us that the US Army's Tenth Mountain Division has sent a thousand men to Uzbekistan to be ready to invade Afghanistan.

Among them might be one extra, although only in spirit. He was a man of such intensity, strength, hope and courage, who, ironically, could be quietly forgotten. But that very act of forgetting him would be, not just pitiful, but horribly wrong.

I have written about Bruce Adams. Shortly after Bruce's death this year, Mathew Sturdevant wrote a fine piece in *The Post-Star* about Bruce's life. This column will not be a restatement of his history, rather a statement of what makes a man great.

That most of you may never have heard of Bruce Adams does not take away from that greatness. Some heroes are unrecognized in their own time by the mass of people.

But a hero he was and it's time now to write those things that couldn't be expressed before, when Bruce was alive, as they would have embarrassed him. You cannot understand the stature of this man without knowing of the promise life held for him before World War II or knowing of the hideous wounds he incurred in battle so near to the end of that war, a war that devastated him and his family.

Cervantes said, "There is nothing so subject to the inconstancy of fortune as war." It was Bruce's worst fortune to suffer near fatal injuries only months before war's end.

He was near Mount Belvedere, Italy, in early 1945, part of the ski troops of the Tenth Mountain Division. German troops fired down on him. His head was torn open, shrapnel ripped through his brain. My understanding is he was left for dead. When he was recovered and taken to hospital, his brain was irreparably damaged. A plate put in his head to replace skull bone caused seizures. It was replaced several times in his life, leaving a permanent depression in his skull.

At first, in Italy, he could understand, but not speak, move somewhat, but not walk. He would learn to walk again, speak to some degree, but never read again. As he said to me, "Me understand, no speak." He'd point to his head, "Words in here." Then his mouth, "but not here."

He told me that on the ship home, "Me get up, fall down. Get up again, fall down." All the way across the Atlantic. His drive was extraordinary. He didn't feel self-pity, only anger. His crowning phrase, which he used constantly, was "All things possible," reflecting his religious belief, as he said it, "the body nothing – spirit all."

Bruce befriended me when I worked at the Chapman Historical Museum, just across the street from his Glens Falls home. He had a scrapbook of family photos that his closest friends, Edna and Tom Harrison, had helped him assemble. He would tell of his family as we looked through the photos.

The album showed an all-American family of four, Claude and Vina Adams and their two bright, athletic, handsome boys, Bill and Bruce. I always loved the look on Bruce's face as he showed me those pre-war photos, especially those of him as a ski instructor at West Mountain, and a tennis instructor at the Sagamore Hotel. I'd kid him, saying, "Hmm, always seems to be good looking women in all these photos." He'd laugh and blush.

The Depression wiped out his father's huge construction business and fortunes. Bruce would always point out the photos of his father's projects, like the NiMo[xxviii] building in Glens Falls or a bridge in Warrensburg, and say, "Daddy, contractor. Buildings and bridges. Famous." Somehow, the family made ends meet and love obviously prevailed in the Adams home.

When Bill and Bruce enlisted, it separated brothers who were so close. Bruce went to Camp Hale, Colorado, as a ski instructor with the Tenth Mountain Division. Bill went to Panama. Bill's letters, now at the Chapman, tell of his hopes and dreams. Bill's plane went down over South America in 1943.

When Bruce was wounded, Vina and Claude lost both sons, in a way. Two sons, bright and beautiful – neither ever to marry, have children or live the life their parents had dreamed for them.

Bruce would be angry with me for saying that, for he never would have. "God's way," he'd say instead. He bore his injuries and disabilities with a smile, in the belief he would triumph. "All things possible," he'd say.

In truth, Bruce did regain a life. With one side paralyzed, his speech nearly gone, he still managed to ski again, to drive a car, and to speak a language of friendship, love and hope. And to build a family – hundreds of people like Edna and Tom – all of us who loved him. "All things possible," he'd say.

Now Bruce is gone, and we say, sleep now, good soldier. But, if you can, Bruce, hold for a just a while longer. Watch over those of the Tenth Mountain and remind them, "All things possible."

"OVER MY SHOULDER" COLUMN FOR JANUARY 6, 2001
Charting history of Glens Falls' buildings

Take a building on a site and trace the history of the building. Better yet, trace the history of the site itself. Not easy, but a wonderful idea. It's one the Chapman Historical Museum is undertaking in what it calls "The Corners" project.

As Robin Wright and Stan Malecki[xxix], the Chapman's education team, explain it, "the idea of the project is to teach the culture and history of a community through the use of public records, primary documents and oral histories." All ages are involved, from high school students on up.

Glens Falls High has been collaborating with the Chapman on the project. On the nights of January 8, 9 & 10 the public is invited to be at the Chapman at 6:30 p.m. as the high school's students share the results of their research.

What grabbed my attention about The Corners is its long-range plan to create a "street-by-street, building-by-building record of the community's development and make it accessible to the public on the Internet." Wonderful! May it become a model for every community.

Here's an opportunity to take research and centralize it via computer, tracing the evolution of military roads and cow paths to streets, buildings going up, street lighting, water and sewer. You could track a single building lot, and link the information to photographs and maps.

Here's an example. On the southeast corner of Exchange and Glen Streets in Glens Falls is Davidson Brothers Brewery and Restaurant. When I was a kid, it was Erlanger's[xxx], an upscale clothing emporium. But what was it originally?

Here the project is fortunate. Pages 58 and 59 of *The History of the Town of Queensbury* [xxxi]relate how Henry Ferguson of Halfmoon bought the site, moved the wood frame structure off and built a new brick one in 1840-1. Good thing it was built of brick, too, as it was spared incineration in the fire of 1864. Ferguson's son remodeled it in 1871-72.

Not to be accused of favoritism, let me mention that Glens Falls' other brewery, Coopers Cave Ale on Dix Avenue, is in a building with a very distinctive shape. I know that Jim Minnick knows the building's history, but do you? The Corners project will be able to record that – as well as link both breweries to a South Street brewery that no longer exists.

To my knowledge, this is the first effort to catalog all of Glens Falls this way, a project that will greatly benefit the history of Queensbury, of which Glens Falls was a part until 1908. However, it is not the first time someone has sought to pull together a coherent picture of the buildings, streets and roads of early Glens Falls, from its early settlement in 1763, when it was called "Wing's Falls" and "The Corners," up to the Civil War.

Researchers would do well to look in the Crandall Library's collection of the voluminous notes of Alexander and Irene Miller,[xxxii] two unsung heroes of local history, who even constructed maps of Glens Falls in those early years. For later times, consult published maps, especially the Burleigh Birdseye maps and the Sanborn maps.

Beyond the Chapman's own collection and the Crandall's, the resources are too numerous to mention. Of course, the most important resource is people. But check out the wonderful records at City Hall, Queensbury Town offices, and Warren County and even Washington County, as Queensbury was a part of it until 1813.

Okay Corners researchers, I'll end with this quiz. Where was the former OMA's Pizza building that was razed this year? What world record is associated with it? When was it built? What was its original use? What building stood there before it?

Pencils only for this exam. Those of you in other towns, don't smirk. You're next.

[AUTHOR'S POSTSCRIPT: Just before this book's publication, I spoke with the Chapman' Historical Museum's Executive Director, Timothy Weidner about the project. Sadly, it went into dormancy around 2010. Tim would like to revive it, as advances in computer power, storage capacity and graphics software could provide users with "virtual downtowns" from all different eras." However, it would be expensive for the Chapman, especially so now. During this Covid pandemic the Chapman, like most nonprofits, struggles to meet operating expenses.]

"OVER MY SHOULDER" COLUMN FOR JANUARY 12, 2001
History buffs get chance to raise grade

Last week we left off with a quiz inspired by the "The Corners" project of the Chapman Historical Museum.

Class, no one correctly answered the quiz. In fact, some people from other towns were snickering because Glens Falls was chosen. So, we're rewarding those snickerers with another quiz.

First, the answers to last week's quiz: the former OMA's Pizza building, which stood just south of Glens Falls City Hall and was razed in 2001, was built in 1937 as a gas station. It replaced the Ridge Street firehouse, which was relocated north to its present site. For a while, OMA held the record for creating the world's largest pizza.

Regarding last week's column, I owe thanks to Judge John Austin[xxxiii] for catching my mistake on Ivy Miller. I should have written Irene Miller.

I picked on Jim Minnick[xxxiv] of South Glens Falls about the Coopers Cave Ale Company building on Dix and Sagamore Street because he had owned it. Jim and his Dad[xxxv] had told me about the building and Ed and Patty Bethel,[xxxvi] the current owners, confirmed that it actually consists of an early barn moved to the site and then added onto.

The building's odd shape comes from a triangular addition that fronted the former railroad tracks on its west side. It made the building fit the v-shaped intersection of Sagamore Street and the tracks.

Ready for another quiz? It's open to all, but if a question pertains to your town, extra homework awaits you if you don't know the answer. Here we go:

1. The Fort William Henry Corporation plans to recreate the 20th century "edition" of the Fort William Henry Hotel. What year was the 20th century version built? When was it razed?

2. Saratoga Springs is famed for its mineral waters. Can you name another

Saratoga County town famed for the same? And a town in Washington County? And a town in Bennington County, Vermont?

3. What was the first major hotel built in Saratoga Springs? In what year and by whom?

4. The train came first to which 19th century village: Fort Edward or Glens Falls?

5. Is Rogers Island in the Hudson River at Fort Edward named for the famed Rogers Rangers?

6. The first Sagamore Hotel in Bolton Landing opened in what year? And the current one first opened in what year?

7. Hague, New York, was named for what place?

Answers

1. The 20th century "edition" of the Fort William Henry Hotel was built in 1911 and razed in 1969. I can't wait for the new one.

2. Ballston Spa was famous for its mineral waters a decade before Saratoga Springs. In Washington County, Whitehall had a mineral water bottling plant, and Manchester, in Bennington County, Vermont, had both mineral baths and bottling works.

3. Saratoga Springs' first major hotel was the Grand Union, built in 1800 by Gideon Putnam. (No, the Gideon Bible did not take its name from Gideon's hotel.)

4. The train first came to Fort Edward in 1854. It was another 14 years before Fort Edward allowed the train to go to Glens Falls.

5. No, Rogers Island in the Hudson River at Fort Edward is not named for the famed Rogers Rangers. It is named for a later owner, also a Rogers, but not a Ranger.

6. The first Sagamore Hotel in Bolton Landing opened in 1883. The current Sagamore first opened in 1914.

7. Hague was first named Rochester, but no one knows why it was named either name. Perhaps the early settlers were indecisive people who gave up after two tries.

I close with a question having nothing and everything to do with our history. How long has it been since appointment of a permanent state historian?[xxxvii] The answer: 7 years. But who's counting?

Certainly no one at the state.

"OVER MY SHOULDER" COLUMN FOR APRIL 6, 2002
Looking back — and ahead

What does 1944 Glens Falls say to today's child?

Ask Jennine. Or Shauna. Or Bill. They were among Ms. Cormie's and Ms. Donohue's fourth graders of the Glens Falls Sanford Street

School visiting the Chapman Historical Museum's new exhibit, "Hometown, USA, A Second Look."

They found common ground with their World War II counterparts. I was in to see the exhibit, based upon the 1944 *Look* magazine series of six stories on Glens Falls, which *Look* dubbed "Hometown USA." I watched museum educators Robin Wright and Stan Malecki walk these kids through the exhibit. Honestly, the students looked like the children in the almost 60-year-old exhibit photographs. The boys' haircuts, especially, were so similar - short.

The exhibit's approach is different, embodying quotes from interviews done with people who lived in Glens Falls and Queensbury in World War II. It also takes in more of the whole war and postwar era of the 1940s.

Those students reacted beautifully to differences between then and now. Stan asked how much a soda, like a Pepsi, would cost in World War II. The kids shouted, "Fifty cents," trying to get that price as low as the "olden days."

"Five cents," said Stan. There was a millisecond of stunned silence, a reverential awe mixed with palpable disbelief, suddenly followed by a wavelike roar of "whoaaaaaa," and all such exclamations of unbridled envy.

Of course, as the exhibit points out, your average yearly income was around $1,800 - so you earned 43 cents an hour. You're really going to think about buying that soda. Oh, and if you could buy a car, the average price was $900 - half your yearly income.

The *Look* magazine 1943-44 reality clashed head-on with 2002's reality for those kids. Shauna and Jennine made two wonderful observations on 1943-44 downtown Glens Falls. Jennine said the streets were "so full of people." Shauna observed that the police patrolled on foot, as opposed "to riding in a car" today. Hmm.

There was the issue of war rationing and recycling and "collecting fat." The exhibit has great black and white and color photos of memorable images, including those famed salvage drives. Glenna Shanahan is quoted as recalling saving tin foil inner wrappers for chewing gum. This was how, she explained, a small child helped the war effort.

The war brought food and gas rationing, shortages of all kinds, and ingenious solutions, including Sunny Buchman's priceless memory about stockings. Women put pancake makeup on their legs and drew a pencil line up the backs of their legs to simulate the look of stockings, which had seams then. In that way, they kept from wearing out their nylon or, if lucky, silk stockings.

But, back to the issue of collecting fat. Animal and vegetable fat was rendered to produce a chemical used to make explosives, vital for victory. So, when Robin Wright brought up collecting fat, she got an interesting suggestion. One boy responded that they could get it by doing liposuctions.

I have this image of a patriotic poster with Uncle Sam in a surgical gown … Never mind.

The way kids responded to this exhibit was great. That's important. It was nice, too, to be able to buy a book called *Hometown Memories* that includes reprints of black and white photos from the *Look* series.

But honestly, the exhibit's color photos made me wish some philanthropist would underwrite a book to reprint the stunning color slides the Look photographers took in 1943. This exhibit's presentation could be the book's theme. The color slides are housed at Crandall Public Library.

For anyone who wishes to see what Mayor Regan's dream of a tree-lined Glen Street would look like in color, the *Look* color photos would fill the bill. And I believe the book would sell like hotcakes.

So, while some philanthropist ponders that, I'll be mulling over liposuctions and Uncle Sam in a surgical gown.

SECTION 2: AREA HISTORY

"OVER MY SHOULDER" COLUMN FOR FEBRUARY 3, 2001
Book was 4-year labor of love

Mama mia, *Con Amore, The Italian History of Fort Edward* is finally done! The 162-page history of the Italian community in Fort Edward is a model of how a group of people can write a much-needed history. I hope you'll contact the Fort Edward Historical Association to get your copy. It will provide you with inspiration to write your community's history. All profits from the publication go to the association.

There were 18 of us who volunteered for what can only be described as a four-year experiment in community book-writing – although sometimes, like family, we got pretty raucous about what was going to happen. Here, in alphabetical order are the volunteers: Leo Altizio, Anita Amorosi Arcuri, Nicholas "Chuckie" Cantiello, Andrew "Jerry" Cimo,[xxxviii] Pauline Massaro Corsall, Joseph Cutshall-King, Sadie Trackeno Dean, Andrew Esperti, Fanny Sarchioto Gaulin, Joseph Giorgianni, Josephine Cardinale Harris, John Mandolare, Joseph Munoff,[xxxix] Anne D'Angelico Murray, Christine Catone Murray, Mary Ann Choppy Nicholas, Mary Casini Smith,[xl] and Frank V. Williams (Francesco Vincenzo Guglielmini).[xli]

The committee is from all over the Tri-county area and had people ranging in age from their forties to their nineties. Its two oldest members are 90 and 96! Sadly, one of us, Christine Catone Murray did not live to see the book published.

All but one member has roots in the Fort Edward Italian community – me, the committee's only non-Italian. Happily, the rest of the committee did not hold that against me. Incidentally, my new name is Giuseppe.

If we all gave our time, one among us was our shepherd: Mary Cassini Smith. Thank you, Mary, for the travails you faced and the triumph you achieved.

The book has three sections: an introductory narrative, a second section of photos and text, followed by a third section of 33 pages of genealogy. The inspiration for the book's start is beautifully narrated in a section Mary wrote and I won't spoil that for you. However, once the Italian Heritage Committee of the Fort Edward Historical Association first got together in 1996, somehow it seemed things would flow quickly. If anyone had said it would take four years, there might not have been a book!

The committee sent a questionnaire to Fort Edward people of Italian descent. The information took a long time to retrieve. Not everyone responded. Wonderful genealogy and written narratives came back. They're on file at the historical association. On and off for four years Joe Munoff and Jerry Cimo collected genealogical data and entered and corrected it on computer. Two guys with no computer experience became pros and the product of their activity is on pages 127-159.

We were swimming in information and in photos from the community and the historical association. We constructed a database from state and federal census records and city directories spanning from 1875 to 1915. Sadly, it was so huge it could not be incorporated, but exists on computer. Jerry also constructed a list of Italian men and women who served in World Wars I and II. That is in the book.

When I wrote the first section, I incorporated some narratives from the questionnaire and others written by committee members. Some narratives were also used in the second section with the photos. Anne D'Angelico Murray did a stupendous job of pulling that photo section together.

In late 2000, Mary Casini Smith spurred us to finish. The committee met several times and it was like a family preparing for a new baby: lots of laughter, memories, tears, debating and fun. I'll miss those meetings.

While artist Dan Zollinger, a Cimo family member, produced a stunning cover, Joe Munoff provided the most needed but unsung jobs in the process, editing and proofing. We lost count of how many drafts Joe read and corrected!

Obviously, it's impossible to summarize four years' work in a column, and proper credits are expressed in the book, which I hope you'll read.

But let me just say to my fellow committee members, for the joy of working with you: "Grazie, con amore."

[AUTHOR'S POSTSCRIPT: This is a book that certainly needs to be updated.]

"OVER MY SHOULDER" COLUMN FOR FEBRUARY 10, 2001
Slavery, Confederacy cannot be separated

When is enough truly enough?

In a past column I responded to syndicated columnist Charley Reese,[xlii] who in this newspaper continues his promotion of the Confederacy and the Antebellum South as a noble cause. His cause grates at my guts.

Normally someone's living in what I consider a state of self-delusion wouldn't be an issue for this column or this newspaper. However, when that self-delusion deals with the misuse of history, it is rightfully an issue for this column. When that misuse is untruthful and hurtful to people, then it is rightfully an issue for this newspaper.

When one uses history to avoid the mistakes of the past, then it is good.

But when one perverts the facts of the past to avoid the past itself, then it can pollute the present.

On February 6, Reese wrote in the *Orlando Sentinel* on freedom of speech: "There should be no topic – and I mean no topic – that Americans cannot discuss and debate publicly and in full without being subjected to attempted intimidation by character assassination."

True, but at some point when what you say is not the truth, then someone has to trace the words to their creator's character. Words do not float out somewhere on their own. They do not come from seahorses or stones. Words come from people, spoken because of people's beliefs.

In the same article Reese wrote: "If there is one thing that should be totally absent from American life, it is fear on the part of an honest citizen to exercise his rights."

Absolutely. Reese, as an active member of the League of the South, ardently defends the Confederacy. The Confederacy upheld slavery. "Slaves," by the very definition of the word, have no rights to exercise. People who own slaves deny other people's rights.

The Constitution of the Confederate States of America, adopted March 11, 1861, refers to slavery and slaves several times, but the most powerful reference is Article I, Section 9., Paragraph 4: "No bill of attainder, or *ex post facto* law, or law denying or impairing the right of property in negro slaves shall be passed." The lower case "n" on Negro is an exact quote.

The same Confederate Constitution was modeled closely upon the 1789 United States Constitution, which itself upheld slavery. But even the US Constitution didn't outlaw the possibility of laws that could prohibit owning Black people. Interestingly, the Confederate Constitution preamble stated it was being created to "secure the blessings of liberty to ourselves and our posterity." Whose posterity?

Reese continued: "In truth there is no reason why any topic, however contentious, cannot be discussed in a civil manner, except for the malice of certain groups." Shall we civilly discuss, Mr. Reese, my contention that you deny what was done in the past? Shall we discuss that you publicly romanticize the Confederacy, thereby encouraging millions to deny a very sad, shameful, heinous and regrettable part of our nation's past?

Reese continues: "Whenever people reveal themselves to be uninterested in discussion, they should be shunned by civilized people."

Civilized people today don't own people. Yet Reese's hero, Robert E. Lee, was a slaveholder, a traitor who sought to destroy his country to uphold the right of people to own people. Because Reese denies the past, he promotes the Myth of Lee as a model for civilized behavior today.

Reese's article accuses those "uninterested in discussion" as "following the totalitarian model in which one's opponents are not bested in arguments but shouted down, intimidated and, in the end, coerced into silence."

Yet Reese's January 22nd column in this newspaper reverentially quoted Confederate president Jefferson Davis, whom Reese called "Jefferson Davis, my last president" in an article titled, "Confederate History Month: South just waiting to rise again..." What "negro slave" did Jeff Davis, the Stalin of the South, ever NOT coerce into silence?

Charley Reese cannot defend the right of personal freedom and defend the Confederacy in the same breath. Slavery was and is the death of personal freedom. The Confederacy was the political embodiment of that death and should be dead but is kept alive by monstrous lies that harm every citizen today.

Lie to yourself, Charley Reese, but not in this newspaper.

"OVER MY SHOULDER" COLUMN FOR FEBRUARY 24, 2001
Speaking up about the painful past

The other night, I was privileged to speak at the Greenwich Free Library about the great Frederick Douglass having spoken throughout the Greenwich area and having hallowed that ground with his presence.

I've written about him before, but he needs revisiting. By way of introduction, I'll paraphrase my talk from the other night, but express some of it in a way I may not have that night. Unlike Douglass, whose amazing career began with his rising to speak extemporaneously at an antislavery rally in 1841, I'm not much of a public speaker. That's not false modesty, just a fact. Often the thoughts I have take better shape for me in written form.

I began with a bit of background on Douglass, who was born Frederick Augustus Washington Bailey in 1817 or 1818 in Maryland. Today we might say that his parents were a Black woman and a white man. But Douglass described it best in his 1845 autobiography: "My mother was named Harriet Bailey. She was the daughter of Isaac and Betsey Bailey, both colored, and quite dark. My mother was of a darker complexion than either… My father was a white man. He was admitted to be such by all I ever heard speak of my parentage. The opinion was also whispered that my master was my father; but of the correctness of this opinion, I know nothing; the means of knowing was withheld from me."

He suspected his father to be his owner, Captain Aaron Anthony. But Douglass was not allowed to know. Nor was he allowed to know his birthday nor even what kind of person his mother truly was. Right after his birth, as was the system with slaves, she was sent far away and saw little of her son before she died. He was 7. He wrote later that her death meant as little to him as that of a stranger.

Deprived of the basic right to information, to freedom, to education, to any kind of life considered "normal" in that era, Frederick Augustus Washington Bailey managed to escape, take a new name, and begin a new life that ultimately made him an American hero.

I said that, to me, Douglass' parentage and his dual race symbolize the story of America's relationship with slavery. For slavery was more than an institution. It was more than a part of society. Slavery was a part of the family.

I might have misspoken that last sentence. What I meant and mean is that slavery was a part of a family called America. And today the family of America, like all families, denies or has a hard time talking about painful parts of its past.

My great-great uncle viciously beat his wife to abort her pregnancies. It was always "whispered" in the family, but never spoken aloud for the shame of it. Until now. And now there is a relief in its being spoken. The shame is exposed. The awful act is confronted.

If we as members of the family of America can speak openly of the painful things about slavery – and how it continues to infect our family today – we have a chance to go in a different direction. Otherwise, the hurt and shame embodied in the awful act of slavery will continue to pollute tomorrow.

We have one country, this "family of America." It has one history with many parts, some of which hurt like hell to discuss because, like wife-beating, they are disgusting and shameful. If we start to view one another as members of this family, with a common family history, we might see a time when we view one another as people first – rather than as "Black" people, "white" people, "whatever color" people to the exclusion of our common humanity.

It's hard, bitter, angry, frightening work to talk about a painful past with honesty. But it's all we have if the future is to be different.

Next week, Frederick Douglass' visit here and the need for its commemoration.

"OVER MY SHOULDER" COLUMN FOR MARCH 3, 2001
Washington County should honor Douglass

Between 1841, when Frederick Douglass first rose to speak extemporaneously before an anti-slavery rally in Nantucket and 1854, the year of his visit to Greenwich, New York, Douglass had already confirmed his place in American history.

Although his life after the Civil War brought presidential appointments, an ambassadorship to Haiti and further fame to the end of his life in 1895, I'm concentrating on his activities before and during the Civil War. Those built his reputation as author, lecturer, and fighter for the rights of all human beings, regardless of race or gender. His presence in Greenwich, I feel, merits plaques and markers being constructed to memorialize his presence, which confirm the importance of Greenwich and the region in the struggle against slavery.

Frederick Douglass spent his first 20 years in slavery and his escape to Massachusetts in 1838 meant only partial freedom, for as a fugitive slave, he was pursued relentlessly by bounty hunters. On the strength of his oratory,

William Lloyd Garrison hired Douglass to lecture for the American Anti-Slavery Society, which he did until 1845.

But accusations were made. Detractors said that his eloquence meant that Douglass was no runaway slave, but obviously a "freeman" born in the North. Douglass responded in 1845 with his first autobiography, the *Life of Frederick Douglass, An American Slave*, compelling reading that holds a permanent place in American literature.

He fled capture by going to Great Britain in 1845, where he lectured extensively. In 1846, his friends purchased his freedom for £150, about $600, and gave Douglass the ownership of himself. Imagine buying your friend, like buying a car, and then giving him the ownership papers?

The year after, he returned and moved to Rochester, New York, where he established a weekly newspaper, the *North Star*. Later that became *Frederick Douglass' Paper* and finally the *Douglass Monthly*.

In 1848, he attended the Women's Rights Convention in Seneca Falls, New York. Interestingly, not every abolitionist favored women's rights. Unlike most 19th century prominent activists, Douglass unconditionally supported the rights of women.

Though I don't have record of it, I assume that Douglass knew that Susan B. Anthony, one of that convention's cofounders, had spent part of her life in the Greenwich region. He must have thought about that in 1854 when he came to Greenwich, then a major stop on the Underground Railroad.

Douglass, who was writing his second autobiography, *My Bondage and My Freedom*, which came out in 1855, spoke extensively throughout the region, especially in Greenwich.

Greenwich had two totally separate abolitionist societies; one a Garrisonian society led by Dr. Corliss, the other the Free Democratic League, which had sponsored Douglass' visit.

On March 1st, 1854 Douglass spoke at the Congregational Church of Greenwich Village, and in the following days spoke again in Greenwich, in Galesville, Shushan, Cambridge and Easton. I know of at least two places where he spoke existing today: the Lakeville Baptist Church in Cossayuna and the Society of Friends meetinghouse in Easton. Standing or not, all those places where the great Frederick Douglass spoke should be memorialized. They were hallowed by his presence and by his cause.

In 1859, he assisted John Brown in planning a slave insurrection, but did not join the raid on Harper's Ferry. He fled to England to avoid prosecution.

The Civil War began, and Douglass was a recruiter for the Fifty-fourth Massachusetts, a Black regiment. Two of his sons served in it. In another connection to our region, Black volunteers from the Tri-Counties served in that regiment as well.

There is so much connecting Frederick Douglass with our region.

Let us immediately seize upon Governor Pataki's Freedom Trail initiative to see if grants can be secured to memorialize wherever Frederick Douglass appeared in our region, in order to remind ourselves and our children of the cause of freedom for which he stood.

"OVER MY SHOULDER" COLUMN FOR MARCH 24, 2001
1816: the year of no spring

Being an ardent "spring" person, the recent snows, still measuring a foot in my yard, are getting to me. I'm eating the grapes off the wallpaper.

However, I have to take heart from the lesson given in the story of the Cold Summer of 1816, the year there was no spring or summer.

Here's a bit of background. The Cold Summer of 1816 (sometimes called the Long Winter of 1816) began with dismal weather in 1815, a year of great triumph for our young country. The US was celebrating its victory over England in the War of 1812.

That war was actually the by-product of the European Napoleonic Wars, during which both England and France kidnapped American sailors. The neutral United States was dragged into war with England in 1812 only 29 years after it had signed a peace treaty ending the Revolutionary War.

The United States and Great Britain finally signed a peace treaty in late December of 1814, but news of that took so long to arrive to the US that the last battle fought was the Battle of New Orleans in January of 1815. Two months later, Napoleon was captured for a second time – and this time for good.

Although the winter of 1815 started out normally, the entire year had been bad and, according to the Warren County History of 1886, there had been a devastating crop failure in the summer of 1815.

When the weather went awry in 1816, people placed the blame for everything on what happened during the wars in Europe and the United States, blaming all the cannon firings for disrupting the atmosphere.

Here's why. When it came time for the 1815-1816 winter to end and change into the spring of 1816, nothing happened. It just kept snowing – through April, May and right straight through June.

It eased off in mid-July and stopped completely during August of 1816. There was some time to get crops in for planting, but then it began to snow again in September.

And it snowed right through to mid-Spring of 1817, by which time the weather returned to normal. Essentially, the region had almost a straight year and a half of winter.

Things throughout our region and up through parts of Canada and New England were terrible. Thousands starved to death in spite of massive efforts by the government and individuals to help. There were no canals through this area at that time, and the railroads had not been invented, making an awful situation even worse. Many endured horrible hardships to travel beyond the famine area to buy and bring back food for both humans and animals. Not everyone was so generous. The Warren County history noted, "many who possessed the means of relieving the less fortunate declined to do so except at such exorbitant rates as to practically shut out the poor."

Now, going back to people's theories on the cause of it, some thought it was divine wrath. Others, as I mentioned, thought that the enormous wars in Europe and the United States, especially Europe, had altered the weather by the huge amount of cannon firings and gunpowder used.

They actually were on the right track, for the truth is that Mother Nature had provided the "cannon" that caused it. That cannon took the form of the Indonesian volcano of Mt. Tambora, which had erupted in April 1815. It was the world's largest volcanic explosion in 10,000 years and it threw so much dust up into the atmosphere that it altered the weather in many parts of the world for almost three years.

So, in light of the Cold Summer of 1816, and putting things into perspective as a mature adult should, I suppose I shouldn't complain of the snow we're having now.

But if it goes on into June, I'll be writing this column from Brazil.

"OVER MY SHOULDER" COLUMN FOR APRIL 21, 2001
Mettawee or Mettowee

My daily planner has a "grass catcher" section, where you put ideas that defy definition.

Two recent topics suggested to me are like that. But they're related enough that it seemed they'd make a good column.

Credits are due to Jack Wiberg of Glens Falls and Don Tripp of Hudson Falls for puzzles thrust my way. Jack's was offered first.

A bit of background. I have a fascination with old words and sayings thanks to my mother, Jane, who collected them like antiques. That is to say, by the cubic yard. She'd see a wagon load of hay and say, "Make a wish!" Or, on some days yell at me "You're not going to traipse all over hell's half acre today!"

Because of some research, I was discussing with Jack about some words and phrases used today that come right from the Revolutionary War period – and how many relate to guns. I'd found the phrase "shooting iron" in the book *The Sexagenary – Or Reminiscences of the American Revolution*. Its author, John P. Becker,[xliii] had been 11 years old when the Revolution began in 1775.

Becker and his father had been helping General Knox haul Fort Ticonderoga cannon to Boston in early 1776. They passed through a Massachusetts village where the people had never seen a huge cannon before. Those folks called the cannon a big "shooting iron." Surprise! I thought "shooting iron" was a Wild West term.

Of course, those villagers had in mind a big flintlock, or musket. And it made me think of a phrase associated with flintlocks so much a part of our language today: "lock, stock and barrel." That refers to parts of a musket. The lock is the part where the explosive charge is detonated. The stock is the wooden frame. The barrel, of course, is the barrel. If you have the "lock, stock and barrel," you have it all.

Well, on that explosive topic of gunpowder, Jack said that as a boy growing up in Brooklyn, people there always said that a no-good person "wasn't worth the powder to blow him to Whitehall."

To Whitehall? I'd grown up hearing that said, "wasn't worth the powder to blow him to hell."

Whitehall is a street in Manhattan. Also a street in London with so many government offices that Whitehall is a synonym for the British government. And, as Jack said, when he moved up here he discovered there was a Whitehall, New York.

But we certainly can't be thinking that anyone would associate our Whitehall with a certain hot region "down below." The saying must refer to another Whitehall.

And Whitehall leads me to Don Tripp. My wife and I were dining out one evening when we saw Don and his wife, Mary. Don came up to our table and asked, out of the blue, how I would spell the name of a particular river that flows through the towns of Whitehall and Granville.

Did I spell it "Mettawee" or "Mettowee?" Wiping gravy from my chin, I think I said Mettawee, with an "a" instead of an "o."

Don had noticed in his work that the current spelling is with an "a," as in Mettawee. However, he discovered that the 1853 map of Washington County shows it spelled with an "o."

Uh-oh. Somewhere along the line it appears it to have come to be misspelled. Don, do you realize how many maps might have to be changed now? You'd better watch out. Somebody is probably going to wish you'd "go to Whitehall."

But then, we could treat it like Cole Porter's song, which gets into pronouncing words like either:

"You say 'ee-ther' and I say, 'eye-ther.'

You say 'nee-ther' and I say, 'neye-ther.'"

You spell Mettawee and I spell Mettowee.

Let's call the whole thing off.[xliv]

"OVER MY SHOULDER" COLUMN FOR APRIL 28, 2001
Jane McCrea death still a mystery

Two histories suggested for my reading have cast some doubt on facts I presented in my past columns on the death of Jane McCrea in July 1777. One is the 1993 *White Captives: Gender and Ethnicity on The American Frontier* by June Namias.[xlv] It analyzes tales of women in captivity on the American frontier. One section is on Jane McCrea.

The book has a feminist approach, which is good. There is great need for new methods to reinterpret old facts, but the information needs to be substantiated. Instead, Namias appears to be using history to support a pet theory. Namias starts out with a few paragraphs, ending them by saying, "so much for the facts of the story, many of which remain in dispute to this day."

There she was right. Where she was wrong was in using as a major underpinning of her book that "a woman who had run off with a Tory soldier was transformed into a martyred revolutionary heroine."

Supposedly, McCrea left her house to join her Loyalist fiancé who was in Burgoyne's army, something I'd written as fact. I cannot say now that it is so.

The other book, recently sent me by Bill Richards, is the 1910 *Facts and Traditions concerning the Argyleshire Clan Campbell*, by Katherine Campbell Norton Lewis, the great-great-great granddaughter of Sarah McNeil. It was from McNeil's house that Jane McCrea had been taken just before her death. In it Lewis writes, "the romance connected with the story of Jane McCrea's murder is purely fiction." She provides strong enough evidence to cast substantial doubt on the Loyalist lover theory.

If Namias had only criticized the romantic drivel about McCrea's death – the novels, plays and histories – written from 1784 onward, she would have produced a strong argument to help us draw a clear difference between the solid few facts there are about McCrea and the later romanticized nonsense, especially of the early 19th century. Instead Namias blurred facts of McCrea's time with later legend.

So much of McCrea's life is supposition, something I learned from educator Eileen Hannay[xlvi], one of the best local authorities on the complexities of the McCrea myth. Namias writes that the Jane McCrea narrative "is a discourse on female choice." Unfortunately, we know little, if anything, of what Jane McCrea actually chose.

We do know Jane McCrea actually lived and that she died in the company of one of General Burgoyne's Indian scouting parties, led by a man named LeLoup. Burgoyne reported on her death. General Gates wrote to Burgoyne to protest it. It was reported in Boston newspapers by mid-August.

We know she was sister to supporter of the revolutionary cause [originally written: "a Rebel"], John McCrea, while it appears she was a Loyalist. We know she was at Mrs. McNeil's house on, it appears, July 27th, 1777. Mrs. McNeil stated it was to help sew the wedding dress of her granddaughter, Polly. Other sources say she was being taken to Burgoyne's lines to meet her fiancé, David Jones. As Mrs. McNeil was taken at the same time by the same Indian scouts who took Jane, Mrs. McNeil seems the best witness.

We don't really know why the Indians took the two women, who were separated. Jane died out of Mrs. McNeil's sight, and how, we don't know. It appears she was scalped and if so we are not are sure why. Supposedly someone else was a captive, but that is unproven.

Why does all this matter now? Because, it is claimed, her death so angered thousands they swelled the Rebel (Patriot) ranks and defeated Burgoyne at Saratoga. Possibly the Turning Point of the Revolution itself turned on the death of one woman. Possibly our nation owes its existence, in part, to her death.

That fact would have great meaning. But until we nail down what is certain, and to what degree McCrea's death meant anything, let's start using words like maybe and possibly – and stop confusing 19th century romanticism with 18th century facts.

"OVER MY SHOULDER" COLUMN FOR MAY 5, 2001
Spellings varied long ago

We return to a controversy started two weeks ago, the case of Mettawee vs. Mettowee.

Don Tripp of Washington County's Real Property Department had asked me if it were Mettawee, as in the river, or Mettowee, as in the Granville street? The Real Property folks have given me good-natured grief for not deciding. I'm flattered to have such power and hereby proclaim that everything named Mettawee or Mettowee be renamed Smith. Then there would be no problem.

Unless, of course, you are spelling Smith with a "y" instead of an "i" as in "Smyth." But that word could be pronounced Smith or "Smeyeth," as in Patrick Smyth who in 1772 built what is called today the Old Fort House[xlvii].

Seriously, the issue is complex because even as late as the Civil War, spelling was just more phonetic. It had less to do with educational levels than just a more relaxed attitude toward spelling. If you came close and everybody knew what you meant, – hey, no problem.

General Burgoyne referred to Hubbardton, Vermont, as Huberton. Nobody raised an eyebrow.

Spelling became more formalized and regulated after the Civil War, as two things became more widespread, public education and printed materials. As the public became more literate, it bought more magazines, books and newspapers. And printing became cheaper because of techniques for inexpensively converting wood into paper. Why do you think Finch Pruyn went from being a major lumber supplier to a major paper maker? Exactly.

Back to Mettawee vs. Mettowee. It may be insolvable, as the word was originally Indian[xlviii] – Mahican, I think – and phonetically spelled into English. Holden's 1874 history of Queensbury[xlix] states that the "Mettowee" was the "Indian name of the Pawlet River." Now there's a solution. Substitute Pawlet for every instance of Mettawee and Mettowee.

Think of it this way: if the early settlers couldn't consistently spell something in their own language, how were they going to consistently spell something from another language? I've seen Queensbury also spelled as Queensborough and Kingsbury as Kingsborough.

Glens Falls first started out as Glen's Falls. But you could get around that by reverting to one of the two Indian names that Holden noted for Glens Falls: Chepontuc or Pangasolink. Pangasolink, Hometown USA. Just trips off the tongue.

Admittedly, I'm not being fair. In the colonial days, Saratoga and Ticonderoga, both Indian in origin, each had dozens of English spellings: Saraghtoga, Saraghtogue, Sharlatoga, and Tienderoga, Tiaontoroken, Teahtontaloga, to name a few. Today, they are standardized as Saratoga and Ticonderoga. Saratoga's name, incidentally, was standardized so the handicappers betting the ponies would not have to strain themselves.

It may just be too late to standardize Mettawee but think of it on the bright side. What if we were suddenly to revert to every original Indian name? Schroon would revert to Skaghnetaghrowahna, Fort Edward to Wahcoloosencoochaleva, and Whitehall to Wompachookglenosuck.

As it is, many folks in Whitehall have been agitating for years to rename Whitehall, but in this case to the town's first colonial name of Skenesborough[1]. To which I reply, do you also mean Skeinsboro or Skenesboro? Because I've seen both of those spellings – and more.

Incidentally, regarding Whitehall, I must sadly report no origin has yet been found for the old saying heard by Jack Wiberg about something "not worth the powder to blow it to Whitehall." Bill Richards said his grandfather sometimes called Whitehall "White-hell," making me wonder what was going on up there in grandpa's day and even long before.

One thing's for sure. Nobody way back then ever walked around casually saying something was "not worth the powder to blow it to Wompachookglenosuck."

A final ruling on Metto, Metta-whatever. Use Mettowee instead of Mettawee, except before "River."

Or, except in all months having an "r" in them.

Or during a leap year.

Or in sounding like a, as in neighbor or weigh.

"OVER MY SHOULDER" COLUMN FOR MAY 12, 2001
Revolution through a minister's eyes

Often, when we depict the past, we don't allow the people back then to be human. Thanks to Tom Nesbitt[li], I have a copy of the diary of Enos Hitchcock, D. D., a very human minister, and a Congregational chaplain the Revolutionary army.

Born in 1764, Hitchcock attended Harvard, and then became a minister. He moved to Beverly, Massachusetts. Later he was a fellow at Brown University and distinguished himself in academic circles.

My interest in him is for the little diary he kept during the Revolution, especially in 1777, when he was in our area, ministering to the soldiers fighting the British General John Burgoyne. The diary wonderfully portrays Rev. Hitchcock as a very human person in the thick of a campaign that created our country.

From his first diary entry of April 8, 1777, we know that Hitchcock had human appetites. On that day he departed for Ticonderoga, where he had served in 1776. He usually traveled a day, then would stay at someone's home. Between then and May 23, he went through Massachusetts, Vermont, and then New York, and dined at dozens of places, thankfully listing them all.

On May 11th Hitchcock met a Captain Greenleaf, whom he paid, "ten [dollars] for my share of Tickets No. 3014 & 3015."

Mystified? Hitchcock was playing the lottery, which was a very common form of financing government operations. Sounds familiar…

Hitchcock faced death at Brookfield's hospital starting April 12, when he was purposely infected with smallpox, a procedure meant to inoculate him, but which could have killed him. He writes taking a "mercurial pill," a pill filled with deadly mercury! He details – too graphically for here – the "pock" that rose on him.

On May 1, "Soreness abates." It is "a day of public fasting." But the next two days he "dined freely on boiled chicken." He left the hospital May 15, crossed to Williamstown, then up to Bennington, recording every stop, the weather, even where he "oated" his horse.

Between May 19 and May 23, when he reached Fort Ti, he made good time and dined well, in Bennington at Captain Billings on May 19 and Fay's on the 20th. – then Manly's in Dorset and Latherbees in Powlett (Pawlet) on the 21st. Corees in Granville on the 22nd and "Captain Wakines" at "Skene" (Skenesborough) on the 23rd. He arrived by ship at Ticonderoga that day.

The sole entry for May 24: "Dined upon flowr pudding & Venison Steak."

In early June, he notes having a "head ake" for days, but on June 6, writes that, "after a fine Supper of Vension Stakes, this may seem strange, but it cured my Head ake."

A larger headache loomed. By June 12, after two days of buying lottery tickets, he knew Burgoyne had landed, possibly "10,000" strong.

His diary shows the tension. On June 17, the lines were attacked and men killed. General Schuyler left camp June 22. The enemy now approached Crown Point. By the 26th, he had reported scalpings by Indians moving toward Skene. On the 28th a "Lt. Huax" deserted.

Then calm. On June 30 and July 1, there was "no disturbance."

It was his last "peaceable" moment of the campaign. On July 2, enemy boats shelled the batteries. Men were wounded, killed and captured. Hitchcock wrote, in breathless words filled with knowledge that all hell had broken loose: "they say the Enemy are 5600 strong."

He fled south to Skenesborough, over the next three months going through Fort Ann, Fort Edward, and Fort Miller to Saratoga. He recorded everything: from dinner with Benedict Arnold on July 22, to war's butchery, whether soldier or civilian, such as Jane McCrea, on July 26.

His diary is a marvelous, readable and very human picture of one hero who helped defeat Burgoyne.

By the way, the last words of Hitchcock's last entry, dated September 19, 1777 were: "dined at Headquarters."

"OVER MY SHOULDER" COLUMN FOR JUNE 16, 2001
Schools should keep America first

This past Thursday, *The Post-Star* ran an Associated Press story under the headline "Benedict Arnold's name to see the light of day."

The New York Times ran the same AP story under the headline "Plaque of Famed Traitor on Exhibit."

The article told how, on Thursday, June 14, "exactly 200 years" after Arnold's death, the Saratoga National Historical Park in Stillwater completed "an exhibit featuring a plaque," donated in 1938 by the Daughters of the American Revolution. The plaque "lists the 16 American generals who fought in the two Battles of Saratoga on Sept. 19 and Oct. 7 in 1777." It includes Arnold's name.

In 1938, the DAR felt enough time had passed to honor Arnold's good deeds, without that honor overshadowing that he had turned traitor. It generated such controversy that the plaque was removed in 1978. It is still causing controversy.

Frankly, and I don't mean to be crude, but so few Americans know enough about the Revolution or even give a damn about it, it's a wonder to me that there are enough people around even to be upset. They must all meet in a phone booth.

My bet is that if *The Post-Star* posted a reporter in downtown Saratoga, Glens Falls or Lake George this summer and quizzed the average citizen, but especially the average school-aged child, fewer than 30 percent would be able to state who Benedict Arnold was.

In fact, I'll bet fewer than 5 percent could tell you who any of the generals were who fought at Saratoga, whether British or American. I'll bet most of you couldn't.

In that vein, the AP article's author could have done more homework. While the article mentions the famed 1887 "boot sculpture,"[lii] it ignores the 1877 monument that straddles the villages of Victory and Schuylerville. Also, the article made it sound as if Fort Ticonderoga is the only place having a marker bearing Arnold's name. Hardly.

And get this. In the Times, the article stated, "Among other things, he [Arnold] is credited with building a fleet of ships for the 1776 Valcour Island battle, considered the birthplace of the U.S. Navy." *The Post-Star* story corrected that by noting the ships were built at Skenesborough, which, it correctly stated, is considered the birthplace.[liii]

Going back to the issue of the plaque, I believe that both Arnold stories, his heroism and treachery, should be told. His life illustrates the complexity of the Revolution, and how perilously close we came to losing it. But I also believe that because our children don't know the story of the Revolution, Arnold's story exists in a vacuum.

And our children simply don't know their own history.

In 1914, Glens Falls educator Sherman Williams[liv], then head of the state Department of Education, wrote that the teaching of local history–and American history—should come first. He complained that children learned more about the histories of tiny countries in Europe than of the United States.

We're arriving at that point again. The current state curriculum seems more interested in solving the political issue of whether the British deliberately starved the Irish to death in the potato famine. Meanwhile the history behind the words "The United States" eludes the majority of our children.

The Department of Education should emphasize local and state history first and give more support to our history teachers. It's nice the kids are getting a worldview, but if they end up unable to tell you how many counties the state has and in which county Benedict Arnold fought at the Battle of Saratoga, we have a problem. And we do have a problem.

Agree? Disagree? Drop me a line. Tell me how you feel.

But beware if your answer sounds like this: "I don't care, Joe, and frankly you're full of it. None of this stuff makes any difference."

Because if your answer sounds like that, Benedict Arnold won.

"OVER MY SHOULDER" COLUMN FOR JUNE 23, 2001
Our beloved "ogas" make news

American history's two "oga" places—Saratoga and Ticonderoga—got well-deserved attention this week.

Tuesday, Governor Pataki announced Saratoga Springs would be home to the New York State Military Museum and Veterans Research Center, more about which in a moment.

All this week, the news has centered on Ticonderoga and the French and Indian War re-enactment focused on the death of Lord George Viscount Howe. Lord Howe was killed July 6, 1758 during a fight with the French in the Town of Ticonderoga, at a spot still heavily debated by historians. Organizer Bob Bearor expects a thousand re-enactors to participate.

The event started Wednesday. Thursday, a flotilla of re-enactors sailed northward on Lake George to commemorate Howe's trip to Ticonderoga. Yesterday the re-enactment of Howe's death occurred. Today Fort Ticonderoga hosts battle re-enactments, and the new Boscawen Cup Competition of replica 18th century boats on Lake Champlain.

While Bob Bearor's wonderful event was splashed all over the papers, Governor Pataki's in-person announcement of the new military museum being placed in Saratoga Springs had to be one of the year's better kept secrets.

Tuesday, Pataki officiated over the dedication of the new museum in the New York Army National Guard Armory on Lake Avenue. If success is measured by the number of politicians present, then the new museum is guaranteed. Pataki was joined by Congressman Sweeney, State Senator Bruno, and Assemblyman D'Andrea, among others.

They were impressively flanked by military re-enactors, clothed in uniform from nearly every period. I saw Kingsbury Civil War re-enactor Dan Smith[lv] there, clothed, like the rest, in sweltering woolens. I marveled at his stamina.

An appropriate choice for the museum was the 1889 Lake Avenue Armory, considered the model for similar armories throughout the nation. The 31,000 square foot armory will actually be the museum's largest "artifact" when the 10,000-piece collection is moved in by 2002.

That collection, started in 1863, is bathed in controversy. For years it suffered from poor storage, even theft. Governor Pataki led the way in getting funds to catalog and properly store the collection. Governor, may your attention to that museum's needs also fall upon the state museum and every museum in New York.

A burning issue regards the 1,800 battle flags in the collection, half from the Civil War, including captured Confederate battle flags. Their deterioration led southern states to demand their return. At the ceremony, Michael Russert[lvi], member of the state's commission on those flags, scoffed at that. "Return them? With the blood of all those northern dead on those flags?" he asked. "Never." That point is moot now.

Scott Sandman, of the Division of Military and Naval Affairs, said the building will remain an armory, serving an element of detachment 2, Co. C 2nd of the 105th Infantry. However, Medical Co. C of the 427 Support Battalion will be reunited with its parent unit at Glens Falls. This will leave more than adequate space for a quality museum and the remaining infantry detachment.

Let me offer sincerest congratulations to all who made this dream of the military museum come true—and ask a favor. It's inspired by a comment I heard in Governor Pataki's dedication. He declared that Saratoga was "the birthplace of American freedom." Momentarily, I feared he mistook Saratoga Springs for the Towns of Stillwater and Saratoga, where the Battles of Saratoga actually took place.

But he knew his history and correctly referred to the nearby Saratoga National Historical Park as enshrining those battlefields of Saratoga.

Let me urge you, the members of the new military museum, likewise to remember always where that national park is. For without that "birthplace of American freedom," all the subsequent battles that took place would never have occurred, and the military and country for which you stand today, would never have come to be.

And you readers? Don't just sit there. Call them up and volunteer.

"OVER MY SHOULDER" COLUMN FOR JULY 6, 2001
Revolution took a turn in Whitehall

Two hundred twenty-four years ago yesterday, Whitehall, NY, was the site of what I believe to be the only naval battle of General John Burgoyne's Campaign to end the American Revolution.

It was July 6, 1777. American colonists were slugging it out against the world's mightiest war machine, the British Army.

In our region, General John Burgoyne moved southward from Canada with approximately 8,000 troops. On July 1, the general had attacked Fort Ticonderoga in New York and Mount Independence in Vermont by land and water.

The British seized Fort Mount Hope by July 3rd. Then on July 4, 1777, British regulars were hauling massive cannon up steep Mount Defiance. On July 5, British cannon pointed downward on Fort Ti.

You must visit Fort Ti and Mount Defiance to appreciate the strategic coup the British had achieved. Mount Defiance looks down on Fort Ti. When the British stood atop it, they could hurl cannonballs down the chimneys of Fort Ti. Ironically, both the American Generals Philip Schuyler and Horatio Gates had rejected the advice to fortify Mount Defiance.

The Americans at Fort Ticonderoga, led by General St. Clair, decided to evacuate the Fort during the night and fled into Vermont. When Burgoyne learned of it, he sent General Simon Fraser to pursue them. By the 6th of July, Burgoyne had successfully seized both Fort Ticonderoga and Mount Independence, sealing up one of North America's major water routes.

Leaving a military contingent at Fort Ti, Burgoyne headed south by water towards Whitehall, then Skenesborough, accompanied by the founder of that town, Philip Skene. They sailed on what we today call Lake Champlain. But in 1777, the lake south of Fort Ti was regarded as a part of Wood Creek. Burgoyne sailed south with several ships and hundreds of bateaux. Right ahead of him was Colonel Pierce Long, heading up a flotilla of escaping Americans, also heading south for Skenesborough.

That armada of ships and bateaux came into the harbor where Wood Creek met the junction of the Poultney River to form East Bay. If you look at a map today, this area has been incorporated into the NYS Barge Canal. Still, some of the beautiful landscape remains, including the rock precipices. According to Richard Ketchum's "Saratoga,"[lvii] Burgoyne's fleet sailed in among those precipices along East Bay, so close they could almost touch the rocks. The rebels, as the Americans were called, could have ambushed them, but did not, Ketchum noted.

Probably they were in such a state of disarray and confusion they could only think of trying to save themselves. At the foot of the waterfall near the blockhouse in what today would be downtown Whitehall, Colonel Long[lviii] decided to send the non-combatants, such as women, children and ministers, in boats south along Wood Creek toward Fort Ann.

So, on July 6, 1777, on approximately the site of the present canal, and only a few feet south of Lock 20, General Burgoyne's armada caught up with the American Colonel Long. Even as the American non-combatants were busily readying to head south, cannonball flew at the American fleet.

The Americans gave it back as best they could, but three of their craft were destroyed, the Enterprise, Liberty and Gates. Ironically, the Liberty had been Philip Skene's own ship, the Katherine, which Benedict Arnold had captured and converted to naval purposes in 1775.

Two other American craft surrendered. Between both sides on that July 6th, five ships and 300 bateaux were sunk. The British seized Skenesborough and won the day.

But the Americans fled and ultimately regrouped to fight Burgoyne again. Also, the engagement at Skenesborough was yet another delay for Burgoyne on his fateful trip to defeat at Saratoga.

How fitting it is that Whitehall, which we regard as the birthplace of the US Navy, should have been the site of the only naval battle of the Burgoyne Campaign, which itself turned the course of American history.

"OVER MY SHOULDER" COLUMN FOR AUGUST 25, 2001
Agricultural history at the fair

This week I spent a few days at the Washington County Fair, meeting people in my capacity as county historian. Joyce St. Jacques of the fair's museum committee graciously set me up with a table in the Farmer's Museum.

There, amidst ancient and not so ancient farm machinery, I learned a lot. For example, the Farmer's Museum improves dramatically with every year and its new exhibits give people a sense of the incredible changes in farming, now more accurately termed the agriculture industry.

Those visitors with the greatest interest in the museum, and in my information, were among the over-40 crowd. Many wanted family history. I referred them to a genealogist named Loretta Bates who works in my office.

A surprising number asked for information on dating their homes. I directed them to the county planning department's 1976 historic structures survey.

I was most interested in the range of reaction of the kids and young adults who came through. Most expressed polite interest for thirty seconds, after which they'd begin rapid eye movements that said, "Where's the door?"

The extreme was best represented by a 12-year-old girl, slumping dejectedly in a nearby pew from an old church, while grandma looked with enthusiasm at the artifacts. The girl was aggressively bored and said so. Of everyone, she made me think the longest about what could be done to capture her imagination about the past.

However, a visit from a young Corinth woman showed that an interest in history among our youth is alive and that a cure for "history boredom" is at hand. Anne Clothier[lix] of Corinth stopped to ask a question about the death of Jane McCrea in 1777 and, in a second, I recognized a person passionate about the past.

Anne is a re-enactor, part of a growing movement of people who recreate past events, such as by portraying the soldiers and civilians of the various wars that the US has engaged in. Anne does both French and Indian War and Revolutionary War re-enactment, authentically re-creating her own period costumes and diligently studying the period she portrays.

Some historians dismiss re-enactors as being too narrowly focused, or poorly informed. It's dangerous to tar a group of tens of thousands of people with one brush. Through my daughter's involvement in re-enacting, I met many re-enactors, many of them serious historians who contribute greatly to our understanding and enjoyment of the past.

In fact, as we spoke, Anne was citing several obscure sources she has consulted – quite a researcher. And I was pleasantly surprised to find she's just beginning college this fall. I see a bright future for her and for our history.

But the whole fair itself is an object lesson in the history of agriculture. It is impossible to miss the fundamental connection of farming to human existence when one sees the parade of goats, chickens and other animals, and the displays of prize-winning vegetables, the stuff of life.

Like New York State, Washington County's foremost industry is agriculture. Frankly, I could hear the worry in the voices of those whose lives are in and on the land: rising taxes on their chief "tool," the land, dropping commodities prices, and the suburbanization that is taking farmland permanently out of production.

History has proven every economic up and down can be predicted in our farmlands, making farmers the bellwether of our nation. Oh, incidentally, bellwether is a farming term – a male sheep that leads the flock, usually with a bell on its neck.

But right now the Washington County Fair is on and, whatever their concerns, the farming community is there to show that the among best things our nation has produced, so many have come – and will continue to come – right off the farm.

And it's certainly one of the most enjoyable living history lessons there is.

"OVER MY SHOULDER" COLUMN FOR OCTOBER 13, 2001
Burleigh was a self-made man

The most complex phrase in the obituary was the headline "A Useful Career Ended."

Recently my friend John LaPointe[lx] gave me an obituary of a man named Henry Gordon Burleigh. It actually was an entire supplement to *The Whitehall Times*, published August 23, 1900.

I read it, pondering the word "useful" that appeared several times. It was a Victorian sensibility, describing a person's life as useful. But it was well chosen because Burleigh fit the character of his time. He was a self-made man in a time that valued self-made people even more highly than today, because there were fewer avenues for doing so.

The 19th century was economically volatile, and a person could be wealthy one moment and literally in the poorhouse the next. Staying wealthy was the trick and H. G. Burleigh managed to build and keep wealth, power and influence from the time he was only 18.

Born in Canaan, New Hampshire in 1832, he moved to Ticonderoga with his parents in 1846, the year of the Mexican War. The move, if I read the obit correctly, ended his schooling, although his love of learning continued for life. He went to work in a general store and lumber dealership that failed when Burleigh was 18. Burleigh actually bought the business. It was 1850. By 1860, Burleigh had not only turned the business around, but had brought in his brother Bracket, started building canal boats, and opened a second office in Whitehall, the northern hub of the Champlain Canal. Burleigh began to split his business life between the towns, a 25-mile distance.

The whole region still had somewhat of a frontier quality to it. The main shipping transport from St. Jean, Quebec to Albany, New York was the canal, and that only in the warm season. The railroad would not connect Whitehall and Plattsburgh until 1873. To make the trip between offices, Burleigh had to take the stage, an 8 to 10 hour, bone-jarring trip, especially slow during bad weather. Numerous times "he walked the entire distance, beating the time of the stage by several hours."

He finally moved to Whitehall with his family, the obit states, "because of the natural advantages possessed by the place from a commercial standpoint." And not having to walk 25 miles.

Burleigh was obviously charismatic, shrewd, brilliant in business and a born leader. He entered "hundreds of partnership deals," bought tens of thousands of acres of land, controlling vast stretches along Lake George. He expanded his lumber interests, developing the shareholding Whitehall Lumber Company, eventually buying out almost everyone. He became a major shareholder in literally scores of banks and other businesses, including Ticonderoga Pulp and Paper Company and, eventually, International Paper. His transportation company grew through mergers to become the lead firm between St. Jean and Albany.

As a civilian during the Civil War, Burleigh raised troops in Ti, underwrote the town's allotment to the war, and once even commandeered a steamship on Lake Champlain for his troops. Through his eloquence he convinced the captain and passengers to surrender enough rooms for his men.

That eloquence was applied to politics. Burleigh had served in Ti as Republican supervisor, but upon moving to Democratic Whitehall was severely trounced. He vowed he'd make Whitehall Republican.

He was elected to the assembly in 1875 in "the most aggressive" campaign ever waged in Washington county. His ability was such that none of his bills was ever vetoed by a governor. The bulk of his work centered on canal system reform, rebuilding it, restructuring its debt, bringing equality to the tolls on its various branches, and making the State Engineer's appointment subject to Canal Board confirmation, thereby stopping horrendous fraud and waste.

Unrelated to canals, but affecting another waterway, was Burleigh's bill that prohibited sale of Lake George islands without an act of the Legislature, a radical act for its time.

Next week, Mr. Burleigh goes to Congress, and the conclusion of his story.

"OVER MY SHOULDER" COLUMN FOR OCTOBER 20, 2001
Burleigh was big in politics

We conclude the story of Henry Gordon Burleigh. Having started his career and immense fortune, his married life with Jane Richards, and his political life all in Ticonderoga, Henry Gordon Burleigh moved his family to Whitehall for business reasons. There, Republican Burleigh got his first political shellacking in the early 1870s.

By 1875, Burleigh had trounced his Democratic opposition in a vicious race for the Assembly. His obituary in *The Whitehall Times* of August 23, 1900, noted that "calumny and vituperation reeked in the county press, and charges of fraud and lying were made by both parties." So unlike our wholesome and noble politics of today.

Burleigh's stint in the New York State Assembly catapulted him into the US Congress in 1882. He represented the Rensselaer-Washington District, which included the powerful city of Troy.

Burleigh's obituary repeatedly called him "useful." That was because Burleigh was an effective party whip, getting out the vote and getting bills passed for our region's betterment. He eliminated the "tonnage tax on our northern frontier boats" and got money for Lake Champlain's ports.

Those bills reflected Burleigh's shipping business interests, but he was no "pocket-liner." He fought for the region's betterment and was clever at it. Consider his Troy post office bill. The Speaker of the House would not yield Burleigh the floor to discuss his bill. Burleigh "waited until the speaker went to lunch," then got a Minnesota Congressman to yield the floor. Burleigh orchestrated 100 Troy businessmen to flood the House with telegraphs supporting the bill and it passed within a day.

His power over Washington County politics was legendary. At the Chicago Republican presidential convention of 1884, President Chester A. Arthur was being rejected because he had gone against the party and pushed the Pendleton Civil Service Reform bill. Washington County delegates were behind his opponent James G. Blaine two to one. So great was Burleigh's persuasiveness that he swung the entirety of the votes behind his friend Arthur.

However, Arthur told Burleigh that he would leave the White House and throw his support to Blaine. Burleigh announced it to the hushed convention and delivered the New York vote to Blaine.

Burleigh's worst political fights were actually in Washington County. His most ardent foe was another political warhorse, former NYS Railroad Commissioner I. V. Baker, Jr., of Comstock. For decades Burleigh waged ferocious battles with his political enemy Baker, the fiercest being the "Argyle mob convention" in 1895, something we'll revisit later.

Burleigh developed cancer in 1898. Within two years he was dead, a year after his wife. In August of 1900, he had gone to New York seeking medical help, and stayed in his Manhattan apartment on West End Avenue. But he returned to his Whitehall home, where he died only days later among family. As the obituary stated, "the Waterloo of his life came when the Great Jehovah calmly passed His hand across the forehead of the great Burleigh."

Symbolic of that greatness were the hundreds upon hundreds of people from the United States and Canada who attended his funeral services in Whitehall. Of those, three hundred went with the casket on the funeral train to Ticonderoga for services and burial. They were joined in Ticonderoga by hundreds more.

The paper listed so many of the attendees, prominent people of his day, such as Congressman L. W. Emerson of Warrensburg, Mrs. M. K. Neville of New York, Judge Joseph Potter of Whitehall; T. S. Coolidge of Glens Falls; and George Leprohon of Three Rivers, Canada. Among the mourners were his business partners, people whom he had helped, and his close friends.

And sitting among them all was his lifetime political foe, I. V. Baker, Jr. of Comstock.

To have your fiercest enemy pay his respects at your death?

Now, that is greatness.

"OVER MY SHOULDER" COLUMN FOR NOVEMBER 17, 2001
Ignoring our closest neighbor?

After the September 11th attack, 100,000 Canadians stood in mourning in front of their nation's capital building.

The US news media barely reported it.

Quickly, now, can you recite the name of Canada's capital city and the number of Canadian provinces?

For those who answered Ottawa and 10 provinces, bully for you! Yet most of America barely acknowledges the existence of Canada, the number two nation on earth in terms of landmass and America's number one friend. With all due respect to President Bush, I think the current crisis demonstrated to him that we possess a powerful neighbor, a peaceful giant with which we share a 3,000-mile border – and cultural ties that surpass those with any other country, including Mexico.

For us in this area, the irony of America's ignorance of Canada is only compounded by the fact that so many of Canada's early patriots came right out of Charlotte County. Charlotte embraced all of present-day, Clinton, Essex, Warren and Washington Counties, and part of Hamilton County in New York. It also claimed half of Vermont.

I have jokingly called Charlotte County the "Mother of Canada." I may be right. Noted newscaster Robin MacNeil's book, *The Story of English*, states that the Canadian accent traveled over the border from Western New York.

Poppycock, sir. It poured out of Western New England and Eastern New York State – most especially Charlotte County.

Over a few columns, we'll look at an unusual occurrence in America – our citizens moving to another land. We think of the immigrant experience as people coming here to settle, but never think of Americans leaving here. However, they did and by the thousands, helping to shape modern-day Canada.

America should know and understand Canada. Instead, it has ignored its greatest neighbor, ally and cultural cousin. And that's Canada, not Mexico. American politicians worry to the point of obsession about Mexico and, in the process, further damage a relationship that is unique in the world. Canada – both the French-speaking and English-speaking Canada – is our largest trading partner and best friend. You'd never think it by reading the news or watching TV.

How did this "cultural cousinhood" happen? In part, because of our Revolutionary War. Between 1776 when the United States declared independence and 1783, when the Treaty of Paris was signed, thousands of American Loyalists, often derisively called Tories, fled Charlotte County rather than switch allegiance from the crown. This included people like Barbara Heck of Camden Valley, Patrick Smyth of Fort Edward, the Jessup Brothers of Lake Luzerne and Justus Sherwood of Vermont.

In past columns, we have looked at Loyalists, but never examined what they did with their lives after the Revolution. A good example is Barbara Heck, born Barbara von Ruckle to German Protestant parents in Ireland in 1734. She married a man named Hesct and the name was changed to Heck.

In 1760, many of Barbara's German colony in Ireland went to New York, following the urging of Methodism's founder, John Wesley. There with her cousin Phillip Embury, Barbara created the first Methodist meeting in North America. Eventually she helped design the first Methodist church building there.

Heck, Embury and others then moved to Ash Grove, in the Town of Cambridge, Charlotte County, in 1770 and founded another Methodist meeting. Embury died in 1773. In 1776, the Heck family, all Loyalists, fled to Montreal. Subsequently, they moved to the Brockville area of Ontario, where Barbara formed a Methodist congregation, the first in Canada. She lived until 1804 and her influence was such that Methodism spread from coast to coast.

Heck, who is truly the mother of Methodism in North America, was a Canadian pioneer. She is also our region's gift to the nation of Canada.

Next week, other Canadian pioneers and heroes from Charlotte County.

"OVER MY SHOULDER" COLUMN FOR NOVEMBER 24, 2001
More Canadian patriots

Last week we were talking about the Loyalists of Charlotte County, Province of New York, who remained true to the king of England and eventually left this area to settle in Canada.

Edward and Ebenezer Jessup, about whom I've written before, were two brothers who probably did as much to help the crown as anyone in this region. They are probably among the most maligned people for doing so. The brothers are discussed in both A.W. Holden's history of Queensbury, as well as in *Lieut. Hadden's Journal,* edited by Horatio Rogers,[lxi] who quoted Holden liberally. Holden, like many historians of that era, would treat many of the "Tories" harshly in subtle and not so subtle ways. In recent times, the use of the term "Tories" has been replaced with "Loyalist," which makes more sense, for it states what those people were – loyal to their government.

The brothers Jessup came from Connecticut and settled in what today is Lake Luzerne. The two, according to Holden and others, bought extensive amounts of land from 1772 onward. Charlotte County was created that year. They bought the 40,000 acre Hyde Township, the 130,000 Palmer purchase, and the 800,000 Totten and Crossfield purchase – a good chunk of the Adirondacks. Holden describes them as "sharp and enterprising" but adds that they were "apparently unscrupulous." He relates how they ran up quite a bar tab at Wing's Tavern for "entertainment of a liberal and generous nature." Holden also describes how they lived in "opulence."

Whether the two were shady in their land dealings or not, Holden never offers proof and so the two are painted as libertine land barons. Frankly, they lived as many land speculators did. The same charges could have been leveled against John Thurman, but then, he ended up on the right side of the Revolution.

Ebenezer and Edward's life as Canadian patriots began in 1776 when they declared themselves Loyalists and were pursued for it. They fled to Crown Point, where they joined with Sir Guy Carleton in November, going with him to Quebec. Ebenezer had assembled a substantial number of officers and soldiers into a battalion. The notes of *Lieut. Hadden's Journal* tell of how Sir Guy Carleton was at first confused with what to do with the men, not knowing whether to put them in the regular army or in the Royal Regiment of New York.

Carleton, meanwhile, was trying to integrate Ebenezer's group into the regular Loyalist troops, apparently without much success. As late as April 1777, Carleton is writing General Phillips of Burgoyne's army stating, "I know no such thing as Jessup's Corps" and that it was "improper for Jessup and his men "to straggle about the country."

Burgoyne used Jessup's battalion in his doomed campaign in 1777, which the Jessup brothers managed to survive. As Lt. Colonel Ebenezer Jessup and Major

Edward Jessup, the brothers went on to fight many Revolutionary battles, with Ebenezer leading Jessup's Royal Rangers. By war's end, they were heroes, although not to their old Patriot neighbors in Charlotte County, who had ransacked their homes and stolen their property. As a form of payback, Jessup's Royal Rangers were among the 1780 raiders who swooped through the area burning everything they could torch.

Both brothers settled in Canada at War's end, Ebenezer, it is assumed, in Ontario. Edward settled in Montreal and by 1791 had become Edward Jessup, Esq., Justice of the Peace for the District of Montreal, a man of distinction, wealth and influence.

Canadian Historian Gavin Watt wrote that the Revolution was a "civil war of American against American."[lxii] With the Revolution, our nation had been born. But another nation, Canada, would be born as well, with many of its most prominent citizens coming from Charlotte County – which is today our region. Next week we'll conclude our look at early Canadian patriots.

"OVER MY SHOULDER" COLUMN FOR DECEMBER 1, 2001
U.S. and Canada more than neighbors

This week, we complete our 3-part story about the Loyalists of Charlotte County, Province of New York, who fled to Canada during and after The Revolution.

These "American-Canadians" created a unique cultural cousinhood between our two nations.

Thanks for your letters supporting my views on Canada. Margie Stonner of North Chatham, NY, wrote: "I, too, believe that Canada gets taken for granted most of the time." And very poignant was retired *Post-Star* printer Donald Robinson of Warrensburg, NY, who spent many retirement days in Florida living next to Canadian visitors. He observed, "They were not foreigners." They were family.

The United States lost ancestors in America's first civil war, The Revolution. No census has been done, but I estimate very conservatively our region lost 1,000, taking into account whole families.

The British archives are filled with the stories of thousands who petitioned the British government after the war to be recompensed for loss of property. A book called *American Loyalist Claims* by Peter Wilson Coldham[lxiii] has transcribed hundreds of these claims, many from Charlotte County.

One was Justus Sherwood of the "Hampshire Grants of Charlotte County," that is, Vermont. In 1776, this close friend of Ethan Allen and an original Green Mountain Boy refused to take an oath to the United States (or "to take the rebel oath," as Canadian historians say). Imprisoned, he escaped with others to Crown Point to join Sir Guy Carleton in November 1776.

During Burgoyne's Campaign of 1777, Sherwood served in the Queens Loyal Rangers with Fraser's troops at the Battle of Hubbardton, Vermont. After that, he became a Canadian Patriot, heading the "Canadian Secret Service," according to Watt's *The Burning of the Valleys*. In fact, a 1982 biography even calls Sherwood the "Buckskin Pimpernel."

Sherwood's second in command was Dr. George Smyth. Smyth's brother was Patrick, first Justice of Charlotte County. Both lived in Fort Edward. Today Patrick's home, the county's first courthouse, survives as the Old Fort House. Patrick was arrested in 1777 by Benedict Arnold and imprisoned in Albany. He escaped and made his way to what is now Ontario, where he settled along with his brother. Their property holdings there were extensive. George's lands, coincidentally, ended up next to those granted to Benedict Arnold.

Loyalist Thomas Richardson's story was typical of the thousands who fled to Canada. In his petition, he claimed a "500 acre plantation five miles above Fort Edward," in today's Kingsbury. He shared a sawmill with Daniel Parkes and James Watson, both Patriots ("rebels"). He was so loved by his neighbors that Watson cared for his property, even when other Patriots tried to destroy it.

Ironically, it was incinerated in the 1780 British raid called "The Burning." Watson wrote Richardson: "I confirm the melancholy news you no doubt have from your unmerciful army. I cannot any longer call them your friends. . . You have no signs of mill or house but by the chimneys standing. . . ." Watson says that Richardson's dependence on the British "will fall far short of your expectation, by which means you grasp the shadow instead of the substance."

However, most moving is Watson's reflection on the effect of The Revolution upon their friendships and community: "However, I need not point out to you, only say we have all done what we ought not to do, [and] praying we all may mend. We cannot be poorer."

Thankfully, we have mended – into two nations united by a shared heritage and the richness of a long friendship.

To show your support for Canada's friendship, forward your comments, or this column, to the Canadian Embassy in Washington, DC at: webmaster@canadianembassy.org.

Or write *The Post-Star* "Letters to the Editor" and say that we need to acknowledge our long-time friend.

We in the North Country know where Canada is. Can the rest of the U. S. get up to speed?

"OVER MY SHOULDER" COLUMN FOR DECEMBER 8, 2001
Infamous dates are forever joined

Pearl Harbor's 60th anniversary, December 7, was yesterday, its poignancy restored by September 11.

Many things will forever link those two days. There's the odd, but understandable, coincidence of using the date without the year. We say September 11 or December 7. No year. We know. The latter date has been reborn in American memory because of the former.

As kids, we knew December 7 – "we" being Boomers, born after WW II, but growing up, in a sense, with the war. Veterans of that war – that is, those who fought in World War II or were just simply alive during it – might scoff. But it's true in a way. Our language was saturated with the war. The very fact that people even of my daughter's generation say "The War" and mean by it "World War II" speaks to its power.

My schoolbooks told of it. Often, they were so old they still had the war either going on or just having been won. We also constantly heard references in veterans' everyday talk: "When I was at Anzio….." or "When I was stationed in Louisiana, guarding POW's….." or, in my father's case, "When I was in the South Pacific…"

We heard references in the everyday talk of those who stayed at home, my mother for one. We kids knew of rationing books and points, and heard of how everything was restricted. We heard the story of the forbidden meat that suddenly appeared on the table one day from a cousin farmer and how no one said a word, but ate it to the bone and got up from the dining room table smiling but silent. And never spoke of it.

Those schoolbooks I mentioned urged us to buy War Bonds. I even tried to do that as a little boy. I went to the Post Office and asked to buy a War Bond. The postmaster smiled kindly and sold me savings stamps for a savings bond. The stamps didn't say war bonds, but I felt I was helping "the war effort."

Movies and TV saturated us with "The War." Notice the capital letters: The War. That's how important it was. It was also called "The Big One" and "Double-U Double-U Two."

As kids, our play was saturated with it. We always played war. But *The War* lived in our house, too. As when my father would run screaming from the bedroom, living a nightmare and still commanding his ship under attack. Or when, 17 years after The War's end, he threw away cans of tuna bearing the imprint "Made in Japan," causing a terrible row with my mother.

In those years after the war, I went to the parades and watched wreathes being placed on the monuments and graves. I saw people cry as they remembered those lost. However, it took me well into adulthood to understand the deadness in the eyes of my great aunt, as she looked at me, namesake of her only child, Joseph, and remembered his death in the South Pacific in the Battle of Leyte in 1944.

For only when I had matured enough to know that a parent always wants to go before the child and would willingly, gladly die to make that happen – to go in the child's place and have the child live – only then, did her loss reach into its proper place: into my heart and soul.

Then December 7 became gut real.

Now for so many, September 11 also brought a similar maturity, and gut reality. For the sickening, word-defying sight of those planes going into those buildings took the generation of today and brought its heart and soul back to another day in infamy.

Yesterday became today, today yesterday, and we all grieve.

"OVER MY SHOULDER" COLUMN FOR DECEMBER 29, 2001
Children last hope for saving history

There is hope for the future of history.

Although until yesterday, you could've fooled me.

Whether by accident or design, over this last week *The Post-Star* had published several articles underscoring the devaluation of our nation's historical landmarks and the sad state of history learned in American colleges.

There was the staggering article on a developer's plans to build private condos within the Valley Forge landmark region. I can hear some future mother saying, "Jennifer, here's where Washington and his troops heroically risked starvation and nearly freezing to death for the sake of the American Revolution."

And I hear the child replying, "But, why Mom? They could've stayed in those condos over there!"

If the Revolution had relied upon people like that developer, today we'd be singing "God Save the Queen."

Then there was George Will's excellent column on "national memory loss." Which statistic was more depressing regarding the ignorance of the college seniors from 55 of America's "elite colleges"? Was it that only 22% of them knew where the words "government of the people, by the people, for the people" came from, or that 40% of them couldn't "place the Civil War in the second half of the 19th century"?

The phrase "elite colleges" became an oxymoron.

But the cake's icing came with Thursday's article on student bloopers cataloged by a college professor. Bet you didn't know the Marx brothers invented the airplane. Lord.

Mind you, all the above came on top of my reflecting upon a year fraught with history, for New York State especially, and my fuming at the irony that our state has still not appointed a state historian.

Everyone agrees the Trade Center tragedy is the dominant memory of 2001, having been permanently written across our minds using an exploding airplane as a stylus. And every New York State politician from the Governor on down said, at least once, that September 11th would "go down in history," or "live in history" or made some allusion to the historical nature of this hideous catastrophe.

But we don't even have a state historian? Such irony.

We sell off our national landmarks for big bucks, watch our elite colleges reduced to intellectual kindergartens, and treat our heritage with the same respect we'd give to a week-old sandwich left in a hot car.

So, then, why do I say there is hope for the future of history?

Because I was reminded this week that I know students who know and love history because it is instilled by their families and by teachers who view history as something needed, useful and fun.

Colleen Smith, of Kingsbury, had sent me a photo she'd taken of her son, Ben, and me, at the recent induction ceremony of the National Honor Society of Hudson Falls High School. Ben was inducted that evening. I'd been privileged to be asked to speak, although frankly I was put to shame by every student who spoke that night. They were excellent.

At 16, Ben is out of the ordinary in his love of history, being especially knowledgeable of the Civil War, as is his entire family who participates in Civil War re-enactments. He told me he could even recite the Gettysburg Address from memory. I am impressed.

But then, in addition to his family's influence, he's had good teachers, such as Matt Rozell[lxiv] and George Neisz. Good teachers are the heroes of civilization.

While Ben is uniquely Ben, thankfully he's also one of the many good students of our region who will shape the future of how our history is learned and our historic sites preserved, and how our government remembers the past.

Who knows, Ben. Maybe by the time you're my age there'll even be a state historian.

What am I saying? I think your history class better contact someone in Albany right away. You can't afford to wait that long.

Happy New Year.

[EDITOR'S POSTSCRIPT: Ben Smith is now an Assistant District Attorney for Warren County, NY.]

"OVER MY SHOULDER" COLUMN FOR JANUARY 19, 2002
County court dispute goes way back

When does it pay to shut your mouth?

The "courthouse caper" of Adiel Sherwood is a case in point.

We need a bit of background. I take you back to the late 1790s, those days when Washington County included all of Warren County.

A power struggle over the placement of courts had been in effect since the county had changed its name to honor Washington in 1784. Since 1772, the courts had been in Fort Edward at the home and courthouse of Justice Patrick Smyth, now the Old Fort House Museum. The courts ceased during the war but were resurrected in the same place by 1786. By that time, the place was a tavern owned by Adiel Sherwood, a Colonel in the County Militia who had been commanding Fort Ann when Carlton's troops had captured it in 1780. Sherwood was a hero.

Folks in Salem agitated for the courts being placed there. This was understandable as so much power was represented in the community, especially with the presence of General John Williams. Williams, a physician who had led that Militia, was himself a hero of the Revolution, a member of the legislature and of Congress, among his other accomplishments. He was also very rich, which didn't hurt.

In 1791, Williams and others succeeded in getting Salem appointed the county seat. Citizens of Fort Edward, then a part of the Town of Argyle, were incensed. They managed to get the state to allow courts to be held in Fort Edward, too. So, in effect, a dual county seat existed. As far as I know, today the only other place with this oddity of having two county courts in two separate towns exists in Bennington County, Vermont.

Now to the courthouse caper. As Crisfield Johnson [lxv] so beautifully wrote in his county history, in 1796, Sherwood "now united the glittering dignity of a lieutenant-colonel of militia with the humble duties of a village tavern-keeper."

Evidently the tavern's well-being took precedent. The court was held in the dining room. One day as the sessions had droned on, it apparently looked to Sherwood as if court were going to encroach upon the dinner-hour, impeding service to the taverns' regulars.

Hell knows no fury like a restaurateur kept from serving customers. Sherwood entered the courtroom and ordered the judges to leave. Forthwith!

However, an innkeeper's wrath is nothing compared to that of a judge, especially these judges, three of whom happened to be state senators. As Johnson wrote, that the judges "should be thus dictatorially ordered out of it, even by a lieutenant-colonel of militia, was almost enough to paralyze them with horror and indignation." Perhaps at that moment, but not at the next session.

Sherwood had actually succeeded in shutting down the court to get his food and beverage service going, his motto probably being, "Don't let the ale fail." However, at the next session the judges retaliated against the insolent innkeeper. Let the court record speak for itself: "Adiel Sherwood, having been guilty of contempt, it is ordered that the said Adiel Sherwood be committed to the common jail of Washington county for the space of fifteen days."

Fifteen days in the pokey for one late dinner-hour. Adding monetary insult to civil injury, the offended jurists yanked the court out of Sherwood's tavern and changed the venue to the "hotel of Mary Dean, in Sandy Hill" (now Hudson Falls). Apparently, Mary could juggle serving both judges and tankards of ale.

The change, however, still left the whole issue of the dual court and dual county seat intact, with courthouses in both Salem and Hudson Falls. It would not be until 1991 that the county courts would again be centralized in just one town.

In which town? Ah, yes, in Fort Edward.

It had taken nearly two centuries, but Adiel Sherwood got the last laugh.

"OVER MY SHOULDER" COLUMN FOR FEBRUARY 16, 2002
Region's Black history needs exploring

Never before has there been the need for the research skills of genealogists as exists right now during Black History month.

While researching the Black history of the early decades of Washington County, Ken Perry discovered a huge puzzle in the federal census records. He found some numbers that simply astound and confound.

The bottom line, as long as we're crunching numbers here, is this: in the US Census of 1790 there were 139 Black people living in Washington County, which until 1813 included all Warren County. In the US Census of 1800 there were 397 Black people. In that of 1810, there were 3,130.

However, in the US Census of 1820 there were 398 Black people listed as living in the county – only one more Black person than listed in the 1800 census.

What is going on here? The logical among you will say the drop was due to Warren County's being formed in 1813. With Warren separated from Washington, the numbers had to drop. However, in 1810, there were only 147 total Black people living within all the towns that would become part of Warren County in 1813.

The rise in number of free and Black slaves between 1800 and 1810 is dramatic, but possibly explained in terms of a rapidly growing economy. I also harbor the notion that there were far more Blacks in the county than the 1790 census ever showed. Please note my use of the term "Black slaves." We need to remind ourselves those who were enslaved here were Black.

Ken's figures show an astoundingly rapid drop-off from 1810 to 1820. What happened? Who were those folks? Where did they go? You have an enormous influx of one color of people, which would be interesting enough if the population levels subsequently stayed the same or grew. But to have this spike, where the population expands enormously and then returns to almost the same number, is inexplicable.

The living arrangements of Blacks living in the county at the time of the 1810 census were complex. The census lists households and they have varying numbers of people. There were a total of 11 free Black households and one free Black living alone. Obviously, they were fewest in number. The greatest numbers of Blacks were living in white households where both free Blacks and Black slaves lived, or in white households where only Black slaves lived.

There were 73 white households where only Black slaves lived. However, there were 1,415 white households where both free Blacks and Black slaves lived.

The greatest rise in the Black population in today's Washington County took place in Hartford, which had a 49% increase in Blacks. Cambridge had the greatest number, approximately 20 percent of the Black population. All the towns with the greatest numbers of Black people were those along the turnpikes being built. Ken suggests that the building of these very important highways attracted Black laborers. The Great Northern Turnpike was being built from Cambridge north to Granville. Another, the Lansingburgh to Whitehall turnpike, ran through the Fort Miller section of Fort Edward, Argyle, Hartford, Granville, and Whitehall.

How can we find out more about this? Not surprisingly, our published histories don't offer much on Black history per se. However, there is so much available information from that time period, including town and school records; deeds, mortgages and wills; newspapers; and diaries, journals, family bibles and the like. This is a job for genealogists – those researchers who for decades have been sorting through this same material.

It's a job for us all. As we broaden our knowledge of Black history, we broaden the history of the human race. Who controls the knowledge of the past too often dictates the future. All history belongs to all the people. Knowledge, and the truth it can bring, can set you free.

[EDITOR'S POSTSCRIPT: Please see the column "More data needed on minorities" for more on Ken Perry's discovery.]

"OVER MY SHOULDER" COLUMN FOR FEBRUARY 23, 2002
Blacks' unsung Revolutionary heroes

This year, as we observe the 225th anniversary of Burgoyne's defeat at Saratoga, let us begin it with a salute to its Black veterans, an unsung group of people.

In the past I wrote of one Black Revolutionary War veteran, Lemuel Haynes, of South Granville, but there were so many Blacks who fought with conspicuous bravery in the war that I needed to write more. Before I do, let me start by saying that it has been strongly suggested to me that recent efforts to enumerate the names of these Black Revolutionary War veterans is "convenient" to Black History Month. The implication is, there weren't that many Blacks who participated then, it didn't matter much then and the only reason it makes any difference now is because it's trendy.

My response? It is shameful that it has taken over two centuries to recognize publicly those nonwhites, whether Black or Indian, who fought for the Patriot cause. That shame is one of three. The second shame is that no complete listing has ever been made of the full roster of all who participated, regardless of their color. The third is the lack of recognition of all, who in any way participated on in creating a new nation.

The men and women who suffered and died in the violent transition of 13 colonies into the United States of America are becoming cartoons, parodies, or sketches, more often used as political fodder for some July 4th speech nobody recalls. These Patriots' names and stories are usually unknown, either because they haven't been collected or because they aren't taught in our schools.

Add to that indignity a veteran being ignored because he's the wrong color and you have a sorry situation. It is time to support those museums and institutions struggling to collect, centralize and honor the few who fought for the many.

And I do mean "the few." Lerone Bennett, Jr., in his history of Black America, *Before the Mayflower,* [lxvi] states that despite there being a million men of fighting age in America at that time, the Continental lines "never exceeded 50,000." The Revolution was fought by a few "Rebels," the remainder being either Loyalist or neutral. Bennett cites George Washington's observation on the lack of volunteers and desertions: "Such a dearth of public spirit and want of virtue . . . I never saw before and pray God I may never see again. . . . Such a dirty mercenary Spirit pervades the whole that I should not be at all surprised at any disaster that may happen."

Given the relatively few of all colors who fought, then a complete centralized listing should be easily compiled, and the numbers of Black Revolutionary veterans will suddenly be seen in greater proportion than previously acknowledged.

Although in 1775 the idea was at first resisted by some, violently rejected by others, eventually freed and enslaved Blacks swelled the ranks of many regiments, even comprising the majority of The First Rhode Island Regiment.

The Minutemen, so enshrined in our history, included in their ranks these Black fighters: Lemuel Haynes, Peter Salem, Pomp Blackman and Cuff Whittemore. Salem and Whittemore were at Lexington and Concord, as well as at Saratoga.

Lemuel Haynes, Primus Black and Epheram Blackman were members of the Green Mountain Boys and were with Ethan Allen when he seized Ticonderoga in 1775.

Haynes was born in West Hartford, Connecticut, in 1753 of a Black man and white woman. He was abandoned as a child and almost immediately indentured until age 21 to a family in Middle Granville, Massachusetts. A noted Congregationalist minister of the late 18th and early 19th centuries, Haynes ended his life preaching in Granville in 1833 at the South Granville Congregational Church.[lxvii]

Next week, more on Haynes, Peter Salem, Cuff Whittemore and other Black Revolutionary War veterans.

"OVER MY SHOULDER" COLUMN FOR MARCH 2, 2002
Black patriot soldiers were unsung heroes of Revolution

Images from the American Revolution, and the period leading up to it, are legendary.

Take the painting of the Boston Massacre of 1770, of which John Adams wrote: "The foundation of American independence was laid that night." The painting's central figure is Crispus Attucks, leader of the attack on the customs house and among the first killed. Attucks was a Black man.

Interestingly, if you search through other images of the Revolution done in that period, you can sometimes find the Black soldiers who rightfully belong there. And sometimes you cannot.

I've seen an engraving of the Battle of Bunker Hill with Blacks portrayed. Among the dozen or more Blacks, enslaved and free, who fought there were Peter Salem, Titus Coburn, Alexander Ames, Cato Howe, Barzilai Lew and Cuff Whittemore.

Salem, an enslaved Black freed by his owners to enlist and fight, was responsible for the death of British Major John Pitcairn at Bunker Hill.

However, images of Lexington and Concord don't include the Black Minuteman who fought there, including Peter Salem and Pomp Blackman. There is debate whether Granville resident, the Rev. Lemuel Haynes, fought at Lexington, but he did memorialize it in an epic poem, among the many published works of the brilliant theologian.

Haynes brings to mind another famed image of the Revolution where Black Patriots should be seen but are not – the seizure of Fort Ticonderoga in 1775. You all know the image of Ethan Allen, demanding the fort to be surrendered "in the name of the Great Jehovah and the Continental Congress." We know from different sources that Lemuel Haynes, Primus Black, Epheram Blackman and Barzilai Lew were among the Green Mountain Boys with Allen that day.

Obviously when Haynes fought alongside Ethan Allen and the other Green Mountain Boys, he liked the look of where he was and decided to return to settle. He did and became pastor of the Congregational Church in West Rutland, Vermont in the late 1790s.

Haynes was far from the only Black Patriot ever to have fought in this area and later settled here after war's end. Veteran Prince Taylor also stayed on to become one of Ticonderoga's earliest settlers, co-founder of the Congregational Church and reportedly the man for whom Black Point is named.

As noted last week, 2002 marks the 225th anniversary of the defeat of Burgoyne at the Battles of Saratoga. American Patriot Blacks fought at several key engagements in British General John Burgoyne's campaign. The Battle of Hubbardton, Vermont, on July 7, 1777 is a case in point.

The Battle of Hubbardton by Colonel John Williams[lxviii] notes the presence of four Black Patriot soldiers at that battle. Titus Wilson of Peterborough, New Hampshire, fought with Colonel Cilley's Regiment. Wilson was wounded and captured, and died that same day.

Simeon Grandison of Scituate, Massachusetts, fought at the battle, but it not known with what regiment he served. Asa Perham (also spelled Purham and Pearham) served and fought that day with Colonel Nathan Hale's 2nd New Hampshire Regiment, as did Nicholas Vintrom. Vintrom also spelled Vixtrom, who was captured by the British, but survived.

You've probably surmised that Black Patriots, such as Minutemen Peter Salem and Cuff Whittemore, fought at so many of the pivotal Revolutionary battles. For example, both Salem and Whittemore faced Burgoyne twice: once at Bunker Hill in 1775 and again at Saratoga in 1777. I'll end with a recounting of Whittemore's bravery.

Whittemore fought at Saratoga, where British forces captured him. Brought to Burgoyne's tent, he was ordered by a British regular to take Burgoyne's horse, as if to hold the reins like a groom or some such thing. Whittemore did, indeed, take Burgoyne's horse, but not as ordered. Instead he mounted it and, amidst whizzing musket balls, sped off to freedom on Burgoyne's own steed! Whittemore added an ultimate insult to the overall injury of defeat Burgoyne would suffer at Saratoga.

From this time on, may our images of the American Revolution – whether painting, movie, or computer image – portray our Patriots in all their true colors.

"OVER MY SHOULDER" COLUMN FOR MARCH 23, 2002
Lost items of days gone by

This started out because of a paper straw.

Dennis Lowery, the Washington County Archivist, was among a group of people when someone said, "Hey, we'll have to have a Fifties Party." Meaning, the 1950s.

And Dennis responded, "Oh, then you'll need to get your paper straws." Dennis was immediately transported to "The Anachronism Zone," which is a part of the Twilight Zone.

Apparently, people stopped dead still and looked at him as if an ear had sprouted from his forehead.

"Paper what?" Paper straws, he replied.

No one had ever heard of sipping straws made of waxed paper, rather than of plastic. He asked me if I recalled them. Having grown up in family pharmacy with a soda fountain? Like, totally.

But I haven't seen a box of paper straws in eons. And his question reminded me that "gone missing" are straws with a paper wrapping loose enough to allow you to remove one end of the wrapper, blow into the straw, and shoot the wrapper off like a rocket.

I decided to ask others "what's gone missing in the last 20 to 30 years?" My friend Loretta Bates of Queensbury replied, among other things, "street dances, where young and old joined in the fun" and "square dancing when it was done without short dresses and tap shoes." Hmm. Time for Arthur Murray, or Denny Terrio of "Dance Fever," to visit Mrs. Bates.

Post-Star publisher Ken Tingley said it was "sand lot baseball" when kids hopped their bikes, threw a glove on the handlebar and went off to play 8 hours of baseball with "five players to the side and the right field dead." And everybody got to bat at least 25 times.

What else? Glens Falls Mayor Robert Regan said 8-track tapes, telegrams delivered to the door, corner stores, afternoon newspapers, the milkman, and full service gas stations. And elm trees. He's working on the elm revival.

Washington County Board of Supervisors Chairman Don Cummings said manual cash registers. (And the money to go in them, Don!)

My wife, Sara, and I note that records are missing. The music for our daughter's sixth grade gymnastics program in 1992 was courtesy of a record player. When the record stopped, the teacher handed a little girl an album to put on the machine. The child looked at it like a spinning wheel. She didn't know what a record was. It's all tapes and CDs now.

Saratoga Springs Mayor Kenneth Klotz said, "Life is so full that it's very hard to think of something missing." But he reflected upon pro baseball of a few decades ago. What's missing now? Team loyalty. Back then, "Lots of the good players stayed with the team for their whole professional life."

Jack and Ann Wiberg of Glens Falls said, "5 & 10 cent stores, balloon tire bikes, and penny candy" have disappeared.

Thirty-somethings, Sherry Ankeny of Skidmore College and her husband Kevin of Adirondack Community College responded: rotary dial phones and Pong, an early video game.

And Gen-Xers? *The Post-Star*'s Gretta Nemcek[lxix] said: Atari, the Cabbage Patch craze, Underoos with the Wonder Woman design. And Wonder Woman herself. Also, Beta VCRs. (Gretta's family bet on the wrong style VCR and still have their Beta.)

What else is missing? Gretta said wistfully, "endless summers when your parents let you go out for the whole day and you had to return home when the streetlights went on."

Ah, Gretta. Endless summers are indeed gone for us adults, what with our day schedulers, palm pilots,[lxx] and frantic lives.

However, thankfully, some things forever await the child yet to come. Endless summers being among them.

Want to share your idea of what's gone missing in the last 30 years? Aside from your hairline or your waistline, that is? Let me know via regular mail or e-mail.

If there are too many answers, we'll draw straws. Paper, of course.

"OVER MY SHOULDER" COLUMN FOR MARCH 30, 2002
Readers miss more than beta

Thank you all for bombarding me in person, and via phone and email regarding last week's column on what has gone missing in the last 30 years. Here's a follow up column.

But first, two corrections. Kevin Ankeny of Adirondack Community College noted that the beta VCR is still made, just not used by the average household.

Also, a delightful correction for Glens Falls Mayor Regan. I quote: "You stated that Mayor Regan missed, among others, the milkman. I just wanted to let you know that your milkman is still around! Dobert's Dairy[lxxi] has been in operation since 1931, in Glens Falls. Yes, they still do home delivery though that has decreased in the years since Victor Miner died. How do I know? Well, my husband still gets up at 3:30 every morning to do home deliveries. (Nope, I definitely do not get up with him.) I bet if you called him up, he'd be happy to add you to the string of happy home customers!"

And it was signed, "the milkman's wife, Kelly Dobert."

Thanks, Kelly! But I am surprised you don't get up at 3:30 am just to say goodbye. Gee.

With so many replies, I had to be selective. Again, this is about what has gone missing in the last thirty years, tops. Kerri Lyons said, "nurses dressed in white uniforms," while Jim Dill said "carbon paper." And Sue Peters notes the demise of mimeographs and air raid drills. Good ones!

Kingsbury historian Paul Loding[lxxii] offered pocket instamatic cameras and Burma Shave signs. Somehow, I think those signs were gone before 1972.

Granville author and historian Peggy Jenks thinks that 8 mm home movie film went the way of buggy whips.

Dona Yeskoo of Schroon Lake had 21 suggestions, among which are: "Captain Kangaroo every morning at breakfast time" and "carrying metal lunch boxes (with a matching thermos) and plaid book bags to school. Remember the peculiar, unpleasant smell the inside of the lunchbox developed after a while?"

Barbara LaSelva wrote: "gum machines that not only distributed a gum ball, but also a small toy."

Barbara Brooks of Stony Creek thought maybe she was going back too far, but offered "Pink rubber Spaulding balls" used in jump rope games. "Girls would say a rhyme while bouncing the Spaulding ball and crossing their leg over the ball as it was bouncing." Can you do that now, Barbara?

Perhaps just inside the time limit of 30 years comes this Plattsburgh memory of Stan Wood: "Going to the corner store to buy a bag of Kitchen Cook potato chips…, a 16 oz bottle of RC cola from a container filled with cold water and a Skybar candy bar for a quarter." And a bonus of "a penny back if you drank the soda at the store."

Salem Historian Al Cormier[lxxiii] said the old fashioned, very bitter variety of Moxie soda was gone.

To give equal time to Washington County Board of Supervisors Chairman Don Cummings, I tried to call Don's counterparts. I got hold of Warren County Board of Supervisors Chairman William Thomas. Bill, who'd once worked in a grocery store, said that gone was tallying the amount of the purchase on the grocery bag itself, pop-beads, Tru-Ade and Shaeffer Beer.

Here are some random ones. *Soul Train*. Afros. The Soviet Union. The Berlin Wall. She-Ra, He-Man and Skeletor. PC's that came with two 5.25-inch floppy disk drives and no hard drive. WordStar software. Enable software, made in Ballston Spa. Pee-wee's Playhouse. Wax lips. Guy Lombardo. The "Double Bubble" in the Howard Johnson's in Queensbury.

And only this week gone missing are Milton Berle and Dudley Moore, just a time when we need their humor most.

One last thought on what's gone missing in the last 30 years: the CB craze, thankfully.

And that's a big 10-4 comin' at yuh fer now, good buddy.

"OVER MY SHOULDER" COLUMN FOR APRIL 13, 2002
Let's go, Rangers

This is a call to all in *The Post-Star* reading area who have served or are serving in the United States military units that trace their roots to Rogers Rangers.

This would include members of the Special Operations Forces, the "Special Ops" – United States Army Rangers and Green Berets; United States Marine Force Reconnaissance ("Force Recon"); United States Navy Seals; and United States Air Force Combat Control Teams.

You are cordially invited by your fellow Rangers, Hebron Town Supervisor Kenneth Talkington (Ret. SGM) and Whitehall School Principal Beecher Baker, (former Sgt. US Army Third Ranger Battalion) to gather for a Rangers meeting on Rogers Island, which is the spiritual home of all United States fighting units tracing their lineage to Robert Rogers' famed "Rogers Rangers."

The meeting will be at the Rogers Island Visitors Center at a time in the very near future, to be determined after we hear from you. The meeting is being held in anticipation of a public gathering of Rangers on Rogers Island in mid-May. Rangers can contact Kenneth Talkington and Beecher Baker through either the e-mail address below or by calling the Rogers Island Visitors Center at 518-747-3693. Just tell them you're a Ranger responding to the call.

Now some history behind Rogers Rangers and Rogers Island. We are all aware of "the Rangers" and the whole spectrum of Special Ops Forces today. They are featured so prominently in the news because of the war in Afghanistan, as well as being featured in the movie "Blackhawk Down," for example. But few know of the units' origins with Robert Rogers and Rogers Island in Fort Edward, New York.

John R. Cuneo writes that Robert Rogers was born in Methuen, Massachusetts in 1731. Rogers' family moved north into the Merrimack Valley, where they farmed in the rugged wilderness. By age 14, he was thoroughly versed in the frontier life. When attacks by the French and Indian allies occurred in 1746, young Robert took his place among the men defending the region. After that, farming was never really a desired way of life for him.

In 1755 British and French hostilities again erupted, this time into the French and Indian War. Rogers responded to Massachusetts Governor William Shirley's call and recruited 24 men to serve. A bit later, New Hampshire Governor Benning Wentworth made Rogers Captain of a regiment of the 50 men he'd recruited.

While Rogers did not invent "ranging," a uniquely American activity, he certainly perfected it. Acting much as Native Americans would in combat, his Rangers used stealth, courage, presence of mind and a deep knowledge of the land and of people to their advantage.

Cuneo writes of how in the winter of 1755-56 Rogers' aggressive "scouts and raids on the enemy … laid the basis for his later ranging tactics." Rogers became hero of the French and Indian War. His abilities, successes and fame led Governor Shirley to appoint Rogers captain of an independent company of Rangers. Our modern-day Rangers, in essence, were born.

Rogers Rangers came to be stationed at "the Island" in the Hudson directly across from Fort Edward, one of the largest British military installations in North America. Rogers trained British troops and Colonial Americans in his tactical knowledge. Historian Robert J. Rogers writes notes that Rogers first transcribed that knowledge in a letter written "at Fort Edward, the 25th of October 1757, to the Earl of Loudon." The contents of that letter evolved into what became known as Rogers' "Standing Orders," the first American military manual.

"Standing Orders," first transcribed on Rogers Island, is today still known and used by everyone in the Special Operations Forces. It is a living link. In mid-May, when Rogers Island Visitors Center holds its Family Day, it wants to make an appropriate acknowledgement of the Island's link between Rangers then and Rangers now.

If you're a Ranger, please contact us at the e-mail address below, or by calling the Rogers Island Visitors Center.

"OVER MY SHOULDER" COLUMN FOR MAY 4, 2002
Past comes alive

[AUTHOR'S NOTE: This note is an apology to my friend L. Lloyd Stewart[lxxiv], whom I did not know at the time. As you'll read below, Lloyd was outraged that his ancestors' graves in Salem's Evergreen Cemetery were so overgrown they could only be found with documents. What I neglected to write is that Lloyd is a Black American whose family traces back into Washington County's and indeed New York State's earliest days. The dismal state of those graves was symbolic of the dismal state of the respect for Blacks in the 19th century. Thankfully, through the efforts of then Greenwich Town Historian Al Cormier and Lloyd Stewart the graves were located, cleared. and properly recognized.]

Thursday's *Post-Star* proves that past is a living issue.

Two frontpage articles underscored that. One was Darrin Youker's article "Searching for lost history" on Lloyd Stewart's efforts to trace his roots in Salem's Evergreen Cemetery. The other was John Gereau's "Duo proposes outdoor amphitheater" on proposal to stage live theatrical productions based upon *The Last of the Mohicans* by James Fenimore Cooper.

In Youker's article, Stewart was seen standing in the Evergreen Cemetery with Salem Historian Al Cormier. Stewart had expressed his dismay and outrage at the state of the section of the cemetery that held his ancestors' graves, which were virtually overgrown and would not have been known except for documents on the cemetery.

While I share Mr. Stewart's dismay, I think of how bad it could have been. The glass half-full sort of thing. First of all, he had a good historian to turn to, Al Cormier, a fact which underscores that the community supports the idea of a historian and promotes the work of a historian. By extension, many different people in the Salem community have been fighting to record and preserve their cemeteries, among them David Male and Ann Pongrace, for example. But there are so many others I risk offense by not listing names. Please forgive me.

What I am saying, Mr. Stewart, is that you have joined the ranks. Had it not been for the historically minded in the Salem community, and elsewhere, the records of the cemeteries could have been lost forever and the cemeteries themselves plowed under. But that cemetery, as well as the Revolutionary War Cemetery in Salem have been the subject of TLC.

A lot of times, this doesn't happen and that's life. The past for some people is simply just the past and its artifacts and relics are at best curiosities waiting to disintegrate or be recycled in the ongoing onslaught of time and change. As much as it goes against what I feel inside, I can't fault that logic.

But there many of us who feel that the preservation of certain objects, documents or places serves a value. Regarding Darrin Youker's article, I'd urge him and *The Post-Star* not to drop it at this stage, but to look into the whole issue of our cemeteries, monuments and markers in New York State. It's one festering sore. You have thousands of cemeteries sitting like abandoned children, sinking into the earth, being plowed under, built over or vandalized.

But the story for a good reporter is that our state puts our municipalities behind the 8-ball on this one. State law required municipalities to maintain the ones that are already their own, although they often have so little money for that. But if municipalities move to rescue private cemeteries, by default they become theirs to maintain forever. Catch-22. Understandably, though regrettable, many municipalities turn a blind eye.

The other frontpage news about proposed amphitheater for the Lake George region is interesting in that the concept's originators, Jens Rasmussen and Michael Dufore, have looked to a theme that is being resurrected in Glens Falls with the new Route 9 Bridge: the Last of the Mohicans. The theater productions would be based upon a historical novel, which has itself become historical.

So, we have the French and Indian War being proposed as a subject for live theater. Perhaps the idea can be brought to other local theaters. Perhaps the Glens Falls Community Theater could stage a historical production, as it has in the past. And perhaps that wonderful new theater building in the old Woolworth's[lxxv] will see one, also.

In past times, community pageants, in particular those employing school students, were large affairs. Is this a chance to see some of that come alive again?

Whatever works to make the past a living issue – that works for me.

Nice to see that history is frontpage news.

"OVER MY SHOULDER" COLUMN FOR MAY 11, 2002
Imagining local life during the Revolution

History has "startling dates," upon which occur events so startling and disruptive that they alter the fates of nations.

September 11th is such a date. May 10th is another. May 10, 1775 Ethan Allen seized Fort Ticonderoga. It's not odd to consider May 10th as a "startling date." What's odd about the conflict that became The Revolution is how many startling dates there were over just a few years. This was because The Revolution began as a family feud. No one thought a divorce would occur.

Let's make this personal. As children, you all sat in class with your eyes glazing over as your history teacher, warming to the task, talked about the conflict that erupted when the British Parliament imposed various taxes upon the colonies to help pay for the French and Indian War.

But now you're an adult. You pay taxes, and undoubtedly gripe about it, have a job, perhaps kids, a mortgage—responsibilities. Imagine yourself living here in 1775. Imagine you moved here after the French and Indian War and settled in, say, Clifton Park, Saratoga (now Schuylerville), Skenesborough (now Whitehall) or Wing's Falls (now Glens Falls).

Imagine, too, that you're damned fed up with the British Crown, which is taxing everything to help pay for the French and Indian War. Still, you pay your taxes on stamps, glass and tea. Although you were shocked in 1773 about the aftermath of the Boston Tea party, which you thought was just a good-humored protest against the tea tax. Instead, the British government shut down Massachusetts' government and the Royal Navy blockaded Boston.

You helped by sending food to the Bostonians, including your cousin. You were even more shocked when your cousin wrote that the British army decided to quarter soldiers in his home without permission. "Hello. I'm Major Armbruster. For the time being, my men are going to live with you instead of sleeping on Boston Commons. Please shut up. Thank you."

You thought convening a Continental Congress of the provinces in 1774 was radical, but a good idea. Let's organize and tell the Crown how we feel. But the Mother Country just ignored the Congress and made even more decisions that everyone here hated.

That was definitely disturbing, and tensions were building, but what could you do? Your life here was still going on, running your farm, buying land and fighting with the spouse over the kids. Normal stuff.

Suddenly it's 1775. The news reaches you that on April 18 and 19, shots were fired between colonists and soldiers at Lexington and Concord in Massachusetts. People are dead. The news is sketchy. Who fired first? This is awful! Then barely weeks later, people right here in this region, a rowdy named Ethan Allen and his Green Mountain Boys, seize a military installation in the name of the Continental Congress. "In the name of God," you ask, "what is happening?"

What happens next in 1775 is that your own civil government begins to shut down. By year's end, Charlotte County Provincial courts cease to function. Your neighbors choose sides. Anarchy begins. By early 1776, those against the Crown are trying and imprisoning "loyalist" neighbors for not taking an oath to "the United States." On July 4, your province declares itself part of a separate nation. Your world turns upside down.

If you successfully imagined yourself living here through those startling dates, keep your imagination going. Over the weeks to come, you'll be reading about the 225th anniversary of the 1777 campaign of British General John Burgoyne to end the rebellion here.

Imaginations ready? An army of 8,000 men is about to march through your town, possibly burn down your house, kidnap your spouse, and put you on the run. And you thought it was bad before.

Burgoyne's Campaign: The Empire strikes back.

"OVER MY SHOULDER" COLUMN FOR JUNE 1, 2002
A hero without honor

Could it be possible to memorialize a person for distinguished bravery in one of the world's most crucial battles without ever inscribing that person's name?

It's been done, and on two different monuments.

One of the two monuments, the Saratoga Monument in Victory, New York, stands at 154 feet 6 inches tall, and dedicates a full quarter of itself to a person never named. The hollow niche in the side of the monument should have a statue like those on the other three sides. Instead it remains empty, 125 years after the start of its creation and 225 years after this unnamed person risked life, limb and sacred honor for a cause we call the United States.

Its emptiness had purpose. Its creators could not physically honor this person, although during their dedication speeches, they credited him with helping turn the tide against General John Burgoyne at the Battles of Saratoga in 1777.

The National Park Service has just reopened the Saratoga Monument, closed since 1987 because of safety concerns. What wonderful news! How happy the monument's creators would be. More likely ecstatic, if they knew the restoration had been prompted by a letter from an 8-year old girl, as Victor Spagnoli reported in Wednesday's *Post-Star*. The letter's author, Saara Johanson, now 17, would have been perfect company on October 19, 1877, the day the cornerstone was laid.[lxxvi]

On that day, over 15,000 people crowded Victory and Schuylerville. Houses were decorated in bunting, the streets swathed in banners. This was the second of two major events commemorating the Burgoyne Campaign, the first being on September 19th at "The Saratoga Battlefield," today the Saratoga National Historical Park in Stillwater.

Now many of the same people gathered again, including veterans of previous wars and descendants of Revolutionary war veterans. According to Sylvester's history of Saratoga County,[lxxvii] a parade of three divisions marched the streets: regiments and companies of soldiers and cavalry, marching bands, police units, re-enactors, civic organizations, Masonic lodges, and "orators, poets, speakers, clergy," and "invited guests" march and rode. They came from cities, towns and villages in New York, Vermont and Connecticut.

The Saratoga Monument Association had been formed in 1859 to create this monument. The Civil War had delayed its efforts, as had financial challenges. Reinvigorated in 1873, its members now included such notables as the eminent historian William L. Stone, who had written so prolifically on the Burgoyne campaign. New Jersey architect Jared C. Markham designed the monument, which would not be completed until 1882.

At the ceremony on October 19, 1877, the cornerstone was ceremonially laid by the Grand Master of the Most Worshipful Grand Lodge of Free and Accepted Masons.[lxxviii] It was filled with newspapers and other items and with "relics of Burgoyne's campaign." A cannon actually used by Burgoyne was fired throughout the day. Poets and orators spoke, choirs sang, and bands played. Significantly, the concept of war, the Civil War, was so fresh in the minds of all. One speaker noted that, like those of 1777, those now present had family and friends "killed in battle…" and among the celebrants stood "the mourners…the widow and the fatherless…the poor in heart."

Though started that day, the monument was not completed until 1882. The three statues of Daniel Morgan, Philip Schuyler and Horatio Gates were not placed in their niches until 1887. It would not be deep into the 20th century that a small interpretive sign would inscribe the name of the person who should have been the fourth statue. The person whose name, while openly discussed at the ceremony, could not be inscribed on the monument. The person who, against General Gates' very orders, jumped his horse, rode into battle, electrified his men into action, and while badly wounded, helped lead the Patriot victory against Burgoyne's army.

The person whose very absence makes the Saratoga Monument so historically significant, so oddly unique.

But, then, how does one honor a traitor like Benedict Arnold?

"OVER MY SHOULDER" COLUMN FOR JUNE 8, 2002
Reflecting on the eagle, enlistment center

Then take a moment to reflect on the eagle and the enlistment center.

This weekend you'll be walking around the LARAC festival in downtown Glens Falls, buying your fair share of the arts and crafts, even stopping to get a bag of popcorn from a guy named Jack. As you munch that popcorn, look up to see the beautifully restored Civil War Monument on Bay and Glen Streets.

As you reflect upon the eagle atop the monument, think about why it was built: to represent a community's coming to terms with the Civil War that nearly destroyed their country—a country in existence only 85 years when the war erupted in 1861.

Reflect also upon the fact that, in 1777, troops had raged through this very spot, as family fought family in our other civil war called The Revolution.

In fact, there were people alive in 1861 who'd been alive when the United States was still a colony. A few were actually Revolutionary War veterans.

Now in 1861 this relatively new country built on Jefferson's proposition of 1776, as Lincoln later stated it, was seeing if it could survive. With Lincoln's call for volunteers, young men flowed into enlistment centers all over our region. The result we know. The Union formed "fourscore and seven years" before indeed survived. Monuments were built and a national holiday born, Memorial Day.

But what of those enlistment centers, those town halls, theaters, churches and storefronts that acted as registry places for these new soldiers? Often they disappeared, forgotten, or were at best recorded in a history, having been swallowed by history.

Miraculously, one remains in our region. In fact, Civil War historians like Michael Russert believe it is the only one of two remaining Civil War enlistment centers in New York State, possibly the only one at all.

It is the Howard Hanna Memorial Enlistment Center and Hartford Museum located in the village of Hartford. This building is so original in its construction that you'll step on the same floorboards trod by volunteers in 1862.

The Civil War, called then the Rebellion, just as our Revolution had originally been called, had raged on for a year. In response to Lincoln's first call for volunteers, a fiery meeting was held April 1861 at the Hartford Baptist Church—not surprisingly as the church had gone on record opposing slavery. The rally raised 19 enlistees and over $5,000.

That year, the 22nd Regiment formed in April, the 93rd in November and the 2nd Cavalry that fall. It was the formation of Washington County's 123rd Regiment in 1862 that marked the Hartford's enlistment center's debut. Lincoln had called for 300,000 volunteers. Historians Brayton and Norton [lxxix]wrote, "In response to this call, a great war meeting was held in Argyle on the 22nd of July."

Each town met the call. With Hebron, Hartford put together Company E. A second great meeting was convened, this time in Hartford. People rallied at the Baptist Church across the street and enthused potential soldiers flocked across the street to the shop of cabinetmaker Sylvanus Hatch, who set up his shop as Hartford's enlistment center.

By its fourth rally, Hartford had gone over quota. A total of 65 men had dutifully enlisted at Hatch's shop. Farewell speeches were made at the church. The soldiers marched to Hartford's tiny green, site of the war monument today, where they received a prayer of blessing from "Grandma" Morrison. Onward they went to Salem where they encamped until September 5, when they boarded the troop trains for Washington, DC, some never to return.

Subsequent peace times and intervening wars erased most Civil War enlistment centers. But Hartford's remains. It is a museum open Sundays from 1 to 4 pm in July and August and by appointment.

Why not see a rare, if not unique, historical site in your own back yard and take a moment to reflect.

[EDITOR'S POSTSCRIPT: The Hartford Museum and Howard Hanna Memorial Civil War Enlistment Center consist of two buildings in Hartford, NY. Owned by the Town of Hartford, both buildings are maintained and operated by the Hartford Historical Group, a not-for-profit organization.]

"OVER MY SHOULDER" COLUMN FOR JUNE 15, 2002
Heirloom finds its way home

Here's a wonderful story about the Boston Tea Party that I feel ties in so well with Flag Day.

I know you're saying, "The Boston Tea Party was in 1773. But Flag Day commemorates when the American flag was first flown in 1777." Right you are, star pupil, but without the Boston Tea Party, there might never have been an American Flag created in 1777 and today Starbucks would only be selling tea.

The story begins. Elizabeth Ireland DeLong of Queensbury recently contacted me about a family heirloom she felt should be placed in a museum. Her grandfather, Irving W. Ireland, a contractor in Newton Center, Massachusetts, in the early 20th century, had obtained a piece of wood from

Boston's historic Daggett House, which was being demolished. He carved it into a small urn, which became a cherished heirloom.

The Daggett (or Doggett) House had played a role in 1773 when the Sons of Liberty launched their raid upon three shiploads of tea in Boston Harbor. The British Government had first imposed the tea tax in the 1760s to help pay for the French and Indian War. While other taxes levied for the same reason had been rescinded by 1773, Parliament kept its tea tax to show it still had the muscle.

It all went wrong when Parliament passed the Tea Act in 1773, essentially to help the East India Company gain a monopoly on all tea shipped to North America. Up and down the coast merchants refused to sell tea. Things came to a head in Boston in December. The captains of three ships loaded with tea agreed not to offload it. The provincial governor stated they wouldn't sail until they paid the tax, whether they sold the tea or not.

The impasse was used to perfection by Samuel Adams and others who, by December 16, 1773, had ratcheted up the situation from a problem to a crisis. They held a town meeting that day at Old South Church in Boston at 3:00 pm. Cheered on by 2,000 citizens, Adams demanded the tea's removal. The crowd waited over three hours for the Governor's answer. He refused.

With that Adams shouted, "This meeting can do nothing more to save the country!" and at that, 60 Sons of Liberty "suddenly" burst into the room, dressed as Indians. A grand piece of theatrical staging if ever there was one. As the crowd went wild screaming "Boston Harbor a teapot tonight!" the whole assembly headed for Griffin's Wharf, where the "Indians" threw 342 chests of tea overboard, thereby creating the world's largest pitcher of iced tea.

As punishment, Parliament closed down Boston Harbor and over the next two years the whole situation went from bad to Revolution.

So the little urn had a connection to history. But where, Beth DeLong wondered, should it go for posterity's sake? Beth contacted Rebecca Pelchar at the Chapman Historical Museum, who advised contacting the Charlestown Navy Yard. Beth received no reply.

Now the story takes a wonderful turn. Quite by chance, Beth's niece happened to visit. Beth showed her the urn and her niece replied that her husband, Thomas Bradley, is descended from the same Daggett family, itself descended from Samuel Bradlee of Dorchester, Massachusetts.

Bradlee's house, also called the Daggett house, was a hotbed of conspiracy. There, Bradlees' daughter, Sarah, and his four sons, Nathaniel, Josiah, David and Thomas, all helped in planning the Boston Tea Party. Sarah, also known as the Mother of the Boston Tea Party, helped outfit her brothers as "Indians." She later served as a Patriot spy during the Revolution.

So, quite by chance, a piece of the Bradlees' own home had been secured by Irving W. Ireland, who had carved into an urn, which then waited nearly a century for a Bradlee descendant to marry into the family.

And 229 years later, the circle was completed.

I love happy endings.

"OVER MY SHOULDER" COLUMN FOR JUNE 22, 2002
Look to history for answers

Napkins and paper mills.

This started out as one historian's observation on a very tiny story that ran in *The Post-Star* recently on McDonald's napkin problem. Little did I think I'd rewrite this column to reflect the demise of the Corinth mill, the last of the 20 mills that formed the original International Paper Company, begun here in 1898.

The news is especially bitter in light of paper-related stories in this newspaper. The first was *Post-Star* business editor Maury Thompson's award-winning series last year on the closing of the paper mills throughout the Adirondacks. The second was a recent story on the McDonald's chain cutting back on napkins because of the rising paper costs.

The last of the original IP mills is closing and at the same time we read of rising paper costs?

Historians look for tiny clues in history to see where the cracks in the plaster eventually became fissures. Or, to be more positive, we look for the small actions that changed history for the better, such as in 1905 when Finch Pruyn put in newsprint making machinery. Finch shifted away from lumbering, which was dying out, and toward modern papermaking, which effectively saved the company.

This article about McDonald's napkin scarcity also comes amidst news stories about pulp mills closing because of cheap pulp being imported from Scandinavia. Two questions flashed through this historian's meager mind. First, we are sitting in the Great Northern Forest, spreading from the Adirondacks to Maine and with probably more board feet of lumber than half of Europe, and we are importing pulp?

Second, there is a napkin shortage when we have the world's best papermakers right here, ready and willing to make paper?

Perhaps you don't think this is a proper topic for a local history column and you think I should be musing on summer memories of the `60s when rock meant the Beatles and life seemed endless. But those memories include recollections of working at an International Paper mill humming at full tilt, with good paying jobs for all.

Our leaders now delicately mention that we have "issues" in this region. History, on the other hand, screams that something is radically wrong here. We have a rapidly shrinking paper industry amidst one of the largest forests in the United States. Drive through it from the Adirondacks to Maine and you'll see remnants of once proud communities, buildings empty or gone, people living in housing that would have been considered substandard a generation ago.

That's another paradox. All this wood, yet the cost of a stick-built house is through the roof, and we're in a trade war over cheap lumber with our best neighbor and largest trading partner, Canada.

I mentioned the year 1905. America hit a pivotal point about a century ago. For the first time since freeing itself from European colonial rule, our country started to outproduce any of the major industrial countries in Europe. A half-century ago, thanks in part to two world wars, we were outproducing the whole of Europe.

In this last half-century, our nation has become the dominant economic engine of the world. But our region, which helped give birth to that engine and where the American Revolution was ensured success, now ranks economically among the lowest in the nation. What was bad before is worsening since 9/11.

It's not negative to use history to point that something is out of kilter. It's only negative when we don't use history to face the problem and to try to fix it. We have a problem beyond the power of our state or even a handful of states to fix and we don't need a commission to study the issue and tell us so.

Because the only thing commissions usually do is to paper over a problem.

And we all know that the cost of paper is rising.

"OVER MY SHOULDER" COLUMN FOR JUNE 29, 2002
Fall of fort could have ended celebrations

America's first Fourth of July celebration was nearly its last.

On July 4, 1777, while some citizens celebrated the Declaration of Independence's first anniversary, British General John Burgoyne was preparing his own fireworks for Fort Ticonderoga and Mount Independence.

And John brought about 8,000 others to help light the fuses—British and German soldiers, American Loyalists, and allied Native Americans.

We're so unaware today of the value placed then upon Fort Ticonderoga, Mount Independence and the narrows they guarded. When Fort Ti fell July 5, 1777, Burgoyne came close to ending The Revolution, which by all rights could have collapsed. And today we'd all be singing "O Canada" at ballgames.

On June 26, Burgoyne landed at Crown Point and made a proclamation designed to embellish his biography. The army would "contend for the King and the constitution" to "vindicate the law . . . relieve the oppressed." He warned, "Occasions may occur in which, not difficulty nor labour nor life are to be regarded. This army must not retreat."

He'd live to regret the last sentence. But right now, in the truest sense, he was calling the shots. When he moved south on July 1 to seize Fort Ti and its companion, Mount Independence, no one would have predicted their fall.

Called the "Key to the Continent" during the French and Indian War, Fort Ticonderoga had symbolic and military value when Ethan Allen seized it in 1775. Congress knew if Fort Ti were controlled, New England would be isolated and the rebellion would fail.

In 1776, Congress beefed up Fort Ti and built Mount Independence, a huge fortification on the opposite shore of Lake Champlain. The two were connected by a bridge and boom strung across Lake Champlain.

Burgoyne had gotten close to Fort Ti in 1776. Now, July 1st, 1777, he commanded an armada sailing to a point just three miles north of Fort Ti. Meanwhile his regiments raced along the Vermont shore toward Mount Independence and south along the New York shore towards Fort Ti.

And towards Fort Mount Hope. By July 2nd, it was in British hands. Retreating Americans fled down the LaChute River, burning local sawmills and bridges. It only slowed the machine. Engineers rebuilt the bridges and troops moved through what is today downtown Ticonderoga along, roughly, Champlain Avenue and The Portage. Destination, the top of the 800 foot high Sugar Loaf Hill overlooking Fort Ti and Mt. Independence.

In one day German troops did what most Americans thought impossible— cut a road up Sugar Loaf, built gun emplacements and renamed it Mount Defiance. Cannon looked down American throats.

It was July 4th, 1777.

American General Arthur St. Clair, appointed as commander by General Schuyler only that spring, now assessed the situation. It stunk. For both sites he had only 2,800 men, many green recruits or noncombatants. Mount Independence alone was supposed to have 12,000 men.

St. Clair chose retreat. In the dark of night, leaving most of his supplies and weapons, he and a huge contingent went east. A second group, under Colonel Long, sailed to Whitehall. Burgoyne was hot on their heels.

Fort Ti's fall shocked American Patriots the way 9/11 shocked us. Even though Burgoyne's campaign eventually failed, St. Clair and Schuyler were later court-martialed, and the recriminations lived on. Even justified retreat is seldom forgiven.

This Friday, July 5, Fort Ticonderoga will commemorate this event with "The Evacuation of Ticonderoga by the Continental Army," part of yearlong observances of the 225th anniversary of the campaign. Re-enactors will bring to life the Fort's evacuation by Continental troops and its occupation by Burgoyne's troops.

This is a must, especially for children. Contact Fort Ti at 518.585.2821 or online at http:\www.fort-ticonderoga.org\.

But the story is just beginning. Next week we'll see how St. Clair's flight into Vermont turned into the Battle of Hubbardton, and Long's trip to Whitehall became the campaign's only naval battle.

Happy Fourth!

"OVER MY SHOULDER" COLUMN FOR JULY 6, 2002
Battle of Hubbardton to come alive

On July 6, 1777, British General John Burgoyne found at dawn's early light that Americans had flown the coop.

Fort Ticonderoga and Mount Independence were empty.

American General Arthur St. Clair decided that the 2,800 troops he had at the two fortifications couldn't withstand an assault from Burgoyne's nearly 8,000 troops.

At 2:00 am, St. Clair and troops quietly crossed the Great Bridge and Boom that spanned Lake Champlain and linked Fort Ti and Mount Independence. He marched southeast toward Castle Town, today's Castleton, Vermont. Shortly, Colonel Pierce Long sailed south in darkness with a second group including the many women, children and other noncombatants, his destination Skenesborough, now Whitehall, New York.

But Fort Ti and Mount Independence were not exactly empty. At Mount Independence four Americans had been left to fend off approaching British using cannon. Instead they got dead drunk on Madeira. The British found them passed out. "Have some Madeira, m'dear," indeed!

Burgoyne sent two officers, the British General Simon Fraser and the German General Friedrich von Riedesel[lxxx] after St. Clair.

Burgoyne pursued Long. Americans had thought the Great Boom and Bridge would stop any ship but British warships blasted through it with ease. Unaware of their danger, Long's group played music and sang as they sailed toward Skenesborough. We'll return to their rude awakening momentarily.

Poor St. Clair. He contended with grumbling soldiers who wanted to fight and poorly trained militiamen constantly slowing down, plus sultry heat, rain, and bugs. Following him in a classic rear guard action was Col. Ebenezer Francis of the 11th Massachusetts Regiment. He would slow the enemy, making possible St. Clair's retreat, which he planned to be through Vermont to Skenesborough then to Fort Edward.

Heading for Castle Town, now Castleton, St. Clair paused at the John Selleck farm in tiny Hubbardton, where he left Colonel Seth Warner and the Green Mountain Boys Regiment, and Colonel Nathan Hale and his 2nd New Hampshire Regiment. They'd join Francis' incoming rear guard.

St. Clair then went on to Castle Town, chasing away Justus Sherwood's Loyalist troops from their pillaging.

The Battle of Hubbardton began early on July 7 when General Fraser attacked the Americans. War raged upon Monument Hill, today the Hubbardton Battlefield State Historic Site. Amidst the wild fighting, Fraser was actually almost surrounded. Miraculously Riedesel appeared and saved his bacon. Americans retreated south but left a very surprised Fraser now knowing that Americans were also excellent soldiers.

Today and tomorrow, July 6 and 7, you can experience that battle firsthand at Hubbardton Battlefield in East Hubbardton, Vermont. Over 1,000 re-enactors will portray American, British, and German soldiers in a huge encampment. They'll hold tactical demonstrations today. Then tomorrow morning, July 7, the battle will be reenacted, starting at 5:30 a.m., with other demonstrations to follow. For more information call (802) 273-2282. This is absolutely the way for kids to learn history!

St. Clair learned of British warships breaking through the Great Boom and Bridge. He wisely avoided Skenesborough, where on July 6, Burgoyne caught up with Col. Long[lxxxi]. In doing so, Burgoyne waged his campaign's only naval battle at Skenesborough, now Whitehall.

Burgoyne struck as Long was in the process of getting the women, children and noncombatants up and over falls and into bateaux to head for Fort Ann. Cannon balls and musket balls clogged the air. Three ships and 300 bateaux sunk. Americans took a beating with three vessels, the *Enterprise*, *Liberty* and *Gates* blown up and a galley and schooner captured. Bodies floated in the bay.

Retreating Americans torched harborside buildings, including a fortification, shipyard and sawmill, adding to the blazing ships and bateaux in the harbor. Then forests on Skene Mountain caught fire. The British were victorious, but Skenesborough was an inferno.

Most Americans escaped, heading south toward Fort Ann. There the next battle occurred on July 8.

Next week, the Battle of Fort Anne.[lxxxii]

"OVER MY SHOULDER" COLUMN FOR JULY 13, 2002
Burgoyne campaign moves into Fort Anne

Over the last three weeks we've been watching the progress of the 1777 Campaign of the British General John Burgoyne.

We've now reached the point of the "the Battle of Fort Anne." This weekend you'll want to save some time to get over to Fort Ann, where there'll be a full-scale re-enactment of the Battle of Fort Anne. As you may have read in Darrin Youker's fine article in Monday's *Post-Star*, this re-enactment is a part of Fort Ann's Heritage Days, a weekend of activities which begins with a parade at 10 am this morning and ends tomorrow with the battle re-enactment on Goodman Road at 1:30 pm. Phone 518-639-8869 for more information.

On July 6, 1777, British troops had pursued American General Arthur St. Clair into Vermont, while the British General John Burgoyne himself had chased Col. Pierce Long south on Lake Champlain. He caught up with Long at Skenesborough, now Whitehall, N.Y. Here Burgoyne waged his campaign's only naval battle. A visit to the Skenesborough Museum & Urban Cultural Park Center on Skenesborough Drive in Whitehall is an excellent place to learn more about that.

The Americans fled south from Skenesborough to the fortification called Fort Anne. With Col. Long were the troops under Captain James Gray, who had commanded the blockhouse at Skenesborough. They were all joined unexpectedly by 400 fresh troops. Burgoyne had ordered two regiments to go along South Bay to head the rebels off, but the chaos in the harbor at Skenesborough delayed them.

So, Burgoyne sent Col. John Hill to Fort Anne on July 7. But Hill's passage along the Great Road from Skenesborough to Fort Anne and on the adjoining Wood Creek was delayed by felled trees, destroyed bridges and torrential rains.

Just above Fort Anne, Hill set up pickets by what we call now Battle Hill. Capt. Gray was out with a scouting when he ran into the pickets and a 4-hour fight ensued.

But the Battle of Fort Anne occurred the next day, July 8. That morning Hill learned of Long's 1,000 men from an American spy pretending to be a deserter. And when the spy got back to the Americans, they then learned that Hill had only 200 men! At 10:30 the Americans attacked.

In Darrin's article, I was quoted as saying that the historical significance of the Battle of Fort Anne is that it was the first battle in which the British troops met heavy American resistance. I have to correct myself. Certainly at the battles at Hubbardton and Skenesborough, Americans had shown resistance.

At the Battle of Fort Anne, Americans showed it again. The battle raged for two hours just north of the present village on what is now known as Battle Hill. The British were nearly out of ammunition, as were the Americans, although neither knew the other side's condition. The British were just about to surrender, when suddenly the regiments Hill requested came to his aid. This was similar to the situation at Hubbardton, where relief arrived in the nick of time.

The Americans retreated, setting Fort Anne afire. They had significantly slowed the British and showed the British some real American mettle. In the retreat, the British captured a flag, which a British officer named Digby described in his diary as "a flag of the United States, 13 stripes alternate red and white, [with thirteen stars] in a blue field representing a new constellation." Historians still debate if this flag were Old Glory, adopted by Congress on June 23, 1777, and whether the Battle of Fort Anne was the first instance of its being flown in battle.

Postscript: During the 1927 Sesquicentennial celebration of the Burgoyne

Campaign, an enormous plaque was erected on Battle Hill in Fort Ann and unveiled at a fitting ceremony. At the ceremony there was an 8-year-old Fort Ann boy, James Goodman. Now 75 years later, that same boy, just a wee bit older, will ride in today's parade through the heart of Fort Ann. Congratulations, Jim!

And congratulations to everyone in Fort Ann for a remarkable celebration of this remarkable piece of American history, the Battle of Fort Anne.

[EDITOR'S POSTSCRIPT: Through the efforts of many, Battle Hill in Fort Ann, NY, the American Battlefield Trust was to purchase 160 acres of Battle Hill in 2020.]

"OVER MY SHOULDER" COLUMN FOR JULY 27, 2002
A fresh look at Jane McCrea

When does a murder suit the political needs of the times? To me, it's the basic question regarding the death of Jane McCrea. Some say her murder[lxxxiii] in 1777 contributed heavily to the defeat of British General Burgoyne in his bid to halt the American Revolution.

Others say such a claim is nonsense.

But I believe rebellious Americans used the brutal murder of a young, unarmed Loyalist woman solely for political gain. I further believe the best information is from sources written at the time of her death. Many later eyewitness testimonies, and histories from the 19th and early 20th century, seem only to have generated contradictory stories, conspiracy theories and nitpicking that have diminished the importance of her death.

Using 1777 sources effectively eliminates a lot of what I've previously written in this column about her death. So be it. Better to give you now what I comfortably feel is the truth.

Born in Lamington, New Jersey[lxxxiv] in 1754, Jane McCrea was living with her brother John McCrea, in 1777, in today's Town of Northumberland. John, a lawyer and farmer, was an officer in the Albany County Militia. Jane was of Loyalist sympathies.

Jane was single and by most accounts physically attractive and personable. She was betrothed to a Loyalist officer in Burgoyne's army, David Jones of Kingsbury. On either July 26 or July 27, 1777, in the company of John McCreas' African American slave, Dinah, and Dinah's child, Jane went to the home of Sarah McNeil, at or near the present building called "The Jane McCrea House" on Broadway in Fort Edward. The well-to-do McNeil was first cousin to British General Simon Fraser, who was encamped about a mile to the north. In that encampment was David Jones.

On the morning of July 27, more likely July 26, Jane McCrea and Sarah McNeil were seized by Indians while hiding in the cellar of the McNeil house. They were taken up the hill where, just south of the present Fort Edward Public School building, the two were parted at a fork in the road, McCrea being taken up one road and Mrs. McNeil up another to Fraser's camp. McCrea was murdered and her body thrown down an embankment, where it was later found.

The American General Horatio Gates wrote Burgoyne and accused him of having paid Indians "to scalp Europeans and the descendants of Europeans" and of paying for the scalps. He wrote that "Miss McCrea" was "engaged to be married to an officer" of Burgoyne's army and "dressed to receive her promised husband."

Burgoyne's venomous response denied only hiring Indians to scalp people, nothing else. He wrote, "two chiefs who had brought her off for the purpose of security . . . disputed who should be her guard." Instead, in their dispute Jane was murdered by one of them. Otherwise his letter confirms everything else Gates wrote.

Other letters confirm and amplify these facts. Patriot Ivory Hovey wrote from Fort Miller on July 27, that McCrea was "Shott, Tomihawk'd and Scalp'd." He learned of it from Dinah, the "Negro wench who hid in the cellar."

In reality, Jane's death seems to have been a random act of warfare, only one of many unrelated murders and massacres done by Burgoyne's Indian allies—horrible, but not rare. Jane's death was also a mistake because she was a Loyalist. Gates used her being a young, betrothed Loyalist woman, to political advantage by sending copies of his letter to newspapers. Within a month it was published from Massachusetts to Virginia! In September Burgoyne was at Saratoga. He was defeated there in October.

Did Gates' use of Jane's murder contribute to Burgoyne's defeat? I believe so. Burgoyne, already short-supplied at Fort Edward, then suffered humiliating defeat at Walloomsac. He arrived at Saratoga to find thousands of Patriots waiting, no longer in retreat but itching for battle.

News of her death helped rally Americans to defeat Burgoyne, and so turned the tide of the American Revolution.

"OVER MY SHOULDER" COLUMN FOR AUGUST 10, 2002
Fortunes – or misfortunes – of war

We return to those sultry days of August 1777.

The British General John Burgoyne is in Fort Edward with enormous supply problems. They would be among "the fortunes of war" that would lead to his first defeat, the Battle of Bennington.

Burgoyne was headquartered at the commandeered home of Patriot William Duer[lxxxv] in Fort Miller. His troops, spread from there to the Battenkill River, consumed food as it arrived. There were no reserves. All necessities of war, sent south on Lake George from Fort Ti, were slow in coming.

For reasons no one understands, Burgoyne sent German Lieut. Col Friedrich Baum—who spoke no English—into Vermont for supplies. Burgoyne and Baum's superior, Major General Friedrich von Riedesel, had planned a lightning strike into Arlington, Vermont.

But Burgoyne expanded it, ordering Baum south to capture the munitions at Bennington. Oh, and while Baum was at the store, he was to pick up horses, cattle, flour, grain and any other supplies he could find.

Perhaps the rerouting was due to another motive, Burgoyne's desire to move into New England to stop those pesky colonists once and for all. What a lesson he'd learn.

On August 13, Baum marched from his camp in the Thompson-Clarks Mills area in the Town of Greenwich, picking up about 500 Loyalists from the region. Baum's total force was 1,200 men. Now began those "fortunes of war" I mentioned, those inexplicable bits of chance that no one foresees. I'll dub them "FOW."

While Baum went through Greenwich, Easton, Cambridge, White Creek and Hoosick toward Bennington, FOW #1 occurred. The newly created Republic of Vermont took a totally unilateral action and petitioned New Hampshire to send troops. General John Stark arrived at Manchester with 2,000 troops and marched to Bennington on August 9.

Now General Philip Schuyler, parked in Stillwater, had sent an escort to bring Stark to the Hudson. FOW #2. Stark instead marched to Bennington, where he combined forces with Seth Warner's Green Mountain Boys. By chance it was the right thing. Had the Americans lost the Battle of Bennington, Stark would have been considered an idiot.

Stark sent a Col. Gregg north to intercept Baum at Cambridge. On August 15, Gregg and Baum battled at Sans Coick, now North Hoosick. Gregg was routed, but it was only round one.

Suddenly a driving thunderstorm erupted that turned everything to mud. Baum sent back for reinforcements while his troops dug entrenchments on a hill overlooking the Walloomsac River. Stark's sharpshooters picked away at them.

FOW #3 now occurs. Burgoyne had sent Philip Skene to administer the loyalty oath to local people. But Skene could not tell the difference between Patriots and Loyalists and to devastating effect, Patriots infiltrated the defenses.

August 16, 1777 was sunny. Stark's troops executed a brilliant assault and overran Baum in a brilliant victory. Now the last FOW occurred. The replacement forces sent were either inordinately slow marching or hampered by roads that were a mud soup. Or both. Whatever, they arrived too late and were routed.

Burgoyne lost in so many ways. Over 900 men are killed or captured. Baum died of his wounds. Burgoyne did not get his supplies.

The Americans, by contrast won a dazzling victory that crippled the enemy and gave Americans a psychological boost of unparalleled dimensions. The battle became a lynchpin for the victory at Saratoga.

From August 16 through 18, the 225th Anniversary of the Battle of Bennington will be celebrated at the Bennington Battlefield State Historic Site in the Town of Hoosick; the New York State Museum in Albany; at the Bennington Museum and Bennington Battle Monument in Bennington, and at the Scarecrow Farm along Route 67 in Shaftsbury.

Watch *The Post-Star* this week for news on reenactment encampments and battles, presentations and other activities. Or go online to website for the "The Northern Campaign": http//:www.thenortherncampaign.org.

Enlist now for the Battle of Bennington!

"OVER MY SHOULDER" COLUMN FOR AUGUST 24, 2002
More data needed on minorities

[AUTHOR"S NOTE: In this column, I apologized for a "mistake" I made in the column "Region's Black history needs exploring" (February 16, 2002). I wrote that historian Ken Perry[lxxxvi] had discovered that Washington County had an enormous African American population between 1800 and 1820. As it was, Perry was correct, and eleven years later he was vindicated. In 2013, L. Lloyd Stewart published incontrovertible proof of that population increase in his excellent history, *The Mysterious Black Migration 1800-1820: The Van Vranken Family and Other Free Families of African Descent in Washington County, New York*. The book traces the mass migration of thousands of African descendants to Washington County, New York at the beginning of the 1800s.]

I've taken some time to write this column, because it's going to offend some people and I want to make sure that it does so in the right way.

A while back, I wrote several columns on Black Revolutionary War veterans and on African Americans living in the region in the late 1700s and the early 1800s. The columns evoked a greater response than I ever anticipated.

On the one side, both Blacks and whites urged me to rethink my interpretation of the population statistics for Washington County in the early 1800s. They said that the 1810 census, showing an immense spike in the Black population, had to have been either a miscount or a misprint. They must be correct.

And for the record, I must be wrong. Nothing I've found supports the census' huge increase in the Black population from 1800 to 1810, nor the subsequent and equally huge decrease in that same population by 1820.

That said, I think more scholarship needs to be done on the overall population in the late 1700s and early 1800s, but especially the African American, Native American-, and mixed-race populations. Frankly, most of the standard histories and genealogies for this region are inadequate.

Having issued this "mea culpa," the other reason for this column is to address those other responses to those particular columns.

Now, some readers responded positively, saying they appreciated a different look at area history, while others were negative, ranging from being annoyed to being obscene. It's a free country. If I help reduce your blood pressure, go to it.

One citizen wrote that I'd betrayed the white race and claimed I'd cheered for the arming of the Black race against the white. Letters like that are filed under "I" for imbecilic. Nothing I write will change that mind.

For me, the most bothersome responses were from bright, well-educated, seemingly open-minded people. One person in particular dismissed the columns as "politically correct." Only after issuing that pontification did the reader then challenge the data.

If by "politically correct" it was meant that I took the occasion to discuss what cannot be found in local histories, I'm guilty. Black soldiers did participate in the Revolution. Black people did live here before, during and after the Revolution. Some intermarried with white and Indian people. Some thrived here and died here, and generally most went unrecorded because of their color.

It's the truth that you don't find in this area's standard histories, because many were written in the 1800s, when it wasn't "convenient" to have too many Blacks or Indians – or women of any color – sharing in the early history.

It's the sad truth that for many people the past means nothing until it impinges upon their here and now. Have your property ownership threatened or your pet notions questioned and then, by golly, history is important!

To me, anyone thinking that the columns were "politically correct" had a racial agenda of his, her own. Oh, and for the record, a "politically correct" column from me would suggest that every Black or Indian who ever lived here was perfect and only the whites were bigoted. From my personal experience, bigots exist in every size, shape, gender and color. Bigotry is an equal opportunity employer.

What is truthful is that in the late 1700s and early 1800s whites, Blacks and Indians lived here, about 47 percent males and 53 percent female judging by today's ratio. Together they created the history of this region, and what they did then makes a difference now.

How many of each group were here at that time? Who were they? What exactly did they do? That's what I want to discover today.

And if discovered, that information won't be politically correct. It will be, for the first time, simply and only correct. At least, I hope it'll be correct. If you want to challenge my data, feel welcome to do so.

But if you're bothered by my motive for searching out that history, here's my advice: Tell somebody who cares.

"OVER MY SHOULDER" COLUMN FOR AUGUST 31, 2002
Working to provide a little dignity

[EDITOR'S NOTE: Pleasant Valley Infirmary in Argyle, NY, is now Washington Center for Rehabilitation and Healthcare. It began its life in 1827 as the Washington County Poorhouse. In 1963 it was renamed Pleasant Valley Infirmary. Washington County privatized it in 2000.]

Richard Wilson is on a "Mission Possible."

Dick Wilson,[lxxxvii] as his friends know him, is seeking to bring a new dignity to a group of people who, until recently, were all but forgotten. You'll recognize his name from the fine article written about him by *Post-Star* reporter Gretta Nemcek. Dick is author of the new book, *Deaths at the Washington County Poorhouse* published recently by Washington County.[lxxxviii]

What's special about this 53-page, illustrated history book is that all the net proceeds of its sale will go to the refurbishment of the cemetery that lies on the grounds of the Pleasant Valley Infirmary in Argyle, the site of what was called the Washington County Poorhouse, when it was first created in 1827. Dick has given up any profit so that the sales receipts can help restore broken stones, provide new fences, whatever it will take to bring new dignity to this final resting place of, until recently, a forgotten group of people.

Pleasant Valley Infirmary, for those not familiar with it, is a county-run facility, dedicated to providing a quality nursing home facility as well as a place a person can proudly call his or her final home. Dick Wilson's connection with it began when he was contacted by Linda Crannell, who was seeking assistance with her publication, *Portraits of Poverty*, which is a history of the residents of the Washington County Poorhouse between 1875 and 1900.

Dick, a long-time historian with several books to his credit, researched the names of those in the cemetery. After he finished helping Linda, he decided to create a complete list of every person who died at Pleasant Valley.

It was a daunting task lasting several years. As he gathered the names, Dick decided to write an introductory history to the "Poorhouse," and include some older photos of both the buildings and grounds, as well as modern day shots of the cemetery.

The cemetery itself is maintained by Pleasant Valley. But, like many of our region's cemeteries, it has broken stones and other problems—a big job for a facility with many claims on its resources.

Dick's hope is that his contribution will spur others to help with repairs and with improvements, such as further onsite identification of those buried there, using the information Dick has gathered. He has listed the names of hundreds upon hundreds of people who have lived and died there. And the institution has been there since 1827, when it was started to accommodate the poor, the destitute, the elderly who had no one to care for them, and the mentally disabled.

Dick lists names, places of origin, dates of death, nationality, and race. Some have headstones with names, while others have headstones with only a number. Some who died at the Poorhouse were buried elsewhere. Dick's book lists them all and, for the genealogist, it's a must.

Dick's way of reasoning regarding these people is particularly appealing: these were human beings who should be accorded the same respect that each of us would wish for ourselves and our family. To me, his view becomes even more fundamental in light of the tragedy of September 11th.

I feel the purchase of one of Dick's books will go a long way toward making the statement that we as a society value the lives of every person, as it will contribute to the betterment of this final resting place.

Copies of Dick Wilson's book are for sale at the Pleasant Valley Infirmary in Argyle and the Old Fort House Museum and Washington County Historical Society in Fort Edward.

And here's a treat for you. Go to the Pleasant Valley Infirmary this coming Friday, September 6, from 1 to 4 pm, and not only can you purchase your own copy, but you'll get to meet the author, who will autograph it for you. As a bonus, Dick Wilson will be giving a tour of the cemetery itself.

Now, there's a man with a mission. Thanks, Dick!

"OVER MY SHOULDER" COLUMN FOR SEPTEMBER 14, 2002
When America left its childhood

Look at your life and chose the two most pivotal instances that catapulted you from childhood into adulthood.

Now look at your country and do the same.

You're probably hard-pressed to say with certainty what might even have been the single most pivotal instance—that "turning point" in your life—when you began to put behind the things of childhood.

So, then, you can appreciate the difficulty in choosing two instances from the beginning of the United States, as it was just emerging from a childhood spent under a distant monarchy into its first moments of young adulthood as an independent nation.

In those early times of the rebellion there are two instances that define for me that moment. The first would be July 4th, 1776, when we proclaimed our adulthood, in some ways like all adolescent rebellion, with the flourish and the awkward, yet cocky defiance.

The second would be to the Battles of Saratoga, in 1777, appropriately called the "Turning Point of The Revolution." After them the young United States was recognized as an adult. There were two battles. Yet they're inseparable and therefore often referred to in the singular, as the "Battle of Saratoga."

The past is always inevitable. That is, we always know what has happened. But standing in the present there is little inevitability in the future to come. So, when the British General John Burgoyne crossed the Hudson on September 13, 1777, into what was then called Saratoga, there was no inevitability of his defeat. No inevitability of the American rebels' victory. No inevitability of the 14 month-old United States of America even existing past December 1777.

True, Burgoyne had just lost nearly a sixth of his army at the Battle of Bennington. True, his counterpart General Barry St. Leger had been driven back at Oriskany. True, subsequent desertions of Loyalists, German and British soldiers and Indians would continue to deplete his army. True, he had lost a month at Fort Miller building up his supplies.

And, true, when he crossed the Hudson, Americans were starting to rally rather than run—partly because of Bennington, partly because of their rage at the Indian and Loyalist raids that left the countryside burning, and people slaughtered like cattle.

But as Burgoyne crossed the Hudson, marching through Saratoga toward Albany, he did so with a highly trained, well-disciplined army of about 6,500, armed with 133 cannon. It was a war machine.

Opposing that machine were between 7,000 and 7,400 Americans, mostly farmers and shopkeepers formed into militias with little or no training. The percentage of rebel Americans who had been French and Indian War veterans was not large. Moreover, American turnover was astounding. American generals faced the wholesale departure of militia when three- or six-month enlistments were up. For example, on September 15, General Stark and his troops, the heroes of the Battle of Bennington, told General Horatio Gates that they were going home. And they did, in spite of bonuses offered!

Gates himself was a pretty dismal general, so cautious his men called him "Granny." He had only just shamelessly politicked his way into his being appointed commander of the Northern Department in place of General Philip Schuyler. Gates seized on the fall of Fort Ticonderoga on July 6 to give what help he could to get Schuyler fired from the job. He then treated Schuyler's allies, such as Benedict Arnold, like poison.

Our region was actually providing Burgoyne with help, as it was pretty evenly split in its sentiments between Loyalists, Patriots and those who were neutral.

And Burgoyne's war machine? Though wounded it was still moving, still very lethal. If anything were inevitable, it was Burgoyne's reaching Albany, as planned.

But the only true inevitability was chance in the form of an utterly paradoxical American, whom Burgoyne's machine would meet on September 19, 1777, during the first Battle of Saratoga.

Next week, the first Battle of Saratoga —the Turning Point of The Revolution begins.

"OVER MY SHOULDER" COLUMN FOR SEPTEMBER 21, 2002
Burgoyne's troubles started in Ti

We come to the first of the two Battles of Saratoga, the Battle of Freeman's Farm on September 19, 1777.

When Burgoyne had crossed the Hudson into Saratoga on September 13, he off cut off his lines of communication with Canada. He had also just suffered a huge loss at the Battle of Bennington. But I believe too much credit is given to those events in contributing to Burgoyne's defeat at Saratoga.

I believe one event had already done, and would continue to do, more to begin Burgoyne's defeat—the fall of Fort Ticonderoga in July 1777. Fort Ti's abandonment shocked and enraged our new nation and Congress replaced General Philip Schuyler with General Horatio Gates as head of the Northern Department.

But frankly, Gates, the embodiment of mediocrity, didn't suddenly lead Schuyler's army from retreat to victory. The Battle of Bennington did rally Americans. The slaughter of innocents like Jane McCrea did ratchet up American wrath. But it was the fall of Fort Ti that first turned the tide. Only after Congress had sacked Schuyler did it now begin pouring troops into the region, not before. Without Congress' sudden infusion of troops, it's likely Burgoyne would have made it to Albany.

But here, chance had stepped in, too. For how could Congress have afforded to send those troops waiting for the attack of British General William Howe? Because Howe had sailed for Philadelphia, instead of sailing to Albany to meet Burgoyne as planned. Howe got waylaid at sea and ended up stuck in Maryland. Suddenly George Washington knew that American troops being held in readiness could now be safely released to Gates. And they were.

Now to the Battle. Burgoyne seized lands in and around Schuylerville,[lxxxix] but he was late. Schuyler, remember, had delayed Burgoyne between Whitehall and

Fort Ann in July and now denied Burgoyne food through a scorched earth policy.

Gates moved the American army north from Stillwater[xc] to the Neilson farm[xci] on Bemis Heights. Here, reinforced by Thaddeus Kosciuszko's new entrenchments. Gates commanded the river and helped block the road to Albany.

Moving south to Dovegat, now Coveville, Burgoyne learned the Americans had tried to re-take Fort Ti—unsuccessfully, but now they knew how weak his supply lines were.

Burgoyne split his army into three columns under Philip von Riedesel, Simon Fraser and himself. They headed southwest for the American lines. Learning of the movements, Gates sent the fierce Virginian Col. Daniel Morgan's forces northward. Morgan ran into Fraser's troops at around 12:30 pm and the Battle of Freeman Farm began. Now part of the Saratoga National Historical Park, this land is scored by huge ravines, in and out of which the battle raged. It ebbed and flowed over Freeman's Farm for hours, the cannon and musket shots roaring in near constant thunder, their lead shredding humans, horses, even small trees with ease.

Space prohibits describing the battle in depth, but though the British won, it was a Pyrrhic victory. Hundreds of his troops lay dead and dying. Burgoyne had led his men in the thick of battle, as did Fraser and Riedesel. Gates stayed in his tent, letting valiant officers such as Morgan, Ebenezer Learned and Enoch Poor inflict devastating assaults upon Burgoyne. And this battle showed the British the reckless, sometimes insane bravery Benedict Arnold would display at the second Battle of Saratoga, where he would play a pivotal role.

After the Battle of Freeman's Farm, Burgoyne dug in and waited for Henry Clinton to sail north and save him. He was still waiting when the Second Battle of Saratoga began on October 8. We'll look at that in two weeks.

Over the coming weeks, there are numerous programs and events observing the 225th anniversary of the Burgoyne campaign. Contact the Saratoga National Historical Park at 518-664-9821 for information.

Visit the battlefields. Contemplate the making of America. There isn't a better story for you to know.

"OVER MY SHOULDER" COLUMN FOR OCTOBER 12, 2002
Arnold emerges as hero of Saratoga

British General John Burgoyne had decided to launch a reconnaissance force, to determine whether to attack the American General Horatio Gates on the 8th or to retreat back across the Hudson on the 11th. What follows is taken from original sources, Richard Ketchum's *Saratoga*, and from tour information graciously supplied by the Saratoga National Historical Park.

Burgoyne himself led 1,500 British and German troops, plus another 600 Canadians, Loyalists and Indians, west on October 7. He sent his others, including Major General Simon Fraser, to weave their way around the Americans and distract them while Burgoyne came up on them with the majority of the force.

As the British moved west from Freeman's Farm to the fields of Barber's Farm, the Americans secretly watched Burgoyne's every move. Deputy Adjutant General James Wilkinson informed Gates that the British were "endeavoring to reconnoiter your left and I think sir they offer you battle." Gates pondered, then said, "Well then, order on Morgan to begin the game." Gates had begun war against a man with whom he had trained to be an officer.

Benedict Arnold, all but chained to a chair, said more troops were needed. Gates said, "I have nothing for you to do. You have no business here." Gates shamefully dismissed Arnold. However, Gates was persuaded to reinforce Morgan with General Learned Poor's brigade. Like Arnold, Gates stayed back in camp. Arnold paced and fumed. Gates sat.

Burgoyne's end and America's beginning started at 2:30 on October 7, 1777. Snapshots must do to convey the confusion, horror and joy that mingled that day. Remember, Gates now had 12,000 men at his disposal, 6,000 of which were trained Continental soldiers. Americans come north to meet Burgoyne at Barber's field. Col. Morgan's Corp of riflemen and light infantry under Major Henry Dearborn hit the British Fraser's light infantry and the 24th regiment. While General Enoch Forest's brigade of New Hampshire men and New Yorkers attacked British Grenadiers and General Hamilton's division, General Ebenezer Learned's brigade hit the Germans.

The American battle veterans overran the British Grenadiers whose commander Major John Dyke Acland, was shot through both legs. James Wilkinson brought American reinforcements, Abraham Tenbroek's Albany militia Brigade and a regiment from Jonathan Warner's Massachusetts militia Brigade. Wilkinson found British dead littering the field, Joseph Cilley sitting on a captured cannon and screaming for joy, and an American surgeon glorying in having British blood on him. Wilkinson rebuked the surgeon sternly then went to rescue Acland, who was about to be shot by the 14-year-old American boy standing over him.

Morgan and Dearborn made Simon Fraser's troops retreat in a hail of cannon and musket fire. Arnold, meanwhile, bolted out of camp against orders and flew onto the field to the cheers of Learned's troops. Arnold actually seized command of Learned's regiment and led them against the Germans who now retreated with the British.

Burgoyne, like Arnold, was riding through it all, musket shot tearing his clothes, killing his horse. Then came a fatal break. Burgoyne's beloved Simon Fraser, on horseback, was rallying his men and making the Americans pay with blood for the British retreat. Col. Morgan ordered sharpshooter Timothy

Murphy to shoot Fraser and the gallant Scot went down. Taken to a nearby house, he died a day later.

Amidst smoke and lead thick in the air and bodies strewn on the ground, Burgoyne's troops broke and ran to the Breymann and Balcarres redoubts.

And in came Arnold on horseback. Refusing to let them have a chance to retreat, Arnold, the smell of blood now like an aphrodisiac, led the charge against the Balcarres regiment, screaming and cheering his troops on. The defense was too tough and Arnold was retreating when he saw Learned's men advancing on Breymann's redoubt. Spurring his horse, Arnold charged between the American and British lines through heavy fire and helped lead in the defeat of the British line.

Arnold's charge was stopped when he was shot in the leg, but he had saved the day. Through maniacal bravery, Arnold fought in concert with Colonel Morgan, Major Dearborn and Generals Poor and Learned to defeat John Burgoyne. The man who would be traitor was the hero of October 7, the British defeat at the Second Battle of Saratoga.

Next week: the surrender.

"OVER MY SHOULDER" COLUMN FOR OCTOBER 19, 2002
Capitalize on Saratoga's history

And so we come to an ending, which is for the United States a beginning: the surrender of Burgoyne.

On Oct. 7, at what is now the Saratoga National Historical Park, the reconnaissance force of the British Gen. John Burgoyne was attacked and driven back by American forces under Gen. Horatio Gates. Burgoyne's army hemorrhaged able officers and men on that day. Retreating into the night, Burgoyne attempted the next day to regain Breymann's redoubt, a log and earth defense structure.

The only result was the American Gen. Benjamin Lincoln being badly wounded and Burgoyne buying enough time to retreat north, toward Saratoga, now Schuylerville.

Cold, driving rains drenched his troops that moved overnight to avoid discovery. They went only 4 miles, arriving on the heights overlooking Dovegat house, today the Saratoga Sod Farm on US Route 4. Finally, on Oct. 10, Burgoyne and his troops crossed the swollen Fishkill[xcii] to encamp at the heights overlooking Saratoga, where the Saratoga Battle Monument is today.

Burgoyne tried one last gamble. Assuming Americans would come at him as the fog lifted, he prepared to charge them, and burned every impediment to his line of fire, including Philip Schuyler's summer home and buildings. But two deserters betrayed Burgoyne's plan, by tipping off the Americans. Gates' troops avoided Burgoyne's fire only at the last moment as a result.

Burgoyne learned that escape was cut off to the east by Gen. Fellows in Easton and Capt. Furnival at Clark's mills in Greenwich. To the north, by Gen. John Stark at today's Stark's Knob. To the west, by Col. Daniel Morgan's riflemen and to the south, by Gen. Gates.

Gates also sent troops to Fort Edward to prevent the rebuilding of a bridge for escape north. Gates had 12,000, possibly 20,000, troops to Burgoyne's remaining 5,000. At a meeting of Burgoyne's generals on Oct. 11, the conclusion was to surrender.

The campaign to end the American rebellion itself ended Oct. 17, 1777, in moments so uniquely American. Gates allowed Burgoyne to save face by calling the surrender a "convention." Americans marched into the British camp playing "Yankee Doodle" – until then a British taunt. Burgoyne surrendered his sword to Gates, with whom, ironically, he had served in England. Then Burgoyne's troops marched to the site of old Fort Hardy in today's Schuylerville to surrender their arms. Gates ordered that only one American officer should witness it, an American military first.

As the defeated British army surrendered, its musicians played "The World Turned Upside Down." It had indeed. A "rabble in arms," as Burgoyne had described Americans, had done more than defeat a major British army. The Battles of Saratoga brought our nation foreign recognition, especially that of France, whose troops turned the tide in Washington's defeat of Cornwallis at Yorktown in 1781, the Revolution's concluding battle.

From Crown Point, Fort Ticonderoga, Mt. Independence, and the Hubbardton Battlefield in the north, south to the Saratoga National Historical Park in Stillwater, every community touched by Burgoyne's campaign shared in making the glory of a history uniquely ours, the Battles of Saratoga.

This year's wonderful 225th anniversary observance called "The Northern Campaign" is ending. Thousands gave time and talent to create re-enactments, ceremonies, and other observances, which in turn brought us tens of thousands of visitors, who spent hundreds of thousands of dollars. It was a vision of what could be.

If my wish could be answered, it would be that all of our political leaders at every level would see that our region's history is not dead, but is a living force waiting to be unleashed with their help, yielding a power that would work wonders for our region, as it has in Williamsburg and other places.

And what is a vital part of this history? The Battles of Saratoga. For plainly and simply, Saratoga changed the world, and its effect has been felt ever since.

With all due respect to my birthplace Saratoga Springs, the first thing the word "Saratoga" should bring to mind throughout the world is neither horses nor water.

The first thing "Saratoga" should bring to mind is freedom.

"OVER MY SHOULDER" COLUMN FOR NOVEMBER 2, 2002
Pies symbol of an end of an era in Corinth

I t was the blueberry pies that got to me.

The local news was too perplexing. Actor Toby Maguire was taking bows in Saratoga Springs and International Paper was bowing out of Corinth.

And my friend was baking farewell blueberry pies for the last gathering among the electricians at International Paper Company in Corinth.

The other day my friend Loretta Bates[xciii] said that her husband Grover had asked her to make a couple of her pies for a farewell dinner among the men in his department. He's an instrument electrician at the Corinth mill. By the time you read this, he will no longer be that. Every wife, she said, was making something. It would be a bittersweet meal.

"The guys like my pies," she'd once said a while back when Grove, as she calls her husband, had inveigled her to make a couple for him to bring to work. She grumbled about it in that way that cooks do when they are pleased to the depths of their mixing bowls. Now, I realized, these pies would be the last she'd ever make for them.

As I write, there's been no announcement of the purchase of Corinth mill, the founding mill of the International Paper Company that began here over 100 years ago. Another town ends its life as a papermill town.

Ironically, my first "Over My Shoulder" column, published in this paper on October 24,1994, was about a mill closing in Fort Edward, another mill town where one of IP's founding mills had been. History is repeating itself. I wish it weren't.

When I asked Loretta if she'd mind if I wrote something about the Corinth mill, specifically mentioning her and Grover, she said it was okay. But she very quickly reminded me that she and Grove are "just one of 290." As she said, "There's 290 in the same boat and a hell of a lot are worse off than we are." My condolences go out to all of the 290 workers and their families.

Loretta expressed it so succinctly when she talked about the mill's closing. "The mill has always been part of our life. I played out in front of it as a kid. I never lived more than 20 miles from it. Grove has worked there 31 years. Grove's father worked there in WW II." Loretta's mother had also worked there during the war. And her oldest son now works in the mill.

Or did. She said, "I have a heavy feeling in my heart for Grove. There is just this incredible sadness for what we have lost. It's not just a job, it's a way of living. But we're a tough generation. Instead of just sitting around and whining…we'll make it."

Yes, the people here are tough, but they aren't superhuman. It doesn't take a historian to say, this area is in trouble, like most of the northeastern US, except for some affluent strips. But historians can offer this perspective: having our national leaders labeling the Northeast the "Rust Belt" and leaving part of it—including this region where our country began—to fend for itself is shameful.

Historians can also offer the perspective that, in past times of trouble, national government took a rightful place in bringing relief. Some will call me a liberal for that. Guilty. But it hurts me as a small "L" liberal to have to ask how we as a nation can justify sending billions of dollars abroad to build countries, when our own is in such shape.

So, what now? Life will go on, with newspapers duly recording that Toby Maguire was here filming a story about America during one its worst financial times, the Great Depression, while simultaneously a nearby papermill closed, one of many recently. And might that ironic tidbit even show up in some history written 100 years from now, leaving people open-mouthed? Probably not.

But at least one history will have recorded the blueberry pies.

"OVER MY SHOULDER" COLUMN FOR NOVEMBER 9, 2002
Son of the USA

He was an immigrant who founded a chapter of a very American organization.

Morris Rote-Rosen's story is the immigrant's tale "writ large." It would take a book to do justice to it. Only an America could an immigrant boy arrive at age 13, speaking no English, then go on to college, then serve honorably in the First World War, and finally return to found a branch of the newly created American Legion. And all this before he turned 30.

Many know Morris Rote-Rosen for his weekly column in *The Granville Sentinel,* "Main Street," on the past and present of Granville and neighboring Vermont. He wrote that he started it "in 1919." He was still writing when he died in 1983. His hundreds of columns survive in beautifully kept scrapbooks that grace the Washington County Historian's Department.

Others remember him for being Granville Village Clerk from 1924 to 1974, or for his six decades of being a Freemason, or for his charity work for the fire department and for every religious organization in town—although, as he would have rightly insisted, he was not religious.

His life was filled with the achievements of a man of intellect and energy. Yet in my mind I associate him with Armistice Day, now Veterans Day. This is because Morris Rote-Rosen, to use his words, was "instrumental in forming the Granville Post of the American Legion[xciv] and its ladies Auxiliary." An immigrant founding an American Legion Post? How perfectly American.

He "was born in Mariampole, in the Baltic state of Lithuania, February 12, 1890," as he wrote later. Mariampole was a district of Warsaw under Russian control. He was the only son of Avraham and Haia Reizel (Mevzos) Rote-Rosen. He had four sisters.

Life works its strange miracles. His father was a contractor to the city and his grandfather a prominent importer-exporter. His family gave him a good education. He passed the exam to enter junior high, but was barred because only five percent of Jewish children were allowed in.

His father moved to West Rutland, Vermont, in 1901 to join his brother. Morris, with his sister Gittel, followed in 1903. Morris nearly didn't make it into the American Army, because, as he had just turned 13, he was eligible to be drafted into the Russian army! Telling border guards they were going to a doctor in Germany, Morris and Gittel instead steamed off to America.

Morris arrived West Rutland reading and speaking fluently in several languages. Just not English. He entered Kindergarten at 13. In two years, he had advanced to the sixth grade, having mastered English, which he spoke with no accent.

His whole family now together, they moved in 1905 to Granville, a place he forever called home. He went on to Albany Business College and was pursuing a business career locally when World War I erupted.

He enlisted and served almost two years with the U. S. Base Army Hospital No. 33 in England and France. About to muster out in 1919, he was ordered to Russia, where the Revolution was still on. Not a place for a man who had evaded the Russian draft! Miraculously he talked his way into a transfer stateside.

Back in Granville, he resumed work and, to Polish and Russian, now added the language of the new Slovak immigrants, becoming their translator and friend. His basic instincts were egalitarian. He treated every person as a friend.

The American Legion had only just begun in 1919 and proud veteran Morris Rote-Rosen helped organize the Granville Post No. 323 and Women's Auxiliary Unit. He then started a Washington County branch of the Legion and was elected first Commander.

Yet, when the national American Legion rejected women as full members, he lashed out in his veterans' column that he wrote in *The Granville Sentinel.* He called the act as "indecent and a cheap insult" to the American women who had served so honorably.

It is said that John Philip Sousa's surname is an acronym, S.O.U.S.A., for "Son of the U.S.A." How perfectly descriptive of Morris Rote-Rosen—Son of the U.S.A.

Happy Veterans Day.

"OVER MY SHOULDER" COLUMN FOR NOVEMBER 16, 2002
Helping piece together a puzzle

This story spans 6,000 miles, two nations and one family.

Last July, I was in the county historian's office and took a call from Sandy Huffer, up in the Board of Supervisors offices.

A man was on the phone, she said, asking for family information. She having a trouble understanding what he wanted and thought I should speak with him. My impression that he was probably doing a rapid-fire succession of "who begat whom" and that it was confusing. Sandy transferred the call.

"Hello?" I asked and within seconds realized the nature of the confusion. From the other end came the lyrical tones of a heavy Italian accent. Adjusting my ear, I listened as the gentleman explained his plight.

Mr. Carmen Stroscio, of Massachusetts, was trying to find information on his grandfather, Francesco Perdichizzi, killed in an accident in 1914. Ever since Mr. Stroscio's family had come to live in the US, he'd wanted to find out more about his mother's father. She was old. He wanted to do this for her before she died. I envisioned her bed-ridden and dying, whispering her final words, "Papa, papa."

"But how can I help?" I asked, appreciating Sandy's confusion.

Some understanding came as he said, "Francesco Perdichizzi died in Fort Edward." Ah! Perdichizzi had come to Fort Edward with his family, was employed by the Delaware and Hudson Railroad, and was killed either August 14th or 15th of 1914, while getting off a train. A freak accident. His wife was pregnant at the time. The baby, born shortly thereafter, eventually became Carmen Stroscio's mother. Could I get more information? For her?

This was a good news, bad news situation. Good because I'd worked on the book *Con Amore, The Italian History of Fort Edward*. Bad, because the name Perdichizzi wasn't ringing a bell.

Did he know anything about his grandmother? Yes. She was Anna Munafo. Every bell rung. "That's the Munoff family!" I exclaimed.

"No, no," he replied, politely correcting me, "Munafo. Anna Munafo." I explained to him how "Munafo" had become "Munoff" and how a Joseph Munoff had even worked on *Con Amore*, and added, "I'll call Joe immediately." Mr. Stroscio was most grateful.

I did call Joe and called Mary Casini Smith, who had headed up the committee that produced *Con Amore*. Could they help?

The results? *Meraviglioso*– marvelous! Joe realized instantly that Anna Munafo Perdichizzi was sister to his grandfather, Frank (Francesco) Munoff. Joe is Carmen Stroscio's second cousin.

Joe provided even more information, and he and Mary also got copies of news stories about the tragic accident, which had occurred as Francesco

Perdichizzi stepped from his train and was struck by an oncoming train. He died shortly after, on August 15, 1914.

I combined their information with naturalization papers that County Archivist Dennis Lowery copied and sent the bundle to Mr. Stroscio. A subsequent, happy call from him revealed the rest of the story. Here's a thumbnail sketch. Born and later wed in Furnari, Messina, Italy, Francesco and Anna Munafo Perdichizzi came to Fort Edward with their children around 1910. They lived with Anna's brother Francesco Munafo. After the accident, Francesco Perdichizzi was buried in the Union Free Cemetery.

Upon the birth of Carmen's mother, Anna decided to return with her children to Furnari in March 1915, on the ship "Roma." However, it was wartime. The Roma was torpedoed! Thankfully, everyone in the family was saved. They completed their trip to Italy. Carmen's mother grew up and later married a man named Stroscio. Carmen was born in 1940 in Furnari. In 1954, his family moved to Massachusetts. His mother had come full circle, back to the land of her birth.

Oh, by the way, about his mother's health? I'm afraid I misunderstood her condition. Carmen said mama and papa live in Florida now. And she's doing one can as well expect for a lady of 88.

Only in America.

"OVER MY SHOULDER" COLUMN FOR DECEMBER 14, 2002
A birthday worth noting

Here's a salute to Dr. Joseph Feingold to say "Happy 90th birthday" to the Good Doctor.

In a 1996 column, I'd fleetingly sketched his history. While this column won't be of any length his life deserves, it offers a bit more detail, particularly of his war service. That's fitting for a man with a passion for history, and for a physician who affected our local history with a family medical practice of more than four decades.

Although I'd recalled some information Dr. Feingold had told me, I am indebted to the Good Doctor's wife, Natalie, who graciously helped with additional vital details, and also to the Old Fort House Museum for its help.

Joseph Feingold was born December 12, 1912 in Fleischmanns, NY. At about age four, his family moved to Brooklyn. He attended the University of Michigan for both his undergraduate and medical degrees, graduating in 1937. He was interning in Brooklyn, when a colleague, Dr. Charles R. Barber of Glens Falls, suggested he move to this area. He set up practice in Fort Edward.

Immediately after Pearl Harbor, Dr. Feingold volunteered, but was not called up until August 18, 1942, and only then assigned duty in the territorial United States, because of his eyesight problems.

He was assigned first to Texas, then to the Army Industrial Ordnance Depot in Gallup, NM, where it turned out he was the only Army physician. While there he cared for some of the Navahos. As casualties began mounting in the Pacific Theater, he met troop trains returning wounded to the East coast.

He convinced the Army to assign him to the European Theater and went ashore at Marseilles, France in August 1944. Natalie wrote that Dr. Feingold "tells of being terrified as they went ashore under enemy fire but decided he could not live like that." My father had said that in combat you had to believe you'd live otherwise you couldn't function.

Dr. Feingold established mobile hospitals, serving with the Third General Hospital, the 103rd Evacuation Hospital and 238th General Hospital in France, Belgium, Luxembourg and Germany. He was at the Battle of the Bulge, the Nazi's last counteroffensive. It forced the Allies' temporary retreat and entailed evacuating the hospital. I recall him saying that he was within 12 or so miles of the German lines—particularly harrowing as, being Jewish, capture would have meant either immediate execution or later death in a concentration camp.

During the evacuation, his train was sidetracked to allow Patton's Third Army to pass. Dr. Feingold froze his feet climbing off the train to pound free the frozen track switches.

He crossed the famed bridge at Remagen, shortly after its liberation at the cost of many lives. At Fulda, Germany, he cared for both American and German wounded and helped secure food for the Germans. His familiarity with Yiddish, a form of German, helped greatly. I imagine his Yiddish helped, too, when later he was attending inmates at one of the concentration camps. But about that, he is understandably silent.

At some point, his jeep came under fire and his leg was broken. He did recuperate and, with the war ending in Europe, was rewarded by being sent to the Pacific Theater. He went via transport ship, carrying cans of sardines just in case rations got low. Mid-voyage, the first atomic bomb was dropped. His ship was rerouted home and he celebrated by throwing his sardines into the sea.

Discharged in the fall of 1945 with the rank of major, he re-established his practice in Fort Edward in the home of the late Dr. Silas J. Banker, where he was until retirement in 1985. He has deeply touched the lives of so many of us and I urge him to record his autobiography, both to improve upon this meager column and to leave a legacy, particularly for a new great-grandson named Joseph.

Happy birthday, Dr. Feingold—and many, many more.

"OVER MY SHOULDER" COLUMN FOR JANUARY 11, 2003
Time to rename Broad Street?

The recent news of a gentleman being mugged on Broad Street in Glens Falls makes me think that maybe it's time to rename the street. Again. The first time it was renamed, as a street, was in the 1890s as part of civic improvement for the street, which was in heavy competition with its cousin, South Street, for having "a reputation." This is understandable, as every generation has tried to deal with civic problems through programs of social improvement, wholesale civic rebuilding, or, sometimes more simply, by calling a place by another name.

Let me clarify something. With any mention of the Victorian era, especially the 1890s, some readers conjure up Disney-like images of the past, pure Judy Garland "Meet Me in St. Louis" movie images out of the 1940s. Streets filled with trolleys, horse drawn carriages, hoop-skirted ladies, and well-behaved, apple-cheeked children.

Of course that image is as fake as the streets in that movie. Life then could be as exceedingly tough as it was beautiful. Every generation has had "rough edges" that civic leaders and planners will seek to smooth.

Glens Falls already had its rough edges before the 1890s. From the 1830s onward, East Canal Street, now Oakland Avenue, was a, rip-roaring place of wild taverns, canal toughs, brawls and prostitution. The book *Bridging The Years*[xcv] notes that in 1835 a Presbyterian minister, Dr. Ephraim H. Newton, proposed a huge re-building project to go from Canal Street[xcvi] up to Warren Street, combining "elegant stores, shops and offices," with Glen Street being the center "of business and wealth, accessible to every species of trade and art." Like so many visionaries, Newton was ignored, although in the 1960s, Urban Renewal had a similar dream. Unfortunately, Urban Renewal concentrated on demolition. The re-building phase got lost.

In the boom times after the Civil War, Glens Falls grew like Topsy, growing even through the huge depression of the 1870s. The sins that accompany prosperity also grew with the village. By the late 1880s, the area around Glen and South Streets was sprouting new business buildings, including saloons, like dandelions in spring. Gangs of young men, fueled by testosterone and alcohol, vigorously practiced street fighting and mugging. Young women hung out, accused by the gentry of licentious behavior. One reaction was a positive social movement to create the Glens Falls YMCA in 1887. It was so successful that a YMCA building was built in 1892. (Today, it houses Godnick's Grand Furniture and the World Awareness Children's Museum.)[xcvii]

In earlier columns on South Street, I noted how in the mid-19th century South Street between Monument Square and Union Square was a beehive of economic activity in the then Village of Glens Falls. Union Square was where South Street intersected with the road to Luzerne. Before the Civil war, with prosperity driving the village's development, that road became a thriving street with a growing Canadian French population. It was renamed West Street.

By the 1880s, commercial development was so heavy that the village approved the removal of a cemetery on West Street and the creation of New Pruyn St., something Glens Falls Cemetery Superintendent Christopher Anderson[xcviii] is attempting to document (so please give him a call). Still, for all West Street's positive development, the section of it nearer to Union Square remained a rough and tumble area that gave the village a headache. By the 1890s, civic leaders decided that "West Street" brought to mind all the wrong connotations. So they renamed it Broad Street, figuring that with a new name would come a new image of gentrification.

Apparently Broad Street is now reverting to its old ways, so I'm suggesting a name change, again. Perhaps the city might want to give it an altogether new name, but my suggestion is that they revert to the old name, but add a word to it.

They could call it "Wild West Street."

"OVER MY SHOULDER" COLUMN FOR JANUARY 18, 2003
Collective memories go way back

What happens when a historian follows only his notes and doesn't check up on that "troublesome date"?

He ends up writing a column to say: "I goofed."

And that's the case here. For last week's Over My Shoulder column on Broad Street in Glens Falls, I consulted my own files. In those I have notes I've taken, copies, news clippings, references to books and newspapers, and so on. But my "Broad Street file" had only my note stating that West Street had been renamed Broad Street in the late 1890s, actually in 1899 or 1900. If it's only my own note, my rule is to check it against a source.

I broke my rule and Dr. Orel Friedman[xcix] wrote to say that he'd grown up in the area and distinctly recalled that in the 1920s Broad Street was still being referred to as West Street. How right you are, Dr. Friedman. Crandall Library's Albert Fowler consulted the Glens Falls city directories for me. The name was changed in 1925.

As I had written, the change was indeed sought to give a more elevated aura to West Street, which city leaders felt suffered image problems. In 1925.

My apologies to you, the reader, and my thanks to Dr. Friedman.

Dr. Friedman said he assumed the name change had occurred after 1925, for his family continued to refer to Broad Street as West Street well after 1925. But that's common. We retain "collective memories" of places and names, referring to them long after they've ceased to exist. My wife, Sara, said a fellow faculty member at ACC, Kevin Ankeny,[c] used the old Joy Store in South Glens Falls as a landmark. She got a kick out of it, because Kevin had barely moved here in 1998, when the Joy Store, at that time long out of business and only an empty building, was demolished. However, it's part of a collective memory.

Here are other examples. When I say the "Boxer's Drugstore corner," what does it mean to you? To many, it means the SE corner of Warren and Glen Streets in Glens Falls, where Boxer's Drugstore stood. Burger King is there today. To many, the "Mike's Submarine corner" in Lake George Village means the SE corner of Canada Street and Beach Road.

Sometimes a collective memory is a business name. Teri Podnorszki Ulrich[ci] says that to her and her mother, the Price Chopper Supermarket on Cooper St. is still "the Central Market."[cii]

Glens Falls City Historian Wayne Wright[ciii] suggested "Bank Square," where Glen, Warren, Ridge and Hudson Meet. The last bank in that square was Glens Falls National, which moved northward on Glen Street in 1949.

Wayne, who was from Hudson Falls but had his passport approved at the border, knows that "where St. Paul's Church was" means the NE corner of River Street and Park Place in Hudson Falls. It burned in 1975.

For Saratoga Springs City Historian Martha Stonequist[civ] says that a collective memory for Saratogians is "the railroad station" Today Price Chopper occupies that spot at Railroad Place.

Region-wide, folks still know that the Glens Falls Insurance Company Building corner was the NE corner of Glen and Bay Streets. That building went down in 1976.

North Creek residents know where I mean on the west side of Main Street when I say, "Where the Farrells had their restaurant."

Many Ticonderogians can mentally locate the American Graphite Joseph Dixon Pencil factory near the NE corner of Champlain Avenue and Rogers Street, although that's been gone since, what, 1962? I'll ask Karl LaPointe the date.

And now, your turn. Email me or write me care of *The Post-Star* and give me an example of a collective memory. You'll have to go down the collective memory trail to do it. But, you know the way:

Hang a right at the corner where the old Esso station used to be.

"OVER MY SHOULDER" COLUMN FOR JANUARY 25, 2003
Let's play 'remember this'?

Last week I was writing about "collective memories." These are memories we retain through several generations of places and names, referring to them long after they've ceased to exist. It is each generation's rediscovery of the past that holds our greatest hope for society's memory being saved—and our greatest fear of its being destroyed.

Judging from how many commented on the article, apparently society's memory is safe! Many offered examples of things that used to be that might not be remembered. To be a collective memory, it has to stay with us in some form after it has disappeared or after its original use has ceased to be or after it has a new owner.

A good example is "the Big Boom," offered by Queensbury Town Historian Marilyn Van Dyke.[cv] For those who don't know it, this is a place name, not a fireworks factory gone awry. The Big Boom area is that spot in southern Queensbury along the Hudson River where the Northway crosses between the Town of Moreau and the Town of Queensbury.

Dr. Austin W. Holden states in his 1874 history of Queensbury that the Big Boom was "a structure built by the associated lumbermen of Fort Edward, Sandy Hill and Glens Falls" to snag logs being floated down the Hudson to sawmills in the region. It was "situated at the Big Bend, about three miles up the river from Glen's Falls." It's interesting that the term "the Big Bend," used in Holden's day, gave way to a structure built on it, the Big Boom, which itself disappeared decades ago.

Post-Star editor Mark Mahoney wrote about a yearly event that he still calls by its original name. Mark wrote, "I always refer to the Christmas parade in South Glens Falls as the 'Joy Parade.'" Mark is remembering back to when the parade's original sponsor, The Joy Store, was still in existence in South Glens Falls. Evergreen Bank today sponsors the parade.

Teri Podnorszki Ulrich wrote about a phenomenon common in many cultures: calling a house by the name of its original builder. She wrote, "I babysat for years for the Reinbolds, who lived in Wilmarth's house on Glen St., near Horicon. Then AND now, we've always called it "Wilmarth's." Martin Luther Wilmarth was a prominent Glens Falls man whose family was renowned for generations for its fine furniture. Wilmarth's furniture-making company and Mr. Wilmarth himself are gone, but his name lives on.

Teri, who grew up in Glens Falls, offered other collective memories of Glens Falls, most of which I think will fade within her generation: She wrote, "We call the corner of Maple and Ridge 'the Paramount corner' " This refers to the Paramount Theater, which stood from 1931 to 1978 at the northeast corner of Ridge and Maple Streets. There are still thousands of people who'd recognize 'the Paramount corner' and those same people would recognize "Shangraw's corner." That is the southwest corner of Glen Street at Grant Avenue, where Shangraw's Pharmacy was. The building still stands. Thanks, Teri!

Reader Greta Rozell wrote, "As for a collective memory, Great Escape will always be Storytown to the locals." You are so right, Greta.

Keith Brannock of Ticonderoga gave me a huge list. Keith, you've got to get going on a book, m'lad! One collective memory he has is of "The Tower," the International Paper mill office block on Champlain Avenue in Ti, to the rear of today's Glens Falls National Bank. It was gone when I moved to Ti but was always remembered. It stood where the "new" number 7 building was, and now that's gone, demolished after the "new mill" was opened in 1971.

Another memory he has is of the "Bloody Bucket," but I'll have to explain that one next week.

In the meantime, how about sending me your collective memory?

"OVER MY SHOULDER" COLUMN FOR FEBRUARY 1, 2003
A wrap on collective memories

All right let's discuss the Bloody Bucket.

Over the last few weeks, we've been exploring collective memory, the remembrance of places and names retained over several generations, still referred to long after they're long gone.

Keith Brannock offered the Bloody Bucket as a collective memory, opening a floodgate of warm memories for some, but fears among others that I'd be discussing hospital procedures. Many people now too young to remember the now vanished Bloody Bucket, or Bucket of Blood as it was alternately known, recall it was the Alexandria Tavern that once stood in Ticonderoga on Alexandria Avenue alongside "the crick," now gloriously known as the LaChute River.

This popular, rambunctious watering hole often saw an excess of fisticuffs when the patrons were "overserved." Karl LaPointe tells of how it was closed once in the early 1920s after the famous strike that closed the adjacent mill. It was in the 1940s, he said, that the term Bucket of Blood came into use.

Many called, mailed and emailed to offer a collective memory. One gentleman, a Mr. Jones of North Creek, wrote to correct my memory: it was Farrell's Hotel[cvi] on the east side of Main Street. Mr. Jones, your letter has become lost amidst the 80 tons of paper on my desk and therefore I cannot properly cite your letter or thank you. Will you accept my apologies for a lousy filing system and write me again? Thanks!

Thanks to Louis Hartman of South Glens Falls for memories from his 85 years relative to the Big Boom, that area where the Northway spans the Hudson between the Towns of Moreau and Queensbury. He also mentioned the Feeder Canal. Canal names are certainly part of collective memory. Originally built in 1823 to "feed" water into the Champlain Canal system, the Feeder was widened in 1832 for horse or mule drawn boat traffic. Today's towpath is the path those animals followed.

Mr. Hartman writes of the Five Combines in Hudson Falls. That name lingers though most residents might not realize the Five Combines was a stone structure combining five locks in one. Today, thanks to the Feeder Canal Alliance, you can walk the towpath alongside, or canoe down the length of, the Feeder Canal that runs west to east through Queensbury, Glens Falls, Kingsbury and Hudson Falls. When you end your trip in Hudson Falls, you will see the remains of the magnificent Five Combines.

Cut Crannell of Glens Falls recalled the logs backed up so thickly behind the actual "Big Boom" that he walked across the river on the logs. He wondered how many people still refer to West Glens Falls as Goodspeedville, its original name. Many do, Cut! Thanks!

Jack Wiberg of Glens Falls shared a collective memory about the present Talk of the Town Restaurant on Hudson Avenue in Glens Falls. To him and many of us, it's still Hart's Cafe.

Native Saratogians such as actor David Hyde Pierce or Saratoga Springs City Historian Martha Stonequist might agree with me that the power of a collective memory is strong in that city. For example, developers retained the name Van Raalte in remodeling the Van Raalte clothing factory on Excelsior Ave. As Martha said, there aren't many of us old Saratogians left – myself included – who recall its original use.

How many Saratogians recall that Bruno's Restaurant on Union Avenue was King's Restaurant and that the restaurant building next door was Mike and Joe's. My brother Michael and I certainly recall that, for as children we thought the places were named for us.

We'll do this again some time, so send in your memories. Meanwhile, let me end by veering off in a slightly different direction with a question: Do you remember the name of the 1970s Queensbury fast food hamburger place on Route 9 on Miller Hill, very near to where McDonald's is today?

"OVER MY SHOULDER" COLUMN FOR FEBRUARY 15, 2003
Time to talk of many things

Did you guess Carroll's hamburgers?

Two weeks ago, I casually asked: "Do you remember the name of the 1970s Queensbury fast food hamburger place on Route 9 on Miller Hill, very near to where McDonald's is today?" I got a barrage of responses correctly identifying the Carroll's stand, which began in the mid-sixties with 10-cent hamburgers.

The question triggered both answers to the question itself and other, different memories. I heard from so many and will be at fault for trying to name them all, because I'll forget a name. But here goes: Loretta Bates, Jack Wiberg, Tony Trello, Judge John Austin, Henry Ashton, Dr. Orel Friedman, Bill Grinnell, Kim Monroe, Martin Morrell, Roger Hogan, Pat Brayton, Joan Champagne, Mary Trainor, John Hogan, William Lee Richards, Mike Armstrong, Judy Scripter, Phillip Smith, Gregory Stoddard, and Barb Smith-Stewart.

Also, to all who have wished me well on my new venture, whether named here or not, thank you so much.

Martin Morrell writes that the Carroll's corporation continues today, as franchise operator of the Aviation Road and Warren Street Burger Kings.

The response showed a generational difference. Instead of Carroll's, Dr. Friedman, Roger Hogan, Pat Brayton, and Joan Champagne suggested Hamburger Haven from the 1930s and 1940s. Phillip Smith recalled "Fan and Bill's nightclub" on Miller Hill.

Ti classmate Bill Grinnell asked if I'd forgotten the Cave[cvii]. Bill, that was in Hague, but are you kidding? A book on everyone's sizzling sixties summer memories at the Cave would have to be printed on asbestos sheets. You know, "Something, Something and Rock'n'roll"?

Speaking of sizzling, Barbara Dehais asked if anyone recalled hearing of the White Barrel on Luzerne Road. (Barbara, talk with Bill Richards of Queensbury, whose encyclopedic knowledge of this region is second to none.) Apropos of the White Barrel, an anonymous reader wondered why I hadn't written about Congress Street in Saratoga. I just haven't gotten into x-rated columns yet.

Another "encyclopedia" I've relied upon over the last five years is Loretta Bates, a professional genealogist, and the volunteer researcher at the Washington County historian's department. We made some fabulous progress in that department on so many projects, such as the computerized catalog of the collection and the expansion of the office.

The job has been a blast because of Loretta's outrageous sense of humor, not to mention total recall of local detail. We speak in shorthand we both possess from having lived locally. She'd say, "Well, you'd go up by where the Hidden Valley Dude Ranch was…" and I'd know she meant the Double H Hole in the Wall. Or I'd say, "Well, it was by the Café Gardens in Lake George Village…" and she knew I meant the northwest corner of Canada Street and McGillis Street. Thank you so much for all the memories, my friend.

Historical facts about Washington County can even come from Glens Falls water commissioners. My longtime friend Jack Wiberg relayed this fabulous fact that there was a communal sauna in Shushan. Around 1900, Finns, Norwegians and Swedes came to live in Shushan, in southwest Washington County, and built a sauna, a part of their culture. That's a book in itself! Get writing, Wiberg! (Jack gets fined when his name appears in the paper, so, for the record, I didn't mention Jack.)

And speaking of books, who will write tomorrow's histories? Who will write the histories for inspiration of that new baby in Queensbury, Lauren Elizabeth, daughter of Mike and Diane Trackey? Who will be the next Marion Chitty, A. W. Holden, William Hill, Harriet Bentley, Don Metivier, Paul Rayno, Louis Hyde, and Morris Rote-Rosen? (When will Rote-Rosen's life be published?) Who will scribe the memories of our communities to tell Lauren how a Katrina Trask, Charlotte Hyde or Juliet Chapman gave her home for culture and learning?

Lewis Carroll wrote" The time come, the walrus said, to talk of many things."

Indeed, the time has come to write of many things.

SECTION 3: PERSONAL AND FAMILY MEMORIES

"OVER MY SHOULDER" COLUMN FOR FEBRUARY 17, 2001
Young bill collector gets the last word

This is the story of the boy bill collector.

For ten years my father had his own pharmacy in the little village of Fort Edward.

Like every child growing up in a family with a small business, I begged to work in the "the store" until, finally, my wish fulfilled, from that time on I begged to be released.

Nothing is so romantic as the dream or as patently awful as the dream made real.

Small stores survive by personal service. A mother would call after midnight for baby formula. Dad would sweetly assure her it was no problem, then mutter down the hallway, "...don't know why she couldn't have breast fed that kid..."

Home delivery was essential. When I was old enough to run errands, like brother Michael, I'd hop my bike like fleet Mercury. Peddling a one-speed American bike was bodybuilding, especially since half the village sat atop a high hill. Riding downhill was the bonus.

In between up and down was the "tender" portion of the transaction. For as I rode off, Dad always bellowed the delivery person's motto: "Make sure you get paid!"

It was difficult at first. How does a boy ask an adult to pay if the adult isn't forthcoming? Father would coach from the 50-yard line of the pharmacy. "Say the amount as you hand them the package." Or "Remember to take change." Amazing how many people only had hundred dollar bills.

Dad was better at instructing than exercising the deed itself. He was great in sales, but collecting wasn't his forte. Although, he was good in a team situation. Once we circled a particularly delinquent customer's house in our car. Unseen, Dad dropped me off at the corner. I approached the house and watched the Venetian blinds drop as I did. Expectedly, no one answered the doorbell. I went off. Moments later the blinds went up. Dad swept in for the kill.

As time went on, things became very dire in our little store's circumstances. It became critical to get the cash upon delivery.

For whatever reason, I excelled at it. I could stare down the best of them, shoving the bill at them with one hand, while tightly holding onto the bag until they paid.

But one particularly recalcitrant customer really tested my mettle. The Gripps, a fictitious name, were truly artful dodgers. Naturally they lived at the most distant and highest point in town. It seemed when I peddled there I was always gasping for breath and Mr. Gripp always had "just stepped out" or had "just gone to your store. Now isn't that funny?" Uproariously, Mrs. Gripp, I thought.

Over and over the Gripps put me in the middle. I'd go back to the store and have to face the music there. I'd deliver; they'd stiff me. Fuming, I reasoned they could somehow see me coming. Finally, desperate, I left my bike down the street, snuck to the house and crept catlike up to the second floor, a spy infiltrating enemy lines.

When I abruptly banged on the door, Mrs. Gripp opened, but Mr. Gripp, caught unprepared, had lamely hidden behind the door. I saw him, though pretended I didn't. She and I went through the usual charade, which I extended far, far longer by negotiating and even offering to wait, savoring her discomfort and his twitching behind the door.

Finally, I went to leave. I sweetly said "Goodbye, Mrs. Gripp," and as the door closed slightly, I sang out, "And goodbye to you, too, Mr. Gripp!"

I heard a gasp, then a "You little son of a b…!" But I was bounding down the stairs as the "itch" portion of that came out. He was right behind me, but old jackrabbit-legs was on the street, on his bike and safely away before the crazed Gripp even hit concrete.

They never paid and the store closed with them owing us.

But, actually, I got paid on that day I just described.

And paid in a way far more satisfying than money.

"OVER MY SHOULDER" COLUMN FOR JUNE 2, 2001
Bag was father's link to peace

My father had a toiletries bag, which he called a ditty bag.

From 1944, until the day he died in 1987, he had this same ditty bag.

It was black leather. Its plastic lining had long since disintegrated, revealing cloth underneath, itself stained from decades of toiletries, but most importantly, from several years of the salt water from the Pacific Ocean, through which he had commanded his PT Boat in World War II.

That Navy experience was pivotal in his life. Though his family never fully understood it, this most terrifying period of his life was his happiest. Until his death, he always used naval terms. His children thought it very natural in the morning to hit the deck, hit the head, then climb into clean skivvies. That is, put feet on the floor, go to the bathroom and then put on clean underwear.

If the language was a part of Dad's war legacy that we knew, so also were his memories, most of which we never knew. We had heard a select few repeatedly. I came to think they were rehearsed, so the others would not slip out, forcing him to relive them.

The ditty bag. I almost said that he'd had it from his enlistment in 1942. However, he'd "lost" one ship, as he always phrased it, in 1944. By which he meant, he had had it blown out from underneath him, killing crew, wounding him. This ditty bag was a replacement and it saw violent action, too.

Those of us who have never been in unremitting combat can never know the mind of people who have dined with death on a daily basis. Even if we've experienced a mugging, or had a gun aimed at our chest, we cannot imagine those solitary instances being repeated daily, forming the expected routine of war.

His family saw the effect of that routine. Early in my childhood, my father still suffered from horrible nightmares, which would bring him from a sound sleep, screaming orders at his crew, on deck again, and screaming. And screaming.

These dreams went away – or at least the sleepwalking reenactments of battle did – doctored in part by time, and, yes, by alcohol. Was he so different? I think not. I rather think he was like millions of service men who returned, so inadequately prepared by their government to resume the most mundane of tasks, their bodies and minds constantly tensed, awaiting the next order, the next attack. The tension had been too often eased during wartime by drinking. That habit only increased when war finally stopped, but the tension never did.

The ditty bag always sat in the bathroom, right next to the sink, filled with his shaving apparatus, toothpaste and other toiletries. Amidst it all – and always there – was a small black leather billfold, about 4 inches high and 3 inches wide. In it was a picture of his wife and their first child.

It never seemed odd to us that a 1943 photo of only two people in our family should be there. It had traveled with him, in the ditty bag, through the Battle of Leyte, when his cousin's ship went down and his did not. Through a second near-sinking. Through the liberation of POW camps on Amboina in Indonesia. Through so much we could never know of, or if we knew, could never understand.

But as an adult, I came to appreciate better the significance of the little photo in the ditty. This had been his link back to the world as he knew it, a small remembrance, a tiny thing to keep him hopeful, a precious keepsake of a day when things would be normal again and he would know peace.

And I thought, after he died, that the little picture and the ditty bag were always there, because they were a symbol of a peace that had been meant to occur much sooner, but in reality was a lifetime in coming, and never truly rested upon him until his death.

In Memoriam to my father, George A. King, Lieutenant, United States Navy, 1942-1946, and to all "that go down to the sea in ships, that do business in great waters."

May you rest in peace.

"OVER MY SHOULDER" COLUMN FOR JULY 14, 2001
Split over store's demise

Brooks Brothers? History?

Andy Rooney writes he's "uneasy about the way things have been going" at Brooks Brothers. Fearing possible changes at the venerable men's store, he says that he's stocking up on boxer shorts.

He writes gloomily that he "harbored the illusion of immortality for Brooks Brothers."

Relax, Andy. Two more movies like Pearl Harbor and wearing button down shirts and boxer shorts will be mandatory again.

Brooks Brothers is safe, Andy, but given my experience I'm not sure it's for the best.

I had several Brooks Brothers suits—all summer suits, all with a distinctive problem.

My first one I bought in the late 1960s when I took a job in a brokerage on Wall Street. Wanting to look the part, I decided to get a Brooks Brothers summer suit, of lightweight cotton, a tad thinner than toilet paper.

It was an incredibly hot summer day. I went to Brooks Brothers, bought the suit, put it on and hit the streets of Lower Manhattan feeling like a million bucks. Feeling like I'd spent it too, but after all it was a Brooks Brothers.

Trouble began in the subway. People were, well, gawking at me. That was odd for New York City, where making eye contact is a punishable offense. The train rushing into the station created a surprisingly cool breeze, especially in my thigh area.

Looking down, I found that the inseam on my trousers had completely unraveled and my pants were falling apart. Rather like a scene from an old silent movie. Fortunately, I had a New York Times and used it effectively while racing back to Brooks Brothers.

I showed the woman at the sales desk the problem. She never batted an eyelash, but merely said, "The tailor can have them ready for you tomorrow."

I blurted out that if I could figure out how to get home in only my underwear, I could as easily walk the city with a sandwich board saying Brooks Brothers made crappy clothes, too.

The tailor was summoned. My pants were sewn up immediately.

In the early 80s, I decided I'd uncork one of my Brooks Brothers summer suits, partially in a protest against 1970s' styles.

You've seen the 70s' styles. Lapels on a sport coat so huge that a gust of wind could lift you to an altitude that brought an FAA fine for interfering with commercial jet flights. And a fine for flying while color blind, because the combination purple and green jacket made you either look either like a giant eggplant or a bad imitation of Screamin' Jay Hawkins.

One hot summer day I donned the Brooks Brothers suit, checked my attire in the mirror and went to work at the Chapman Museum. Later, I had to go downtown and decided to walk. Purposefully striding along, I encountered many people, several of whom I knew. All smiled broadly.

Now, a bit of background. That morning, I had reached into the dresser for a pair of shorts and, not giving it a second thought, put on a pair of boxer shorts with huge red hearts that my wife had given me as a joke for Valentine's Day.

Entering a restaurant, I sat, swirling on a stool, coming face to face, so to speak, with a woman a few stools down. She suddenly let out a monstrous gasp, blushed to her hair roots, and fled the air-conditioned restaurant. Memories of the subway came to mind.

I looked down and, well, let's just say that I was wearing my heart on more than just my sleeve, and for the whole world to see. Reprising my role as a wearer of newspapers, I grabbed one and wore it out the door.

So, Andy Rooney, regarding your fear of the demise of Brooks Brothers and their style, let me just say again, relax.

Or, to put it another way: keep your pants on.

"OVER MY SHOULDER" COLUMN FOR JULY 28, 2001
Daughter not alone in Saratoga

When my daughter strides along the streets of Saratoga Springs this summer, she'll have unseen company.

Julia has taken a summer job in a place called the Clothes Horse on Broadway. I had asked her to describe for me where it was and she replied opposite Congress Park, on Broadway.

"Where the old Chinese restaurant was?" I asked. My asking her this was ridiculous, of course. It was akin to the instructions I received in Saranac Lake one time, where a man told me to go to the intersection where the gas station used to be and then take a left.

I tried another tack. Was it in a building that at one time had to have been a legitimate theater?

Yes, the building definitely had to have been a theater.

Now I knew it. In the early years of my life I had been by the building a million times. The huge and majestic theater on the corner of Spring Street and Broadway was, at that point, home to a Chinese restaurant. It wasn't that many blocks away from MacFinn's, a pharmacy my father had managed on Broadway. In fact, it was actually closer to the Arcade, a lovely building also on Broadway where my godfather Ned Rowland owned a liquor store.

MacFinn's Drugstore was destroyed in the great fire of 1957[cviii] that obliterated a goodly chunk of lovely buildings, leaving them to be replaced with a far more utilitarian, and a damned site uglier, group of buildings.

So, yes, I did indeed know where she worked. In fact, Grandma Fitzpatrick, my father's mother, had lived on Spring Street for many of her 15 years in Saratoga. She was what Skidmore College called a "house mother" in the Spring Street House, a residence for Skidmore College's students, then all women. The college had a series of former homes turned dorms. It was Grandma's job to keep the house in ship shape, and the girls, too.

Our family – my mother, father and brother Mike, that is – had moved to Saratoga in 1946. Grandma's second husband had died in that same year. She followed our family to Saratoga shortly thereafter, probably around the time of my birth in 1947. We had moved to our house on Lincoln Avenue. Grandma got a job with Skidmore, where she lived.[cix]

Given the, how shall we say, tender relations between my mother and her mother-in-law, Skidmore was still a tad too close – San Diego would have been a tad too close – but at least it wasn't under the same roof.

So, Grandma Fitz ended up running Spring House, as she often sometimes calls it. Her task was formidable. She dealt with a house full of girls with raging hormones, all besieged by young men, most of whom in Grandma's opinion were rather like baying dogs all barking around the house as if they were in heat. Not her words, mind you. Grandma, being born in 1884, was a proper Victorian, and "in heat" would have been indelicate.

But even before my family had moved to Saratoga, it had been a place with family associations. In the 1930s, my Dad worked summers at the Colonial Restaurant and my mother at Brown's Old Homestead Restaurant by Saratoga Lake. And my Uncle Jim Kalbaugh worked summers in the cashier's office of the United States Hotel.

Yes, I know well the area where Julia works, and recall with fondness Congress Park – and will not step into the "Carousel minefield"[cx] thank you.

So, while Saratoga may be new territory for my daughter, as she takes a walk or visits the park, she'll have unseen company as the spirits of her family walk with her.

Especially that of her great-grandmother Fitzpatrick, who will be on the lookout for baying dogs.

"OVER MY SHOULDER" COLUMN FOR DECEMBER 15, 2001
A Dickens of a verse

I n these times that are so seasonable
Holiday wishes do seem reas'nable.

In keeping with a column historical,
The wishes will be – less or morical.

Wishes spread like vast mantle or toga,
From Springs to Fort, both ending in "oga."

For those "Falls" – Glens, South Glens and Hudson,
Downtown rebirth, that is not a dud, son.

For that Crandall Park part known as Coles Woods,
More trees, fewer buildings for its soul's good.

For Abe Wing's offspring, Glens Falls, Queensbury,
To act like cousins, not adversary.

To Saratoga Mayor, the Hon. Klotz,
The carousel's in place, fill it with tots.

Then, no future buildings there do spawn:
Hereafter, Congress Park's Vict'ry needs lawn.

To libraries, we know, Crandall's a symbol.
Give it a home that's more than a thimble.

Henry's fair gift needs a renewal,
Some rich old soul to buff-up that jewel.

Justification? Look at Spa City,
Where new ideas found no pau-city.

Where Sullivan's shade, at home on Lincoln,
Set sensible folks to serious thinkin' –

Inspiring those who'd add one brick or two,
Instead to build a library brand-new.

Crandall's' 10 choices, really quite pretty,
All scattered about the Empire City.

"Use old Clark silk mill," among the ten.
Says Regan: "I have a gap there, on Glen!"

To all friends like Rosoff, Searleman, that's Sandy,
A Hanukkah wish, may your dreidels spin dandy!

Local historians, give them their due:

Bill Gates, Don Metivier – need more from you!

Spirits of Juliet, Gladys, Dot, Gwen,
Watch over the Chapman: Three-Four-Eight Glen.

Dear Fortune, all museums remember,
Canfield Casino, Hartford, Hague, Pember,

Old Fort, Fort Ti, Slate Valley, too.
Whatever the name, they serve all of you.

Or North Creek's train station, where TR gained fame,
And skiers of yore came in on "snow trains."

To Utah's new Winter Olympic game:
No torch in Glens Falls? It won't be the same!

Without the same flame, we sent to Placid,
Here watch our spirits going all flaccid.

For Bruce Adams' 10th Mountain Division,
Olympic flame's path needs a revision.

"Trim Lake George boat speed," says Lou Tessier
"Ere Queen'o the Lakes gets any messier."

With him we agree, but do caution Lou:
Marinas make gifts for old Saint Nick, too.

By pushing those speed boats out of your way,
You'll only "clog up" our poor old Heart's Bay!

A Historian, please, Empire State!
Doesn't the keeper of heritage rate?

"Honor the past," our politicos cry!
But give Hist'ry money? "Aye. Bye and bye."

For a site called Ciba or Hercules,
Imperial…who cares? A buyer please!

For Wiberg, guarding City's water,
Fewer fines, Kiwanis, are in order.

To South Glens Falls, one wish – oh boy, more!
A business where once was the Joy Store.

To South Glens Falls priest, yes, Father Michael,
New knees, shoulder. What next? Unicycle?

New Hudson bridge seven? Eight? Shout "Mayday!"
Bill Richards, he knows old Glen Street's heyday.

Wishes for Dobert's "recipe Patterson":
Cranberry ice cream won't make you fatter, son.

Wishes for Yaddo, Seagle, and Sembrich,
SPAC, LARAC, Hyde, all that make arts rich.

For Pop Peltz and Glens Falls Symphon-eye
A bandshell where we will surely stay dry!

For Skiddies,[cxi] and kiddies at ACC,
Be grateful that those fine colleges be!

Vermont readers take heart! You're surely seen,
From Old Bennington to Lake Bomoseen.

Saratoga, Fort Edward, and my Ti,
These old hometowns bring a tear to my eye.

To you and to places, yes, all revered,
Holiday wishes, oh most sincere.

Galway to Crown Point to Pumpkin Hook,
By the powers that be, you won't be forsook.

Chilson to Thurman to Kingsbury,
Wealth from the "New Economy."

From Rogers Island, first home of Rangers
Prayers our present ones are kept from dangers.

And from this vast region, which we know rates,
As cradle of all these United States,

A wish from us to our nation at war,
We stand with you now, as ever before.

So Merry Christmas from this Nervous Elf,
Who fears shopping hist'ry repeats itself.

Oh Ghost of "Christmas Presents" please mail me
That "perfect gift" for my wife! Don't fail me!

"OVER MY SHOULDER" COLUMN FOR DECEMBER 22, 2001
Oh, the power of Santa

This is a story of a rooftop Santa come alive.

When our daughter, Julia, was a little girl, she, her mother, Sara, and I lived on Harrison Avenue, at the corner of Davis Street, in Glens Falls. The long and narrow older home had a broad expanse of windows providing acres of glass on the west side of the house. They would provide the view for the magic transformation to take place.

Our daughter's bedroom was on the front corner of the second floor, banked on two sides by windows. She was at that special age, around three, her imagination developing prodigiously, certainly fed by parents with equally fertile imaginations. At bedtime I'd spin for her my own tales of fantastical happenings, always starting with "Once upon a time, there was a little girl, just like you, who lived in a house on a corner, just like your house…." Then I'd weave stories of this little girl and her teddy flying out those windows into magic lands.

The concept of Christmas – and presents – was also jelling in her young mind. In all, she was primed for the transformation. Now, some backdrop: Reagan was in office, Sting still with the Police. Both were minor events, for most importantly it was the era of "My Little Pony" and of She-ra fighting the evil Skeletor at Castle Grayskull. Miss Piggy reigned supreme. (How I recall the "easy to assemble" Miss Piggy tricycle, requiring only simple tools and 200 hours of labor.)

We'd take shopping trips to Aviation mall and, in a nod to her parents' childhood, we'd stroll downtown Glens Falls, through stores like Country Fare with its beautiful goodies, and of course through Woolworth's. Fueled by these trips, TV ads and seasonal reruns of "Frosty the Snowman" and "Charlie Brown's Christmas," our child became crazed.

Enter now our story's central figure. Every year our neighbors, Mark and Joy Griffin, placed a plywood figure of Santa and his reindeer atop their roof. Set aglow with lights, the huge display would come alive, sending our daughter into near frenzy. Christmas was official! I can still see her tiny face at her bedroom window, gazing at the jolly elf.

At night when the lights came on, the Griffins' rooftop Santa burst into our home, his image pouring through our windows, and visible, it seemed, in every room. I think perhaps the transformation first happened around suppertime one night, not too long before Julia's bedtime. "The child," functioning at warp Christmas speed, was expressing her litany of "I wants" and definitely not concentrating on food, impending bedtime, or anything her parents said.

Suddenly, Santa began to glow on the rooftop. Trying to calm her, one of us looked over and called out, "Oh Santa! Can you hear this little girl?"

Shocked, Julia stared at Santa. She'd actually gone silent. Then her litany began again. "Santa," we'd call out and again she became silent. Ahhhhh!

During those crazed pre-Christmas days, we had only to call out to the transformed rooftop St. Nick and Julia would shout, "No, don't!" and supper was eaten, bath taken, sleeping done – and all promptly. Each Christmas, until we moved a few years later, the Griffins' Santa performed his magic.

The other night, as Sara and I left the Glens Falls Symphony Orchestra's Christmas concert at Glens Falls High, I drove us past our old home, wondering: would the Santa still be there?

Indeed, he was, glowing through the snowflakes from the Griffins' home over onto our old home. I looked up. I fancied that I saw a little face in the second-floor window, gazing over at Santa. And as we drove on, I could hear again the words, "Once upon a time, there was a little girl, just like you, who lived in a house on a corner, just like your house...."

I'd received my Christmas present early.

Merry Christmas to you all.

"OVER MY SHOULDER" COLUMN FOR MARCH 9, 2002
By 83, she should have been flying

J ane would have been flying now.

That is, she would have been literally flying. Not "flying" as she would describe it when she was in a tizzy.

But let's begin at the beginning. Jane, for the uninitiated, was Martha Jane Kalbaugh King. My mother, simply always known as "Jane."

Although there was simply nothing simple about Jane. This woman was pure energy, contained, if barely, in a vessel five feet two inches tall, and slender, almost wispy in her younger days. Her actions were constant. Her fingers darted. Her eyes moved, as if scanning the horizon for new possibilities. She was incessant motion, fingers drumming like one typing without the typewriter that was almost a born extension of her hands, and legs moving as if wishing for a new errand to run. I've described her as an exposed nerve,[cxii] which some think offensive. "That's your mother you're describing." But those who knew her then, know even now that it's true.

Quickness was her trait. She'd trip lightly, almost springing, across a street, as if in flight. She'd have dozens of projects going simultaneously, a juggler with dozens of balls in the air. As children, we never wanted to say to Jane, as we all called her, that we were bored. "Bored!" she'd almost shriek. And zip! We'd have something to do.

Her "nervous quotient" usually exceeded normal levels. She took tranquilizers for years, often by the handful. What would have knocked a horse to its knees kept her on even keel. Even so, she'd have her days when she was, as she would put it, "flying." It was a word she'd often use. When she'd say, "Oh, I could just fly!" it wasn't metaphorical. You sensed from the nervous energy that, had she wings, she would have flown.

I'd call and ask, how are you? "Oh, I'm just flying!" This often was the harbinger of a migraine, but while doing the usual 12 things at once, warbling in the church choir with Pauline Wardell and others, canning fruit, designing and sewing a dress, and working at Dr. Cummings' office as secretary. Taking care of her mother-in-law. ("Oh that woman! I could just fly when I'm around her!") Taking care of her husband George. (Oh, that man. Sometimes he just makes me want to fly!") And reading. She was a voracious reader. I don't know how many books a week, plus magazines and newspapers, including her beloved *New York Times*.

And writing. She wrote all her children at least one letter a week. Sometimes two. Sometimes more. As well as her sister Carrie, her brothers, and her friends. Over an eighteen-year period, she wrote to me alone over a thousand letters ranging in length from three lines to three pages. All typed, thank God, as her handwriting was worse than mine.

Her letters are her triumph, part of her literary legacy and unfulfilled dream to be a published writer. She was for a while, I must add, a *Post-Star* correspondent. After her death, amidst her belongings I found a rejection letter from a publishing house. We writers savor our first rejection letter. The rest get canned.

To that unfilled dream add her dream of flying, by which I mean flying a jet. She often said, "When I'm 83, I'll fly a jet." Or, "I'll be taking flying lessons when I'm 83." She was absolutely serious.

Jane would be 83 now.[cxiii] When I hear a jet, I pause to think who could have been at the controls, a concept still frightening given her driving skills. But years ago cancer had cheated her of flying lessons and I had wondered for a time if her disappointed spirit had hung out invisibly at airports.

But I gradually came to realize she wouldn't have stayed on to fret. For in life she had always been flying. And on the day she left, Jane got her wings.

"OVER MY SHOULDER" COLUMN FOR MARCH 16, 2002
Relative shows possibilities are endless

John Francis Green's story is typical of many first-generation Americans. John was born February 5, 1855, to Irish immigrants in Oxbridge, Massachusetts. By the time of his death, he had been a railroad engineer, a board of education member, president of his Saratoga County village and initiator of a free mail system for his village, among other credits to his life. Yet the man never learned to read and write until well into adulthood.

When he was a boy, John's family moved to the southern Washington County town of White Creek, possibly to farm sheep. The Greens lived near the Relihan family, who worked on the Boston and Maine Railroad, the B&M as it was known. Railroad families were plentiful in those days.

The Relihans had originally settled in Eagle Bridge, Washington County. However, fairly early on they moved just across the Hoosic River to White Creek, where my cousin Catherine Relihan[cxiv] lives to this day. John Green fell in love with and married Mary Elizabeth Relihan there in 1881.[cxv]

As you've surmised, John is related to me, my great-grandfather to be exact. For among the, at least, seven nationalities that comprise my gene pool, Irish is one.

John went to work for the B&M and he and Mary moved to Mechanicville soon after they married. There they raised seven children, including my father's mother. John had a thriving future with the B&M. He had worked his way up to being a locomotive engineer, not altogether easy for a man who could neither read nor write. My grandmother often told of seeing her mother at the kitchen stove, stirring a stew with one hand, tending a baby with another, while teaching John to read and write.

John's B&M career gained luster in March of 1888. During the famous blizzard, he was first engineer to bring a train through from Boston to Mechanicville. By the time he reached the Hoosac Tunnel in North Adams, Massachusetts, things looked grim. From there and through southern Washington County, the snowdrifts were taller than the engine. John repeatedly backed the engine up and slammed it into the snow, inching the engine forward. His successful arrival became legend, recounted every year in local newspapers.

John's career with the B&M was not to last. One day his excessive speed caused his train to derail, thereby derailing John's job. My father, however, always claimed that John Green was really fired because he was a Molly McGuire, a union man.

Whatever, he found work in the West Virginia Pulp and Paper Company in Mechanicville[cxvi]. Later, he entered Mechanicville politics, became a member of the Saratoga County Democratic Committee and served on the school board.

What irony. The man who only learned to read and write after well into his adulthood now was on the school board. Yet he would also influence "reading and writing" in another way. As a local paper wrote, he was the "father of free mail delivery . . . furnishing the post office department in Washington with the data and street numbering system necessary for free delivery" in Mechanicville. It was instituted in 1905.

In 1910, he was elected representative of the first ward in the, then, Village of Mechanicville. In 1914, as village president and as chairman of the Citizens Committee, he helped draft the city charter, but was defeated in his bid to be the new city's first mayor. He remained active in local and county politics until his death in 1946, only three years after the death of his wife.

His was a typical life. His was a symbolic life. In one generation, this son of immigrants had achieved literacy, as well as prosperity for himself and family, had held political office, and had made a contribution to his community beyond simply being a good citizen.

Amazing what we take for granted, isn't it?

"OVER MY SHOULDER" COLUMN FOR APRIL 20, 2002
Childhood memories of Saratoga

A recent photo of humorist Frank Sullivan reminded me that the Saratoga Springs of my birth is surely different from today's.

I was born in the Spa City after World War II, my parents' having moved there from Mechanicville in 1946. I spent my early childhood on 121 Lincoln Avenue, just down the street from Frank Sullivan's house.

As a little boy, I was too young to know that Frank was the famed humorist and celebrated member of the legendary Algonquin Round Table, an equal of Dorothy Parker, James Thurber and other literary greats. He was to me just "Frank," who lived with his sister Kate. The Sullivan house was my stop for my second or third breakfast. More about which in a moment.

Frank was my neighbor, as he was to all who lived on Lincoln Avenue. Certainly, he was admired for his literary gifts, but, as my parents always were fond of saying, "he was a Saratogian." My mother, Jane, befriended him early on and they corresponded infrequently throughout the remainder of his life.

Being little, my world was Lincoln Avenue. We rented the downstairs apartment from "Downsie," Mrs. Downs, who lived upstairs, which always seemed funny to me. No accounting for a child's humor. My older brother Mike and I played with the neighborhood kids, including the Van Rensselaers, Tommy Berrigan and the Stiegerwald brothers. The Stiegerwalds' father had a filling station that had been at the intersection of Broadway and Route 9. (A sure sign of aging is when one starts constantly referring to buildings that "had been" somewhere.)

We played openly, although not really unsupervised. The neighbors all watched, a special quality of Lincoln Avenue. Like every young mother with children, mine could trust to allow me to play along Lincoln Avenue. I truly believe most of those on our block knew who we were and where we were supposed to be.

Even at age 5, I went out alone to play. I had a regular route that ended at Nelson Avenue. I could not cross any street. Standing on the corner, I'd shout to an elderly man who sat on his porch. He'd shout back. This went on daily until, one day, the man did not appear. He never reappeared. I made my daily trip until finally my mother said he would not be sitting there again. "Is he deaded?" I asked. "Yes," she said sadly. "He's deaded," I went daily thereafter, just in case he wasn't.

Many mornings saw a happier ritual. After breakfast, Dad headed for MacFinn's and Mike for elementary school. Too young for school, I'd play while Jane listened to "Don McNeil and the Breakfast Club" on the radio. Then my friend Tommy Berrigan would come down. We'd set out with my mother yelling, "You had breakfast. Don't be begging people for snacks!"

Tommy and I would drop by the Caplans, Cy and Vicki, whom I called Vichy as I mixed her name up with the spring water. Vichy always had a treat ready. Then we went to the Maddox house. Anne was my godmother. We had a bite there to keep up our strength.

Normally, the last stop was Frank Sullivan's. Kate would welcome us in, somehow just knowing we boys had an appetite. Usually for a full breakfast. Frank was not downstairs, but up writing. Periodically, Kate, the Keeper of the Gate, would allow us to say hi to him. How mysterious he was! He often worked in his pajamas, writing in bed, with his typewriter on one of those hospital adjustable rolling trays. We'd peeked in, say hello, get a smile and depart quickly.

Afterward it was out to play a little and then home for lunch, always being greeted by Jane's questions. "You visit anyone?" Yes. "You didn't ask for anything to eat, did you?" No.

I had answered truthfully. One doesn't have to ask for what's offered.

"OVER MY SHOULDER" COLUMN FOR MAY 25, 2002
Song versions may reveal your age

We come to the serious issue of The Locomotion.

Yes, the same "Everybody's doin' a brand new dance, Come on baby do the locomotion" of your youth. But which version of it you remember will label your age?

Recently my wife and I were at an Adirondack Community College affair at the Hilander. Students and alums were gyrating to the music when the song "The Locomotion" was announced. I was standing next to Kevin Ankeny,

Assistant Professor of Radio, TV Broadcasting at ACC. I asked him, "Which version? Little Eva or Grand Funk Railroad?"

He smiled and said, "Neither. Kyle Minogue. 1988." I was stunned. Kyle Minogue? For those unfamiliar with pop, rock, Kyle was really big in the 1980s and is now enjoying a renaissance. My daughter, Julia, grew up listening to her.

But I'd recalled only two versions of "The Locomotion" – the original by Little Eva in 1962 and the second by Grand Funk Railroad in—what? Was it 1973? I blanked. I was experiencing a "historian's moment." Panicking, I called Gary Gifford at WCKM. He affirmed it was 1974.

The lesson? The memory a word triggers for me is not the memory it triggers for you. Kevin was a little boy when the Grand Funk version came out and not even a gleam during Little Eva's time.

But then, my daughter was only 7 when Kyle's version came out. To her, turning 21 this June 4th, the year 1988 is ancient history. Sorry, Kevin.

I'm returning, in a roundabout way, to a theme I'd addressed this March: what's gone missing. Now, some things keep coming back, especially music. But what's gone missing in terms of those three versions of "The Locomotion" is the record album. It's all CDs now.

Still, there's a substantial difference between 1962 and 2002, compared to the difference between 1988 and 2002. One difference, notes reader Thomas Loding, is "glass milk bottles with the cream in the neck." Yes, and the bottle's paper cap and foil cover—also non-homogenized milk that lets cream float to the top.

Mr. Loding also notes "train whistles at 4:00 am." The sheer daily decibel volume of factory and train whistles, fire sirens, and church bells was an unbelievable cacophony.

How about some other differences between 1962 and 2002? Stan Wood says "playing hide and seek or kick the can and yelling `Ollie-Ollie-in-come-free' when I couldn't find anyone else."

Anita Dingman writes: movie theaters in every small town, flash bulbs for cameras; car tires with tubes, 8mm home movies; Thursday night shopping in Glens Falls-other nights, the stores closed at 5:00; fridges that have to be defrosted; Cadillacs as status symbols; cap guns with roll caps; the neighborhood teen hangout with the juke box to dance to.

The last of which brings us back to music. Music can transcend time, but, honestly, when you hear a song from your youth, don't you flash back to one particular time?

Let me show you. Let's take the musical litmus age test to see what group you're in. We'll use the word "heart." When you hear the word "Heart" do you think of the rock group Heart? A 1980 high school graduate does. You're in the "Kissing the Last of Your Youth Goodbye" group.

When you hear the word "Heart" do you think of Elton John and Kiki Dee's "Don't Go Breakin' My Heart." A 1975 grad does. You're a Responsible Forty-Something!

When you hear the word "Heart" do you think of "Heart of Stone," by the Stones? A 1965 grad does. You're a Boomer!

But what about those for whom the word "heart" evokes Connie Francis' "Don't Break This Heart That Loves You" or Ted Weems' "Heartaches"?

You're called historians.

"OVER MY SHOULDER" COLUMN FOR JULY 20, 2002
Childhood memories of Decora

Plastics, Mickey Mouse, the Erie Canal, and silicon chips.

All these images whirled through my head this week as I read of the closing of yet another plant, Decora in Fort Edward, heard that a major producer of computer chips is moving to Albany, and heard Governor Pataki saying this new plant will be the next Erie Canal, a thought I'll return to in a moment.

Plastics were the computer chip of the post WW II. It's hard to think of plastic as exotic. When I was in college, "The Graduate" was a major movie hit. In it, the protagonist is told that his future was to be found in "plastics." As a Boomer, I was ripe for that image.

When I was little, plastics were starting to be used for everything—toys, TVs, radios, cars, Tupperware, you name it. When my family moved from Saratoga to Fort Edward, plastics were in my new town. A plastic sheet with a gummed backing was produced there, ConTact Paper. It was easy to get rolls of it for next to nothing. And, oh, that sound as you tore the sheet off the backing.

The smell of the Decora plant's chemicals was the perfume of money. We even brought that smell with us to school. We had to cover our schoolbooks, so we'd get ConTact Paper, which we all pronounced "con-tack paper," and cut the sheets to fit the books, like those covers on library books.

You didn't glue the ConTact Paper to the books. No! You left the paper backing on the plastic. In many cases the cover had more durability than the often decades old books, which had seen better times. Some books were so outdated the Second World War hadn't started and the very production methods for ConTact Paper probably emerged after the books' publication.

In the mid-1950s, Walt Disney introduced the Mickey Mouse Club to TV. It was an explosion of Disney and anything Disney, we kids had to have. As I matured, I wanted Annette Funicello, but that Christmas gift never came to be.

In a brilliant move, Decora got the contract to put Mickey Mouse and other Disney characters on ConTact Paper. It had a profound effect in town. Those whose parents worked at Decora got to bring home seconds, so there was always a lot of ConTact Paper in town. We all were pretty blasé about it. But now Mickey and the gang were on ConTact Paper. And the kid who could walk down the street with Mickey Mouse on his or her book cover? A King or a queen, that's what they were. Alas, my father had to be a pharmacist, so we didn't get to have Mickey for a long time.

You saw Maury Thompson's excellent article in last week's *Post-Star*, I know, so I needn't reacquaint you with Decora's history. What's important is that Decora's history has ended, and people are out of work. Plant closing stories are becoming so numerous that the average reader risks becoming numb to the tragedy of them. We've seen it too many times in our region's history.

And history is exactly why George Pataki spoke of the Erie Canal. He knew the Erie Canal's opening in 1825 would trigger New Yorkers' historical memories. They'd recall that the canal had turned New York State into the driving economic engine of the nation. And they'd have hope for this new venture doing the same.

His reference was calculated to inspire the hope that New York State will again boom. There are the cynics who will say Pataki's message was simply calculating. But those without a job today may be forgiven if they ignore the cynics and hope that Pataki is right.

For, right now, they need that "Erie Canal hope." And they are praying that history repeats itself.

"OVER MY SHOULDER" COLUMN FOR AUGUST 17, 2002
A magical day at the track

S aratoga Race Course could never get back what it has paid out to me.
But then, as the payout was in memories, we've both made out well.
It was an exceptional day, those nine years ago, August 20, 1993. My girl, Julia, was 12 and we had a father-daughter day set aside for the track.

Mind you, neither Julia nor I played the ponies. She had, and has, an abiding love of horses, something she gets from her mother. I had, and have, a nostalgia for the track.

Perhaps there is a genetic disposition in me that finds a romance in this big course. And perhaps there might be just a bit of a genetic hand-me-down to my daughter from her Grandmother King, who could play horses with a winning hand in a way that made her husband want to gnash his teeth.

That knack seemed to come into play that special day nine years ago. Although, truthfully, it was hard to lose that day. After all, it was Julie Krone riding.

You needn't be a diehard racing fan to recall that magic day. Krone, diminutive even among jockeys, was a long shot riding long shots. She was a female jockey and for the father of a daughter, it was a thrill to say: "See? Don't be daunted. Women can excel in those bastions of manhood." Not that Julie Krone was welcome in that bastion of manhood, mind you. She wasn't.

However, Krone had entered the track that morning already a success, having won the Belmont that year. She would be even more of a success by that evening.

It was a perfect August day. We arrived early. Walked the grounds. Watched the early morning workouts. Visited the stables. It was lovely. We oohed and ahhed over the horses and the child dreamed her dreams of a large stable chock full of beautiful animals pampered like babies. I prattled on too much about childhood memories of Saratoga, which were received with the same polite smiles and feigned interest I'd given to my parents' memories. It's a rite of passage.

The first race came, and we decided what horse we would play. I still have our partially faded "Pink Sheet" from that day, with our check marks on it. Each check was by a horse ridden by Julie Krone, the female jockey, whose first name was so similar to my girl's. And, oh heavens, the odds on that first horse she was riding were astronomical.

We, pardon me, I bet lightly. Foolishly now, I realized. For every race Julie Krone was in, she won. You could feel the buzz in the crowd. As the races progressed, and she rode in half of them, the odds on the board dropped as she continued to win. The excitement grew. The buzz became an electric current. We cheered her on as if we were her family.

I didn't bet because we liked the horse. I bet solely because it was Julie Krone. On that day, she won all five races at Saratoga, the third jockey ever to do that at Saratoga, but the first woman jockey to do so. It was a screaming day.

What happened next was most fitting. We had waited in a huge crowd to speak with her, but Julie Krone left before my daughter, Julia, had her chance. Julia was disappointed, but a woman with Krone took her name and later in the mail Julia received a personalized memento from Julie Krone, expressing her regret that she had not been able to speak with my girl. It meant so much to her, and to me.

That aside, we'd had a great day. Using our winnings, we even went out to eat, something not too many people can claim after a day at the races.

And we'd shared a second "payoff" that day—a purse full of wonderful memories, all wrapped up now in a fading Pink Sheet.

"OVER MY SHOULDER" COLUMN FOR SEPTEMBER 07, 2002
Summer memories with Kinks and Frank

When I was a child, the end of summer usually meant a stay of several weeks at the Stillwater home of Aunt Kinks and Uncle Frank.

There was a special something between my mother, Jane, and my great-aunt Cornelia, Aunt Kinks, as she was always known. It showed in their faces and embraces whenever we visited.

Jane was much like Kinks. Both had funny little nervous habits, product of a restless personality and inner thought patterns that would have surprised many. Kinks cleared her throat a lot. Her hands moved incessantly, sewing, canning, furniture-refinishing, gardening, and doing the zillion other chores she planned. Like Kinks, Jane had a "to do list" that needed three lifetimes.

Kinks and Frank were different, he large, she small, he reserved, she easy to laugh. He was said to have his family's "German temperament." Some thought him aloof and quite, shall we say, frugal. I do recall that every time they returned from the Mechanicville A&P, he went through the groceries piece by piece. If anything were missing or had an incorrect price, back to Mechanicville they'd go and woe to that checkout clerk!

To us, my brother Mike, sister Martha and me, he was a big, loving man, with his white hair combed straight back, and always a huge smile, so reminiscent of the comedian George Burns. He incessantly smoked cigars and his pipe. His Prince Albert tobacco cans lined his cellar shop walls, all filled with nails and bolts and so on. The cozy shop was his sanctum sanctorum.

Kinks was small-boned, with twinkling eyes and that pale skin that wrinkled so easily when she hugged us. She smelled of a particular dusting powder, which I doubt is even made anymore. Typically kids, we thought they were ancient. They were in their late fifties and early sixties.

Their home was a vision of sameness, upon which we could count year after year. Kinks had spent years decorating the house to her tastes with beautiful antiques, but all used, nothing for show. The antique clocks always ticked the same way. The oriental carpets absorbed all other sound. The walls were hung with her paintings and with 19th century engravings from Godey's Ladies Book, all lending an air of another world and another time. This was only accentuated by our sleeping upstairs where on cold nights we were encouraged to use the "potties" under the bed.

The television usually remained off. Instead we'd play in the house or the gardens. Kinks was surprised once when Mike and I were contented to spend hours viewing the old stereopticon images upstairs. Maybe she didn't realize they contained "French postcard" images of half-clad women. Her old National Geographic magazines served a similar educational purpose.

We'd explore their huge gardens, filled with flowerbeds, ornamentals, hydrangeas, pear trees, and masses of raspberry plants. Our imaginations were always stretched. Once she had three-year-old Martha help the house painter. Kinks gave Martha brushes and plain water. Gradually we all came to see the same vibrant colors and excellent work that Kinks extolled.

I still can see Frank coming home from his coal and grain business at the same time every day, washing, then sitting to dinner. The kitchen at that time of year was always redolent with the fragrance of their garden produce being canned—corn, beans, raspberries, fruits, all stored in the cellar in wooden cabinets, perfumed with years of jams and pickles. Frank always sat in one chair, his left arm cocked in a question mark, used only to reach for bread or for vinegar to pour on his spinach.

After dinner he sat to read the paper by the tall Zenith console radio.[cxvii] Kinks cleaned up then came in to sew. We laid on the huge oriental carpets, whispering or saying nothing, content, safe and happy in the house of Kinks and Frank, on a late summer day many years ago.

"OVER MY SHOULDER" COLUMN FOR SEPTEMBER 28, 2002
Death brings back schoolboy memories

The recent sad passing of David Burroughs, formerly of Ticonderoga, brought back memories of his father, George Burroughs.

I did not know David Burroughs, although I have the privilege to know some of his family and I extend my condolences.

But George Burroughs, past principal of Ticonderoga High School? Ah, yes, I knew him well.

Or I should say, I knew his regime, his techniques, his way of "running the ship." One never really "knows" one's commanding officer. One only knows what one is allowed to see. Having grown up in the home of a former US Navy officer, I know of what I speak.

So, too, with this new commander, Mr. Burroughs. My family had moved to Ticonderoga in that summer of 1962 and I was immediately plunked in summer school to help raise a dangerously low geometry grade. Outside of loving history, there's a reason I am a historian. I am, shall we say, mathematically challenged.

Our house was near Lake George, which beckoned daily. Instead I'd trudge down Lake George Avenue to the halls of Ticonderoga High School, quite barren on those summer days.

My very first day of summer school introduced me to George Burroughs' "hands-on" style of education. I was just about to enter the principal's office to register. I'd already seen this large, balding man, who would address me, as he addressed every other male student, as "boy." I'd heard he was stern, perhaps gruff, but nothing prepared me for what I was about to see.

I was standing with someone, I can't recall who, when a very young male student, perhaps in 7th or 8th grade, suddenly and frantically burst from the office door and began running down the long hallway. Exploding out the door behind him was George Burroughs, principal. He shot me a look that seemed to say, "Are you the offending party?"

Gawking, gaping open-mouthed, I managed to shake my head "no" and he shot his gaze in the direction of the escaping boy at whom he bellowed, roared, "Boy! Come back here!" And the boy stopped for a millisecond and shouted something that for all the world sounded like "Go to hell, Mr. Burroughs!" and bolted for the stairs.

I stood dumbstruck. Unlike today, when the f-word is used as a punctuation mark in most school hallway conversations, what that young boy had hollered was considered the equivalent of an obscenity. Although, I was impressed that he had said, "Mr. Burroughs." It seemed oddly respectful, even in light of its intentions.

I might have been frozen to the spot, but George Burroughs was after that boy in a heartbeat, spurred on to sprint like a gazelle. The pace picked up and we heard the patter of the boy's feet running up the stairs, echoing through the empty hallways, along with the thump-thump-thump of George Burroughs' broad, measured stride. And echoing with both set of footfalls were Mr. Burroughs' bellows: "Stop, boy! Stop!

We could hear it as George Burroughs closed in on the boy, his voice louder, their footfalls meshing, and then, a momentary silence. And then a child's shriek of "NOOOOOOOOO!" that turned into a wail that carried on, seemingly forever.

It was confided to me later that day that Mr. Burroughs had been a tennis star at one point. True or not, it didn't matter. What mattered was that I knew my commanding officer.

In future days, George Burroughs would be the educator perhaps most responsible for my going to college, for which I shall be forever grateful. But that is a story for another time. And I could not know that at the time. For at that moment, as I heard the wails of that boy dying out in the hallways, all I knew was my new commander and his inimitable style.

And that was enough knowledge to absorb on that first day of school.

"OVER MY SHOULDER" COLUMN FOR NOVEMBER 23, 2002
Memories of holidays gone by, via the back porch

My mother, Jane, had a special affinity for enclosed porches that were not winterized. They provided a holding space for a chaise lounge, crockery and other antiques, dried flowers, stacks of books, old New York Times magazines that rose like towers, and once a year, a Thanksgiving turkey.

The porch was her sanctum sanctorum. Of course, the whole house was Jane's to decorate as she saw fit. God knows my father had as much inclination toward interior decorating as a duck has for space travel.

But an enclosed porch was hers alone. My parents' last home in Ticonderoga, actually provided Jane with two unheated enclosed porches. The front porch had loads of window space, providing good sun. Here she had assembled various pieces of antique crockery, and tinted 19th century medicine bottles that cast soft blue light when the sun shone through them. There were a few chairs and even a small bed that a guest could use.

The porch had been painted repeatedly and the chalky white paint took on a particular odor that gradually built into something hauntingly familiar. When dry flower arrangements and a few more antiques appeared, the realization came to me. Jane was carrying on a tradition. Here was a porch much like the unheated porch at her Aunt Kinks' house.

Aunt Kinks, given name Cornelia, occupied a special place in Jane's life and it was fascinating to see Kinks' porch – itself a place of warm memories for us all – re-emerging in our house in Ti.

However, it was the second porch off the kitchen that eventually became Jane's true sanctum sanctorum. The front porch was just too hot in the summer and, with the crockery and dried bittersweet, it developed as more of a room to behold than to occupy. The back porch had more shade. It was more of a cubbyhole, too, holding as it did the freezer and various large oven roasters, as our house sported the world's smallest kitchen.

Packed in there was also a chaise lounge. Summers, when hollyhocks grew tall outside the little porch, Jane would retreat there to read her books and newspapers and take the essential nap.

In the winter – mid-October to mid-April – the whole porch was a substitute refrigerator. It was very much like, I also saw, the back porch off Aunt Kinks' kitchen. It offered excellent cold storage for Thanksgiving and Christmas meals, when the variety and number of dishes Jane prepared surpassed anything offered by Julia Child.

I recall a particular Thanksgiving. It was a bit warmer than usual. Most of us kids were home, packed in the dining room with parents and grandmother. Between the number of bodies, the kitchen stove going round the clock and the fact that my father, George, had the thermostat cranked to 75, the house was unbearable. Occasionally to escape the heat, I'd step on to the front porch, which had received the overflow of relishes and rolls that no longer fit on the table or piano bench, already full with food. The smell would transport me to my aunt's house.

Thanksgiving dinner done, George ensconced himself in "his" chair in front of the football game and was promptly snoring. We kids were ready to go out to visit friends. Mom, who should have been on the couch, was nowhere to be seen. Impulse guided me to the back porch. There, amidst the roaster pan with the turkey carcass, dishes of creamed onions and scalloped oysters, and stacks of magazines, lay the chef, asleep on her chaise with a coat on and a blanket pulled over her.

I let her be but left the door open to let in the heat, allowing the sleeper to dream that it was summer again, with the hollyhocks in bloom.

"OVER MY SHOULDER" COLUMN FOR NOVEMBER 30, 2002
Beefing about food history

Call this gastronomic beefing.

I was fascinated by Gretta Nemcek's fine article on the archeological discovery of a turkey bone at Fort Ti, in which Curator Chris Fox discussed the find, dating to about 1760. He noted the turkey was part of a meal of "some lucky soldier" or an officer. Meaning, the turkey signified the meal was special. Soldiers' rations in those days included large quantities of salted meat and other items not easily perishable. Fresh foodstuffs were a rarity.

How exotic the diet of American colonists must have been to Europeans arriving for the first time in the mid-1700s. That colonial diet is, in a limited way, still expressed today in the traditional Thanksgiving dinner.

And that's what started my beefing—or carping, if you prefer fish. Last Sunday on "CBS Sunday Morning News" a guest commentator pontificated on how boring the traditional American Thanksgiving dinner is, solemnly adding that America only developed gastronomic variety after 1965, when new immigrant groups started to arrive.

How did that chucklehead manage to ignore the millions of immigrants who poured in before 1965, among them millions of Italians? Italian food lacks variety? Perhaps his problem had to do with having lousy cooks in his family.

The traditional American Thanksgiving dinner is to me a delicious piece of living history, embodying the New World's culinary gifts to Europe: turkey, potatoes, corn, squash, and pumpkins, although it's believed vegetables didn't play a major role in colonial diets.

Maybe the archeology done at Fort Ti last year, in preparation for rebuilding an original portion of the fort, might shed more light on vegetables, and tell us what else was eaten with that turkey up at Fort Ti in 1760. The diary of Enos Hitchcock, D. D., would be helpful. Hitchcock, a Continental Army minister, was stationed at Fort Ticonderoga in 1777 when Burgoyne's Army invaded. He was writing only 17 years after the turkey bone in question had been part of someone's meal.

The good Reverend loved to eat and on his way to Ti often recorded his meals, such as "roast beef," "boiled chicken" and "Sallet" (salad?).[cxviii] On his first day at Fort Ti, May 24, 1777, he "Dined upon flowr puding & Venison

Steak." On the 25th it was "roast & stewed Venison," and the 26th "Pudding, Veal &C." Fish played a major dietary role, but venison was king: "Venison Stakes," "roast Venison Stuft," and "Venison Soop &C." His abbreviation "&C," for etcetera, tells us there was more than just venison.

But nowhere does Rev. Hitchcock record having eaten turkey. How odd! Unfortunately, cookbooks don't seem to have been prevalent in the late 18th century, so perhaps Chris Fox will tell us more about the culinary life at Fort Ti in the form of his own cookbook.

And in mentioning cookbooks, I return to my beef with the "CBS Sunday Morning News." By the late 1880s, cookbooks were plentiful. My grandmother's, from 1901, tells a lot about tastes then. While its suggested "colonial Thanksgiving dinner" menu stretches the limits of what was truly "colonial," what's important is what is acceptable for Thanksgiving dinner in 1901: clam or fish chowder; lobster bisque; highly spiced puff pastries with fish; roasted turkey with pumpkin sauce; all different turkey stuffings, made with bread, corn bread, nuts or oysters, among other things; a "cloved ham;" potatoes, mashed with heavy cream and butter; succotash; green beans cooked in milk and butter; corn pudding; fresh, stewed, creamed or scalloped oysters; turnip casserole; creamed onions; pickled and Harvard beets; bread and butter pickles; chili relish; New England baked beans; squash (or sweet potatoes) baked with brown sugar and maple syrup; fresh fruit; Indian meal pudding; mince, pumpkin and apple pies (with cheddar cheese); lemon cheesecake; frozen custard; and punch, both high test and low test.

That menu is boring? Get me my fork!

And to "CBS Sunday Morning News": get a culinary life.

"OVER MY SHOULDER" COLUMN FOR DECEMBER 7, 2002
Thoughts of a Christmas couch

Frankly, George was not a devotee of Christmas.

Which might be the most egregious understatement ever written in this column.

Jane, on the other hand, was Mrs. Christmas, the embodiment of the season, ultimate holiday cook, ultimate decorator, and—yes!—ultimate shopper. By the late 1960s in Ticonderoga, she was now free from dragging a gaggle of children store to store and, finally possessed of a driver's license, she became a Christmas dervish, whirling among the downtown shops.

I see her now, exiting J. J. Newberry's, with store manager Pat Carney smiling wistfully at the departing figure. When she'd tell me where she'd been, I'd envision merchants strewing rose petals in her path, crying out "Hosanna in the highest!" regardless of religious affiliation. Heaven knows she didn't have a lot of money, but she always seemed to have some kind of a gift for everyone. I'm convinced there are grateful recipients in Zambezi.

Hyperbole becomes inadequate when discussing Christmas and my mother.

Now, every rule has its exception. George excelled in one Christmas activity: partying. His birth must have been so difficult, for I'm sure came in wearing a lampshade, his right hand grasping a drink, and his left a party favor.

While not a shirker, Mrs. Christmas lacked that passion and full-bodied stamina that Mr. Christmas Party brought to one, two, even three parties in one evening. Ticonderoga in those days of the Sixties featured multiple parties on Christmas Eve, Christmas Day, even Christmas night—perhaps an Adirondack custom, but definitely a novelty to our family, just new to the area.

Understand that George was also not a devotee of Christmas shopping. It was normal for Dad to buttonhole one of us grown kids and say, "Go to such and such a store and buy your mother some gifts." Meaning, buy her gifts from him. He usually had one biggie he'd pick out each year and that exhausted his shopping ability.

Beyond us, he'd recruit one of the "girls" behind the counter at Burleigh's Pharmacy where he worked. *Post-Star* editor Maury Thompson's late wife, Nancy, comes immediately to mind.[cxix]

So, on this particular Christmas he decided to surprise Jane totally with a present unusual for him: a couch. Known in his younger, more adventurous shopping days for fur coats, French perfume or jewelry, furniture was considered interior decorating—Jane's turf, not his.

The family couch was a bed and hammock, a campaign veteran worn out by years of snoozes and indelicate floppings by all us kids, several of us now grown and gone. It sat forlornly beneath two gold-framed Currier and Ives reproductions, and positioned so Jane could watch a fragment of TV, then nod off with the newspaper.

Dad secretly ordered a couch from Kirby Wilcox's furniture store,[cxx] which had at its opposite end, in fine tradition of old, a funeral parlor. Kirby could sell you the first and last piece of furniture you'd ever use. This couch, however, was for mid-life passage.

George got Jane out of the house on some pretext. I hope memory serves me, for I recall it was Mike Connery who helped sneak in the couch on Christmas Eve. This was a younger Mike, before being supervisor and, now, the reigning new president and CEO of Capital District Off-Track Betting. Mike masterfully wrestled that moose of a couch, carting out the old and bringing in the new.

As was meant, eagle-eyed Jane saw it immediately upon later entry. She cast a suspicious look at George. Furniture? Her territory! And it was an odd color, not her taste. But she thanked him graciously and they hit midnight services.

The new couch, it turned out, was like fine wine, simply needing to breathe a bit after uncorking. The next few days of parties having left both exhausted, the living room saw the veterans recuperating on the 28th, their wedding anniversary. Mr. Christmas Party was in "his" recliner, snoring.

Mrs. Christmas was on the firm new couch, which was providing its reward: a long winter's nap.

"OVER MY SHOULDER" COLUMN FOR DECEMBER 21, 2002
Christmas unveils thoughts of two lives

This is a Christmas story about "the ten dollars."

When each new December arrives, and that seems to be now in three months instead of twelve, Christmas memories flood over me. Many are from my childhood, some associated with shopping with my family in downtown Glens Falls. But other memories are from the beginning of my "second life," with its images of downtown Glens Falls in the late 1970s and early 1980s.

My second life began on a mid-December night of 1978 in an upstairs apartment at the pointed corner of Glen and Ridge Streets. Oddly, when I think of that night, I see it from two perspectives. One is from the viewpoint of my crossing Ridge Street to a Christmas party.

In the second, more movie-like, I'm looking down at a bachelor in his early thirties, as forgetful then as now, scarf flying as he dashes for a bottle of wine before rushing to his friends' apartment. At that time, Chris and Deborah Scoville[cxxi] [*Christopher Scoville and Debra Vales*] had redone the upstairs over Scoville Jewelers into lovely living quarters, a concept so far in advance of its time for downtown.

The rushing bachelor's plans were predictable that December. There was doing the Christmas opening at the Chapman Historical Museum, where I worked, then later on shopping with what little money I had, and, finally, taking the train to Ticonderoga for Christmas with the family. Right now, I had a party to go to. Pretty much the bachelor life.

The apartment was jammed, noisily festive, and I ended up at the bar, talking with a diminutive redhead with a penchant for martinis. I'd seen her in the North Country Arts Center[cxxii] downtown and, for some reason, assumed she was divorced with two kids. She'd seen me, but assumed that my sole interests were the past, cobwebs, and boring historical stuff.

How wrong assumptions can be. She'd never married and had no kids. I liked the present and looked to the future. It's her version of the story that she couldn't get rid of me that night. I'll let that stand. Whatever the case, we started to see one another.

In fact, I stopped by to see her Christmas Eve, on my way to Fort Edward to catch the train. At that very moment, I realized I was flat broke and ended up borrowing 10 dollars from her. Not an auspicious way to impress a lady.

It was the last Christmas we ever spent apart. Within a short time, we were married, and the second life launched its own Christmas memories. I recall the Chapman's 1980 Christmas opening, where our friend Jack Wiberg looked at Sara's glowing skin and guessed the secret she carried: she was expecting. Then how different the next Christmas was! Sara had started teaching at ACC[cxxiii]. The former rushing bachelor was now the hurrying father, dashing home after working with Dan and Jan Hazewski on their first "Victorian Christmas Past" celebration downtown.[cxxiv]

I paused only to shop, for at home my wife and our new baby awaited me. It was three years and a lifetime from that party where we'd met.

Oh, and about the 10 dollars? Try as I might, I've never been able to repay it, for the "interest" has been growing with every year. You see, my wife, Sara, has always been a better gift giver than I. Each Christmas, when I think of those times when my second life began, I unwrap in my mind those Christmas presents she's given me.

And I unwrap the memory of when we first met at that Christmas party.

And I unwrap the memory of our first Christmas as a couple, and then the memory of our baby on her first Christmas.

And I unwrap the memory of—and experience all over again—the thrill of starting that second life in that downtown of long ago.

And how could I ever match presents like those?

Merry Christmas to you all.

"OVER MY SHOULDER" COLUMN FOR DECEMBER 28, 2002
Bidding adieu to 2002

With this year's end, it seems propitious
For history review and future wishes.
And to tally mistakes we've made—
Bring'em forth in repentant parade.

Ms. Debra Vales[cxxv] of Scoville Jewelers,
Should task me sternly with a ruler!
For though I've known her, yea, for ages,
Her name I mixed up in these pages.
Fool am I—diamond in the rough?
Debra, please just buff, but don't rebuff!

Confession made, let's start our history
And look back `pon Spa City myst'ry
Some nut who fancied theft most tawdry,
Stole equine statues right from Broadway!

Klotz called Regan `bout fiberglas Horses:
"Mayor to Mayor, can you lend the Morses?"
    Yes, he meant Phil and good wife Sue,
Who gave Glens Falls High a field or two.

    Their timing was "keen," offer them cheers,
For high school building's fiftieth year.
    Spa City did fix that horsy mess,
With carousel ponies in Park Congress!

    Johnny Burgoyne made his off-Broadway debut
In battles reprising his Waterloo,
    At Hubbardton, Ticonderoga
Forts Anne'n'Edward, Old Saratoga.

    Restaging Burgoyne's two-twenty-fifth,
Brought alive history, but caused such a rift.
    Counties Saratoga, Washington
Almost faced a "new" Revolution.

    Things now smoothed over amongst them all,
With peace treaty `twixt Pulver and Hall[cxxvi].
    Here's to heritage tourism, sonny!
Surprise, surprise! It brings in the money!

    Again benefactors, like Charley Wood,
Gave to the needy, and spread the good!
    Mary Lou Whitney's "charity prance,"
Helps out the arts, Museum of Dance.

    Fort Ti's sweet gift made Nick Westbrook see stars,
Proved candy is dandy, but best when by Mars.
    The Post-Star said, "Help out? Oh, aye, aye!"
Became St. Nick to the Glens Falls Y.

    `Cause counties are gloomy, in the red,
Poor Warren had to tax every bed!
    It works now, sure, but do beware,
Because next they'll tax your underwear.

    Washington County got check in mail,
Used tobacco bucks to build a jail.

Dollars from those ceasing to inhale,
Left Salem without courthouse or jail.

But plans have the Salem citizenry,
Led by that good man Bill Eberle.
　Working with their planning tools,
They even foresee a swimming pool!

Snuggled right up to Glens' City Hall,
LARAC said, "Let's do have a ball!"
　Pat Joyce smiled. Arts Council's so sturdy,
Can you believe that now it's 30?

New Year wishes for all striving historians,
Museums, centers, and theaters galore-ian!
　Juliet Chapman, Charlotte Hyde do
Guard those museums named just for you!

And shade of sweet Katrina Trask,
Watch over Yaddo, that's your task.
　Sharon and Joe Knipes in good ole VT,
Have you seen Manchester's SVAC?

Hubbard Hall's Garrick, good Benjy White,
Keeps Cambridge theater bright at night,
　By bringing in a thespian live wire,
You know whom I mean, Kevin McGuire.

For Glens Falls theater once a Woolworth,
Of fives and dimes, please, be there no dearth.
　Like belov'd Boston Candy Kitchen,
Fed Martha Stewart—is now enrichin'!

Martha Stonequist, Spa City Historian
Please, a book on bard Frank Sullivan.
　Housed on my old Avenue, Lincoln,
Frank needs a bio, I am thinkin'.

And By Lapham's *Hometown Memories*?
Loved volume two! When will we see three?[cxxvii]
　Come on Joan, tell him we pray:
Just one more on Hometown USA!

And Hannay, that's Eileen, oh my land!
A wish for Center at Rogers Island!
   Here's a hope Rangers make a landing
Where Rogers wrote those Orders Standing.

   Oh, Father Michael Abraham,
Bend those knees when you can,
   Say a prayer for Maury's Nancy,
Whose love lives on, that we fancy.

   And for IP's former Corinth mill,
Casualty of a corporate will.
   Let those workers, two ninety all,
To new work all be recalled.

   Now ending verses, short two liners
Served fast, tasty, like Peter's Diner.
   Our Glens Falls Symphony does inspire.
Buy Peltz, Rosoff, the Theatre Empire!

   Hail to Jack Wiberg, commissioner,
Seeking good water conditioner.
   Daughter Julia, this memento:
Good luck in school in Sacramento.

   And birthday wishes for my sweet wife,
May this one start you a brand new life.
   Well wishes to friends, all family,
For good fortune in 2003!

"OVER MY SHOULDER" COLUMN FOR FEBRUARY 8, 2003
So many columns, too little time

Let's do some business and then get back to history.

So many of you have written in response to the article in Tuesday's *Post-Star* regarding my taking a new position and ending this column. I thank you for your caring comments. They mean more to me than you ever can know.

And a reminder to some: Tuesday's article was not carried on the obituary page. To my knowledge, I am very much alive and well. Life simply offers opportunities that can't be missed. Life's also unpredictable. So, I won't say "goodbye," rather "I'll be seeing you." One just never knows.

This is my newspaper, and I am proud of it. I have been writing this column since 1994 and shall miss my relationship with you. I thank you and *The Post-Star* for the chance to show up on your breakfast table every Saturday. I hope I haven't spoiled your eggs too many times.

Also, I'm grateful to my editors for the latitude given me in these columns. In addition to writing about local history, I've had the very selfish pleasure of being able to reminisce about family and friends, and "my life and times" in Saratoga Springs, Fort Edward, Ticonderoga and Glens Falls. My poor parents, gone now for many years, never have had the option to protest their personal lives being dragged through these pages. It is a different story with my wife, Sara, and daughter, Julia. I'm grateful for their forbearance, especially Sara for the encouragement and reality checks that she gives. She is my rock.

And for the record, I paid back that darn ten dollars I borrowed from her when we first met. No matter what she tells you to the contrary.

If I've grown as a writer and a historian since 1994, it is because of you. You've challenged and inspired me. I thank those of you who have. Some of you have hated me for what I have written. And I thank those of you who have. I'm never sure I've fully defended my principles until someone hates me for them.

As with anyone who loves today and eagerly anticipates tomorrow, I have unfinished projects, and potential columns written in my head but not on paper. With *The Post-Star* having expanded into the Saratoga Springs region, I had a series of articles planned on downtown. My father ran MacFinn's on Broadway. His mother had been a housemother at Skidmore for 14 years and my trove of materials on the Skiddies, over whom she held sway, is vast. And there was my mother's friendship with Frank Sullivan—so many columns, too little time.

A quick note to those who've enjoyed my columns on my mother, Jane, especially her friends in Ti. A book on her letters and life is in the hopper. Jane lives.[cxxviii]

I also have unfinished gripes, of which I will air a choice few. To State Senator Betty Little and Assemblyman Roy McDonald: why can't we have a State Historian? It's the law. We complain our kids don't respect the law, when all the while we adults don't?

To Saratoga Springs: why, in any local supermarket, can I buy a bottle of naturally carbonated spring water from France, but the only bottled effervescent Saratoga spring water sold is artificially carbonated? What the hell is coming out of the ground down there? Root beer?

To Glens Falls: before another budding genius destroys another building, could somebody please take control of downtown's destiny while there's still a downtown in downtown? Have mercy.

To the world: Washington County is not a junk shop from which to move historic houses.

I'll leave off with that one. Thank you all for nine wonderful years. And now, over the next few weeks until I go, we'll talk history and share memories of people, places and things. Like Carroll's 10 cent hamburgers? Saunas in Shushan?

"OVER MY SHOULDER" COLUMN FOR FEBRUARY 22, 2003
Raining cats and dogs, but mostly cats

Cats were vital to my family history.

Dogs were a part of my mother's childhood. My father had no pets while growing up, as his mother did not like them, although he always had always wanted a dog. For years after Jane had married George in 1942, they lived in apartments. So, dogs were not allowed or, at least, not practical.

In 1946, they moved with their little boy Michael to a Lincoln Avenue apartment in Saratoga Springs. A dog just didn't fit, especially with a boy and girl added within four years.

The boys were a handful. Michael and his little friends were found scampering between the legs of a high-strung thoroughbred at the racetrack nearby, sending practically every parent there into cardiac arrest. Michael nearly fractured his skull diving Superman-style into the bathtub.

At age 4, his brother Joseph "painted" the Caplans' white house, using black trim paint the house painter had left uncovered while taking lunch. Another time, he and Tommy Berrigan released chickens from a neighbor's coop to run wild throughout the area. With a child like Joe, one didn't need a dog.

Yet, some pet was desired, so a cat was chosen. Thereafter, it ruled.

Mo-Mo, the first, successfully transitioned in our move to Fort Edward, then went AWOL. Two dogs were adopted, but both died. Jane said she hated having pets, because you came to love them so, and it hurt too much when they died.

Such was the case with the white cat, whose death tested the Kings' matrimonial bonds. Jane had a wicked temper and sharp tongue when she let it go. The white cat's death brought out both. The white cat was an astoundingly loving animal that had entered our yard and our hearts all in one day.

He was also a champion mouser. He fell ill, and Jane lovingly brought him to the veterinarian. Rat poison in the mice he consumed had caused his liver to fail. He was put down, Jane by his side.

In tears, she afterward stopped at our pharmacy, quite crowded at noontime. Now, many who knew George also knew his legendary fondness for toddy. This led directly to the "comment about the white cat," famous in family history. Innocently George asked her: "What happened with the white cat?"

"The cat," she spat out bitterly to George, the noon crowd listening, "is dead of cirrhosis of the liver and it never had a drink in its life. But you? You're still alive!"

It was days before George spoke to her again. That rift, like many others was mended, later laughed about, but never forgotten.

Our move to Ticonderoga saw a succession of cats that fit the family's altering shape, as Martha, then Bill, and finally Scott matured and moved away. Dad made a last bid for a dog one Christmas. But now, having a house without little children, Jane wasn't about to have a dog.

Compounding that was Dad's mother, Annie as he called her, who lived next door and was becoming increasingly frail and dependent. Yet, being a dominant person, Annie would not yield to the realities of being in her 90s. The relationship between the two women was, in the best of times, a truce.

That Christmas, Jane jokingly gave George a stuffed dog. The humor bombed and thus ensued another "silence," also famous in family history.

Throughout it all, however, the cat remained a constant. In fact, my parents' last cat, Sharon, was well suited to them both. It had my mother's love of afternoon naps and matched Dad's very nocturnal habits. An all-purpose animal, loved by all.

Well, almost all. In her 100-plus years, Grandma had never come to like any cat, especially Sharon. Interestingly, Sharon's favorite spot was sitting on the front porch of her house. Sharon could be found there preening in the warm sun, right in front of the huge front window, in full view of Annie's favorite seat.

"OVER MY SHOULDER" COLUMN FOR MARCH 1, 2003
Whispering memories come calling

In life, there are moments of whispering memory.

These memories are always here, so nearby they're like another room, waiting to be entered. The slightest nudge of a familiar sight or sound will open the door. As is often life's way, what's recalled had originally occurred in so small an area, that as we pass through it later, we're overwhelmed by memory piled upon memory. Some are exquisite, and some exquisite in their sorrow.

This happened recently. I was driving through the Glen and Ridge streets intersection in downtown Glens Falls. Whispering memories suddenly became a conversation, then a cacophony. It struck me. So many events in the life Sara and I constructed have taken place within a half-mile or so of that apartment over Scoville's Jewelers where we first met.

I neared the Queensbury Hotel. Whispering memories brought me to a Beaux Arts Ball there in 1979. Sara and I danced. Love grew. Friendship, too, as we met for the first time the man whom our child still lovingly calls Uncle Jack.[cxxix]

I slowed in front of the hotel. Suddenly it was 20 years ago, 1983. Sara and I were bringing our daughter Julia to see Grandma and Grandpa King at the hotel. Jane had been diagnosed with cancer and, over time, the hotel became her sanctuary as she shuttled the short distance to and from the Glens Falls Hospital for chemotherapy. To the same hospital where my wife had been born. Where she would later bring our daughter, Julia, into the world. And where my mother would leave it, not long after.

Whispering memories. See the Queensbury's lobby? Our child is moving toward my mother. There are long tables full of food that Julia wants, but can't have. As the inevitable tantrum arises, I watch Jane's smile spread softly. Her eyes say to me, "Your turn." A 2-year-old is a grandmother's revenge.

My car passed by the Presbyterian Church. I recalled the Caritas meetings there and meeting a man named Father Michael, who helped us understand how cancer affects whole families and how sweet friendships grow out of tragic circumstances.

Without at first realizing it, I could now see that I was driving north along main and side streets, touring parts of my life as whispering memories were calling, calling. They called as I drove past the home of the Adamses, Julia's other family, who cared so tenderly for her. They called as I rounded the corner onto Harrison Avenue, and went on to our old home.

I idled, not really parking. There was our first home. Birthdays and bedtime stories, Christmases and cats, good times and hard times, all whispering. Next door sat Edna Cutshall[cxxx]'s home – Julia's Grandma Cutshall, love on the second story. She lived so close a little girl could dash next door to Grandma's and make her way up that huge flight of stairs to where a cooing laugh so particularly Edna awaited. I can see the two, snuggled together in love in a big easy chair, the light from the TV with Mr. Rogers' show bathing over them.

I looked back to our house. I could see my father pacing our floors, the fear on his face. There would be a funeral. The time Grandma King had with her granddaughter was not enough and, at 3, Julia was too young to understand death. Even that time with Grandma Cutshall, it turned out, would be too short and she, too, would be gone too soon. As would George. All gone.

But I allow those memories to recede as others whisper, then call, more loudly. These are the sweet memories of a little girl and her mother, and those sounds of laughter and stories before bedtime carry me from an idling car and into an antique rocker with a sleepy girl in my lap. And I say the words I said so often, as we rocked, and I made up my stories:

"Once upon a time, there was a little girl, just like you. And she lived in a house, just like yours."

Then, quietly, I engage the clutch and I am off, with the whispering memories calling softly, softly: We'll be seeing you.

Joseph Cutshall-King has been the history columnist for The Post-Star since 1994. This is his last column.

AFTERWARD

Please pause for a moment, would you? These columns could only have come into existence because they were published in a newspaper, *The Post-Star* of Glens Falls, NY. The columns combined history and commentary, but they had to be grounded in fact. That was my editor's rule. *The Post-Star* always has been and is now about the factual, honest presentation of real news.

In my opinion, but one expressed by so many, newspapers are under siege and threatened with extinction. The onslaught of the internet has caused newspapers, daily newspapers especially, severe revenue losses resulting in shrinking staffs and truncated editions. Even publishing online, newspapers still face economic competition from internet advertising, and, far worse, competition from online opinion sites disguised as factual news sources.

The newspaper, on paper or online, remains unique as the central source for factual, vetted, unbiased news.

You could say that, today, I could easily start a "column" via a blog or some other internet format. You could say news is available everywhere on "The Net." But the reality is that no personal blog, no Facebook page, no Instagram, nor any form of social media devised as yet, can provide the newspaper's centralized, professionally edited, fact-based, open-to-scrutiny information.

In rural regions like that *The Post-Star* serves, the newspaper is the **only** central registry for community news—births, deaths, elections, upcoming cultural events, political infighting, school news, building projects, crime, stories of human interest and compassion, etc. The newspaper is not a perfect source. But as a self-governing gatherer and purveyor of facts, the best newspapers operate under ethical standards universally held by all true journalists. When I need the surest source for the facts, I turn first to a newspaper.

We are drowning in a sea of online opinion. We need to defend and promote factual information in all media, but especially the original bulwark of it, the newspaper. In my opinion, there is no replacement for the newspaper—the Fourth Branch of government, after the Executive, Legislative, and Judiciary. It is the guardian of our freedom.

We must support the newspaper—daily, weekly, and monthly—and help publishers find new ways of bringing young readers into the fold.

Whether your newspaper is printed on paper, delivered electronically, or sent by heaven knows what invention yet to come, support it. Agree or disagree with its news; love it or get angry with it; send in your critiques, corrections, commentary. But always cherish, defend, and promote your newspaper.

Your democracy depends upon it.

That is the view from *Over My Shoulder*.

***Over My Shoulder 3* Editor Julia C. Cutshall-King with the co-author of her life, Sara Cutshall-King – 1981**

INDEX

"Bank Square" Glens Falls 116

"Don McNeil and the Breakfast Club" radio program 135

"Hague, Hell and Horicon" and Helen Farrell 32

"Over My Shoulder" column, final 154

"rabble in arms" - Burgoyne quote 107

"shooting iron" phrase from American Revolution 48

"The Corners" project, Chapman Historical Museum's and Robin Wright & Stan Malecki 35

"The Graduate" movie 137

"The Jane McCrea House" Fort Edward 95

"The Saratoga Battlefield," now Saratoga National Historical Park 85

"The Tower," International Paper mill, Ticonderoga 117

"The World Turned Upside Down" Burgoyne's troops play at their surrender 107

"Victorian Christmas Past" celebration downtown Glens Falls and Dan and Jan Hazewski 148

"Yankee Doodle" American troops play at Burgoyne's surrender 107

105th Infantry, detachment 2, Co. C 2nd remains at Saratoga Armory after conversion 57

105th Infantry, Medical Co. C of the 427 Support Battalion returns from armory in Saratoga Springs to Glens Falls 57

Glens Falls, 1835 proposed downtown renovation by Dr. Ephraim H. Newton 114

1927 Sesquicentennial celebration of the Burgoyne Campaign 95

South Street, Glens Falls 114

225th anniversary of the defeat of Burgoyne at the Battles of Saratoga 76

22nd Regiment, formed April 1861 87

2nd Cavalry formed autumn 1861 87

55th Regiment of Foot reenactment group 31

9/11 attack on World Trade Center 28

93rd Regiment, formed November 1861 87

Abraham, Father Michael 129, 151, 155

Acland, Major John Dyke, British Grenadiers commander and Battles of Saratoga 105

Adams, Bruce 34

Adams, Claude, Glens Falls contractor Bruce Adams' father 35

Adams, Joe and Joanne 155

Adams, John on the Boston Massacre of 1770 75

Adiel Sherwood, Colonel at Fort Ann's capture by British Carlton 1780 71

Adiel Sherwood, Colonel, Charlotte County Militia 71

Adirondack Community College aka SUNY Adirondack 78, 135

Adirondack Girl Scouts Florence T. Bromley, Founder and first director .. 6

Adirondack Power and Light Corporation Elmer J. West,-Haviland's Cove 7

Adirondack Regional Chambers of Commerce and Glens Falls Chamber of Commerce 12

Afros 79

Aldrich, Carolyn "Carrie" 132

Alexandria Tavern Ticonderoga aka Bloody Bucket, or Bucket of Blood 118

Algonquin Round Table and Frank Sullivan 134

Altizio. Leo *Con Amore, The Italian History of Fort Edward* 41

America's first temperance society Dr. Billy J. Clark, founder 21

American Anti-Slavery Society and Frederick Douglass ...... 46 and William Lloyd Garrison 46

American General Arthur St. Clair retreats from Fort Ticonderoga and Mt. Independence 94

American generals in both Battles of Saratoga and 1938 DAR plaque 54

American Graphite Joseph Dixon Pencil factory in Ticonderoga, NY 116

American Hotel Corporation and Queensbury Hotel 14

American Loyalists 64, 90

American Loyalists, derisively called Tories.........64

Ames, Alexander
    Black Patriot Revolutionary War soldier...............75

Anderson, Marion
    and the Queensbury Hotel.............................15

Ankeny, Kevin...115

Ankeny, Kevin, of Adirondack Community College..78

Ankeny, Kevin, Professor of Radio, TV Broadcasting...136

Ankeny, Prof. Kevin, SUNY Adirondack.........78

Ankeny, Sherry, of Skidmore College................78

Annie-Ann Elizabeth Green King Ftizpatrick
....154

Arcuri, Anita Amorosi
    Con Amore, The Italian History of Fort Edward..........41

Argyle mob convention....................................62

Armstrong, Mike..119

Arnold, Benedict
    and heroics during Burgoyne Campaign............102

Arnold, Benedict..................................55, 67
    absence of statue in Saratoga Monument.............86
    and DAR plaque at Saratoga National Historical Park...54
    and Enos, D. D. Hitchcock's diary.................54
    monuments and markers to............................54

Arnold, Benedict...102

Arnold, Benedict...104

Arnold, Benedict...105

Arnold, Benedict, and Fort Ticonderoga...........55

Arnold, Benedict, and Schuylerville/Victory monument...55

Arnold, Benedict, and Valcour Island................55

Arnold, Benedict, creates first American warship
....58

Arnold, Benedict, pivotal role in 2nd Battle of Saratoga..105

Ashley, Dominick..................*See* Eugene Ashley

Ashley, Eugene
    Spier Falls hydroelectric dam.........................32

Ashton, Henry..119

Attucks, Crispus
    and Blacks in the Revolution.........................75

Austin, Judge John................................37, 119

King, George & Jane.....................................134

Baker, Whitehall School Principal Beecher, (former Sgt. US Army Third Ranger Battalion)..80

Ballston Spa, mineral waters.............................38

Barber, Annetta E., M.D.
    Zonta Club of Glens Falls...............................5

Barber's Farm
    and second Battle of Saratoga........................105

Bates, Grover..108

Bates, Loretta...77

bathhouse at Haviland's Cove Park
    and Zonta Club of Glens Falls.........................5

Battle Hill
    Battle of Fort Anne.......................................94

Battle of Bennington................96, 97, 98, 102, 103

Battle of Bunker Hill
    and Blacks in the Revolution.........................75

Battle of Fort Anne..............................93, 94, 95

Battle of Freeman's Farm, September 19, 1777
    first Battle of Saratoga.................................103

Battle of Hubbardton, VT
    Black Patriot soldiers at.................................76

Battle of New Orleans
    and Cold Summer of 1816..............................47

Battles of Saratoga, 1777
    "Turning Point of The Revolution"..................102

Baum, Friedrich, at Sans Coick, now North Hoosick...97

Baum, German Lieut. Col Friedrich
    and Battle of Bennington................................97
    and Burgoyne...97

Bayle, George F., president
    Glens Falls Hotel Corporation.........................13

Bayle, George F., president
    Glens Falls Portland Cement Company..............13

Bayle, George, Glens Falls Portland Cement
    and Haviland's Cove.......................................7

Bearor, Bob, organizer of French and Indian War re-enactment in Ticonderoga.........................56

Beaux Arts Ball, 1979
    and Queensbury Hotel....................................16

Beeman, Polly Hoopes..............*See* Hoopes, Polly

Ben Bernie Orchestra
    and Bennie Goodman......................................14

Benjamin P. Burhans, 1st pres.
    Glens Falls National Bank & Trust Co..............21

Bennett, Lerone, Jr., Black historian...............74

Bennington County, VT
    having two county courthouses.........................71

Bennington VT at Captain Billings
    and Enos, D. D. Hitchcock's diary.................53

Bentley, Harriet...120
Berlin Wall...79
Berrigan, Tommy...135
Big Boom area, Town of Queensbury, along
    Hudson River..117
Big Boom spanning Hudson River between
    Towns of Moreau and Queensbury20, 117,
    118, 119
Bigelow, Henry Forbes
    and Louis F. Hyde..3
    architect, 1910 Glens Falls Hospital addition..........4
    designs Finch Pruyn & Co. corporate headquarters
   3
Bigelow, Henry Forbes, Boston architect
    and Hoopes, Hyde and Cunningham Houses
    Glens Falls...3
bill collector, King's Pharmacy........................121
Birthplace of the U.S. Navy
    Whitehall, NY...55
Bissell, Inez M., Librarian, Crandall Library
    and Zonta Club of Glens Falls.........................5
Black Green Mountain Boys
    with Ethan Allen, Fort Ticonderoga 1775............76
Black history anomalies in Washington County
    1810 Census...72
Black Patriot Minutemen Peter Salem, Cuff
    Whittemore..76
Black Point on Lake George
    named for Black Patriot Prince Taylor..............76
Black Revolutionary War veterans....................74
Black soldiers, contemporary images of in
    Revolution...75
Black Swan Image Works
    Michael George King, artist..............................5
Blizzard of '88
    John Green brings first train into Mechanicville
   133
Bloody Bucket, aka Bucket of Blood,
    Ticonderoga...118
Bloody Pond, name origin..................................31
Blow, Dave
    and *The Post-Star*..2
Boston and Maine Railroad, the B&M.............133
Boston Candy Kitchen....................................150
boxer shorts with huge red hearts
    and Sara Cutshall-King..................................125
Boxer's Drugstore, Glens Falls........................116

Brannock, Keith, collective memory of
    Ticonderoga.......................................117, 118
Brayton, Pat..119
Breymann and Balcarres redoubts
    and 2nd Battle of Saratoga.............................106
Bridging The Years
    Glens Falls pictorial history............................114
Broad Street, Glens Falls
    renaming from West Street.............................114
Bromley, Florence T., Director, Adirondack Girl
    Scouts
    and Zonta Club of Glens Falls.........................5
Bronne, Else
    Bronne Shirt Co., Fort Edward.........................6
Brooks Brothers suits, problem with................124
Brooks, Barbara..79
King, William "Bil"..154
brothers Jessup
    self-declare as Loyalists, join Sir Guy Carleton at
    Crown Point..65
Brown University
    and Charles Evans Hughes..............................9
Brown, Louis M.
    Glens Falls Hotel Corporation..........................13
Brown, raid on Harper's Ferry
    Frederick Douglass helps plan.........................46
Brown's Old Homestead Restaurant, Saratoga
    Lake..126
Buchman, Sunny
    1944 *Look* magazine "Hometown USA"...........39
Bucket of Blood, aka Bloody Bucket,
    Ticonderoga...118
Burgey's Cave, Hague......................................120
Burgoyne Campaign's only naval battle, Whitehall,
    NY..57
Burgoyne, British General John, in Fort Edward
    1777..96
Burgoyne, defeat of British General John
    and death of Jane McCrea...............................95
Burgoyne, John, British General
    and Battles of Saratoga..................................102
Burgoyne's "convention" aka surrender............107
Burgoyne's surrender.......................................106
Burke, Maude D., Superintendent of the Glens
    Falls Hospital
    Zonta Club of Glens Falls.................................6
Burke, Maude D., Superintendent, Glens Falls
    Hospital

Zonta Club of Glens Falls.................................5
Burleigh Birdseye maps.................................36
Burleigh, H. G.............*See* Henry Gordon Burleigh
Burleigh, Henry Gordon.................................60, 62
Burleigh, Henry Gordon, and President Chester A. Arthur.................................62
Burleigh, Henry Gordon, NY State Assembly 61
Burleigh, Henry Gordon, US Congress.................................62
Burleigh's Pharmacy, Ticonderoga.................................146
Burma Shave signs.................................79
Burroughs, David.................................141
Burroughs, George
    Principal, Ticonderoga High School.................................141
Call Hardware
    and Haviland's Cove.................................7
Camp Hale, Colorado
    and Bruce Adams, Tenth Mountain Division....35
    and Tenth Mountain Division.................................35
Canadian patriots, American Loyalists.................................66
Canal Street, Glens Falls
    now Oakland Avenue.................................114
Cantiello, Nicholas "Chuckie"
    Con Amore, The Italian History of Fort Edward.................................41
Caplans, Cy and Vicki
    Saratoga Springs.................................135
Caplans, Cy and Vicki, Saratoga Springs.................................153
Captain Speakman's Company of Rangers
    reenactment group.................................31
Carney, Pat
    Manager J. J. Newberry's Ticonderoga.................................145
Carousel, Congress Park, Saratoga Springs.................................126
Carroll's 10 cent hamburgers.................................153
Carroll's hamburgers, Miller Hill, Queensbury 119
Castle Town (now Castleton), VT
    and St. Clair's retreat 1777.................................92
Champagne, Joan.................................119
Champlain Canal at Whitehall.................................61
Chapman Historical Museum.................................2, 32
Chapman Historical Museum, Christmas opening.................................147
Chapman Museum.................................125
Chapman, Juliet.................................120
Charlotte County, NY
    renamed Washington County 1784.................................71
Charlotte County, NY, "Mother of Canada"..63
Charlotte Pruyn Hyde.................................3
Chitty, Marion.................................120
Christmas and the Cutshall-Kings.................................147

Christmas and the King family.................................145
Church of the Messiah, Glens Falls, NY.................................33
Cimo, Andrew "Jerry"
    Con Amore, The Italian History of Fort Edward.................................41
City of Glens Falls.................................12
Clark, Dr. Billy J., founder, America's first temperance society.................................21
Clark, James C.
    and Queensbury Hotel site.................................13
Clark, Robert, English teacher, Ft Edward Junior HS.................................33
Clinton, General Sir Henry
    British commander in chief in America during Revolutionary War.................................104
International Paper Company in Corinth.................................108
Clothier, Anne.................................59
CNA building, now 333 Glen Street.................................33
Coburn, Titus
    Black Patriot Revolutionary War soldier.................................75
Coffin, Marian Cruger, landscape architect
    and Fort Ticonderoga, King's Garden.................................23
Cold Summer of 1816
    aka Long Winter of 1816.................................47
Colonel Nathan Hale's 2nd New Hampshire Regiment
    at Battle of Hubbardton.................................76
Colonial Restaurant, Saratoga Springs.................................126
communal sauna in Shushan, NY.................................120
Community Chest of Glens Falls
    George F. Bayle, co-founder.................................13
Como, Perry
    and the Queensbury Hotel.................................15
Con Amore, The Italian History of Fort Edward.................................41
    and Anna Munafo Perdichizzi.................................111
Condon, Bob
    City Editor, *The Post-Star*.................................2, 177
Condon, Bob, City Editor of *The Post-Star*.................................5
Congress Park, Saratoga Springs.................................126
Congress Street, Saratoga Springs
    renowned for its nightclubs and houses of prostitution until the 1960s.................................120
Connery, Mike, president and CEO of Capital District Off-Track Betting.................................146
Connie Francis, "Don't Break This Heart That Loves You".................................137
Constitution of the Confederate States of America.................................43

ConTact Paper
and Decora, Fort Edward................................137
ConTact Paper with Mickey Mouse.....................138
Continental Insurance
buys Glens Falls Insurance Company.....................14
Cool, Keyes P.
1st exporter of Glens Falls lime..............................20
Coopers Cave Ale Co., brewery & restaurant
Glens Falls...36
Coopers Cave Ale Company.......................................37
Corinth mill, International Paper Company.....108
Cormier, Historian William "Al"................................79, 81
Cormier, Salem Town Historian William "Al" 82
Corsall, Pauline Massaro
Con Amore, The Italian History of Fort Edward............41
Country Fare, Glens Falls
and Dan and Jan Hazewski................................130
Coveville, was Dovegat
in Battles of Saratoga...104
Cowles building, at Warren and Ridge Sts., Glens
Falls
first office of Glens Falls Insurance Company....21
Cowles, Daniel H.
Glens Falls Hotel Corporation................................13
Cram, Ralph Adams
architect for 1932, St. Mary's Academy......................4
Cram, Ralph Adams, dean of American
architecture's Gothic Revival Movement
and First Presbyterian Church of Glens Falls.........4
Louis F. Hyde brings to Glens Falls...........................4
Crandall Public Library
expansion 2008..3
Crandall, Henry
and Crandall Library...3
Crandall, Henry
and Crandall Public Library...3
Crannell, Cutler "Cut," of Glens Falls, collective
memory..119
Crannell, Linda, author
Portraits of Poverty...100
Crocker, Ephraim, Patriot
arrested by Abraham Wing II..................................26
Crown Point
Burgoyne lands at...90
Cummings, Don, Washington County Board of
Supervisors Chair...79
Cummings, Donald "Don, Chairman,
Washington County Board of Supervisors 77

Cummings, Dr. Thomas, Ticonderoga..............132
Cuneo, John R., historian
on Robert Rogers...80
Cutshall, Edna...155
Cutshall, Edna and Harland.....................................16
Cutshall, Edna, past president
Zonta Club of Glens Falls...6
Cutshall-King, Giuseppe
Con Amore, The Italian History of Fort Edward............41
Cutshall-King, Julia......................130, 136, 138, 151
in Saratoga Springs...125
Cutshall-King, Julia C.
and celebration of birth..16
Editor Over My Shoulder Volumes 1-3....................5
Cutshall-King, Julia C., editor.................................2
Cutshall-King, Sara 5, 2, 77, 115, 130, 131,
148, 152, 154, 155, 177
and dance lessons at the Queensbury Hotel........15
D&H Railroad
and Haviland's Cove...7
Daggett House, Boston
and role in Tea Party 1773..88
Daley, Fred
and *The Post-Star*...2
Daughters of the American Revolution (DAR)
and 1938 plaque at Saratoga National Historical
Park..54
Davidson Brothers Brewery and Restaurant
Glens Falls...36
Davis, Jean Wing...25, 26
Dean, Sadie Trackeno
Con Amore, The Italian History of Fort Edward...........41
Dearborn, American Major Henry
and Battles of Saratoga..105
Fraser, Simon...105
Deaths at the Washington County Poorhouse
by Richard Wilson..100
Dechame, Roger
Fort Ticonderoga, King's Garden............................24
Decora, Fort Edward...137
Dehais, Barbara...120
DeLong, Elizabeth Ireland.......................................87
and grandfather Irving W. Ireland..........................87
Hitchcock, Enos, D. D.
Congregational chaplain the Revolutionary army
....53
Dinah, John McCreas' enslaved African
American

captured with Jane McCrea 1777 95

ditty bag, of USN Lt. George A. King 122

Dix, John Alden, 38th NYS Governor 8

Dobert, Kelly 78

Dobert's 129

Dobert's Dairy 78

Doolittle, Will
  and *The Post-Star* 2

Dorothy Parker
  and Frank Sullivan 134

Douglass, Frederick
  spoke at Lakeville Baptist Church, Cossayuna, and
    Society of Friends meetinghouse, Easton 46

Douglass, Frederick and Susan B. Anthony 46

Douglass, Frederick, in Greenwich, NY 45

Douglass, Frederick, in Greenwich, NY area 44

Douglass, Frederick, weekly newspapers 46

Dovegat house, second Battle of Saratoga 106

Dovegat, now Coveville
  and Battles of Saratoga 104

Downs, Mrs. (Downsie)
  121 Lincoln Avenue, Saratoga Springs 134

Dudley Moore 79

Duer, Patriot William, Fort Miller 97

Eberle, William "Bill" 150

Ellington, Duke
  and the Queensbury Hotel 15

Else Bronne
  and Zonta Club of Glens Falls 6

Elton John and Kiki Dee, "Don't Go Breakin'
  My Heart." 137

Embury, Philip, founds second Methodist
  congregation in North America
  Ash Grove, in the Town of Cambridge, Charlotte
    County, 1770 64

Embury, Phillip, created first Methodist meeting
  in North America. 64

Enable software 79

Enterprise, Liberty and Gates
  American warships sunk by Burgoyne 58

Erie Canal 138

Erlanger's
  Erlanger's Fashions 36

Esperti, Andrew
  Con Amore, The Italian History of Fort Edward 41

Ethan Allen, seizure of Fort Ticonderoga 1775
  and Black Green Mountain Boys 76

Evergreen Cemetery, Salem, NY 81

*Facts and Traditions concerning the Argyleshire Clan
  Campbell*
  by Katherine Campbell Norton Lewis 50

Fan and Bill's nightclub, Miller Hill, Queensbury
  120

Farmer's Museum
  and Joyce St. Jacques 59
  at Washington County Fair 59

Farrell, Brian
  on phrase "Hague, Hell and Horicon" 32

Farrell's Hotel, North Creek 118

Farrells' restaurant ...... *See* Farrells Hotel

Feeder Canal built 1823
  runs through Queensbury, Glens Falls, Kingsbury
    and Hudson Falls 118

feeder canal's widening in 1832 20

Feingold, Dr. Joseph 112
  and and Dr. Silas J. Banker, Fort Edward 113
  and degree from Univ. of Michigan 112
  and Old Fort House Museum 112
  and service in WW II 112
  at Battle of the Bulge, WW II 112
  attending concentration camp inmates 112

Feingold, Dr. Joseph, at Battle of the Bulge 113

Feingold, Dr. Joseph, medical practice in Fort
  Edward 113

Fellows, Brigadier-General John, Massachusetts
  Militia
  at Saratoga 107

Fifty-fourth Massachusetts, Black regiment
  and Frederick Douglass 46

Finch Pruyn & Co
  cofounders Jeremiah and Daniel Finch 30

Finch Pruyn & Co.
  and Haviland's Cove 7

Finch Pruyn and Company
  and Louis F. Hyde 3

Finch, Jeremiah and Daniel ...... *See* Orson Richards

Finns, Norwegians and Swedes in Shushan, NY
  120

first Battle of Saratoga, first, September 19, 1777
  103

First Presbyterian Church of Glens Falls
  and and Samuel Yellin's wrought iron 4
  and Louis F. Hyde, architectural committee 4
  and Ralph Adams Cram, architect of 4

First Rhode Island Regiment, Revolution
  majority Black Patriot soldiers 75

Fitch, Dr. Asa 26
Five Combines in Hudson Falls
　　at east end of Feeder Canal 118
flag of the United States captured at Battle of Fort
　　Anne 94
Forest, American General Enoch
　　and Battles of Saratoga 105
Fort Edward6, 5, 6, 22, 26, 30, 38, 41, 52, 54, 64,
　　67, 71, 72, 73, 80, 81, 92, 107, 108, 111, 112,
　　117, 121, 129, 137, 147, 153
　　plays major role in French and Indian War 81
Fort Edward Historical Association 6, 41
Fort Edward, Jane McCrea murder 95
Fort Mount Hope, Ticonderoga 91
Fort Ticonderoga23, 24, 48, 56, 57, 58, 76, 83, 90,
　　91, 92, 102, 103, 107, 144
　　and Major General Arthur St. Clair 58
　　archeological discovery of a turkey bone 144
　　Burgoyne seizes 91
Fort Ticonderoga, Burgoyne invades Jul 6, 1777
　　and Enos, D. D. Hitchcock's diary 53
Fort Ticonderoga, May 23-Jul 6, 1777
　　and Enos, D. D. Hitchcock's diary 53
Fort Ticonderoga, NY, Mount Independence,
　　VT
　　Burgoyne attacks July 1, 1777 57
Fort William Henry Hotel 37
Fowler, Albert, Crandall Library 115
Fox, Chris, Fort Ticonderoga Curator 144
Francis, Col. Ebenezer, 11th Massachusetts
　　Regiment
　　rear guard defense of St. Clair's retreat 1777 92
Franklin D. Roosevelt
　　and Fitzgerald's Restaurant, Glens Falls 9
Fraser, British Major General Simon
　　in Battles of Saratoga 105
Fraser, Simon
　　in Battles of Saratoga 104
Frederick Douglass speaking engagements in
　　Southern Washington County 46
French and Indian War
　　and Robert Rogers 80
French and Indian War being proposed as a
　　subject for live theater, 2002 82
Friedman, Dr. Orel 115, 119
Funari, Messina, Italy
　　and Francesco and Anna Munafo Perdichizzi.112
Furnival, Capt. Alexander, Maryland Militia

at Saratoga 107
Gates, American General Horatio57, 85, 103,
　　104, 106
　　accuses Burgoyne of complicity in Jane McCrea
　　　murder 96
　　in Burgoyne Campaign 102
Gates, Bill 128
Gates, Horatio, aka "Granny" 102
Gates, Horatio, commander of the Northern
　　Department 102
Gates' use of Jane McCrea's murder in
　　Burgoyne's defeat 96
Gaulin, Fanny Sarchioto
　　Con Amore, The Italian History of Fort Edward 41
Gideon Putnam
　　Grand Union Hotel, Saratoga Springs 38
Gifford, Gary, broadcaster at WCKM 136
Giorgianni, Joseph
　　Con Amore, The Italian History of Fort Edward 41
Glen Street fence
　　and home of of William E. Spier 33
Glens Falls Boom Association
　　Orson Richards, co-founder 30
Glens Falls Cemetery Superintendent
　　Christopher Anderson 115
Glens Falls Chamber of Commerce
　　and The Queensbury Hotel 12
　　beginning 1914 12
Glens Falls City Charter 1908
　　signed by Charles Evans Hughes 11
Glens Falls Community Theater 82
Glens Falls Community Theatre
　　and Little Theater Group of the Glens Falls
　　　Operetta Club 6
Glens Falls Country Club
　　and Governor's Day 1933 9
Glens Falls Elks Lodge #81 11
Glens Falls High School 18, 36, 149
Glens Falls High School Class of 1961 18
Glens Falls Hospital 6, 155
　　and Henry Forbes Bigelow, architect 4
Glens Falls Hotel Corporation
　　and The Queensbury Hotel 13
Glens Falls incorporated as village 20
Glens Falls Insurance Company
　　and Glens Falls Chamber of Commerce 12
Glens Falls Insurance Company created 20
Glens Falls Lyceum 17

Glens Falls National Bank & Trust Co.20,   21, 116, 117
Glens Falls National Bank and Trust Co. co-founders................................21
Glens Falls National Bank and Trust Company history of...............................20
Glens Falls Railroad
    Orson Richards, co-founder........................30
Glens Falls Recreation Commission
    and Haviland's Cove Park..........................5
Glens Falls Sanford Street School.................39
Glens Falls Symphony.................129, 151
Glens Falls Symphony Orchestra.............131
Glens Falls theater once a Woolworth
    The Wood Theater...............................150
Glens Falls YMCA founded in 1887.............114
Glens Falls Zonta Club *See* Zonta Club of Glens Falls
Glens Falls, City of................................12
Chapman Historical Museum........................6
Godnick's Grand Furniture......................114
Goodman, James
    at 1927 Sesquicentennial celebration of the Burgoyne Campaign.......................95
Governor's Day 1933
    list of Governors.................................9
Grand Funk Railroad, The Locomotion.........136
Grand Union Hotel, Saratoga Springs
    and Gideon Putnam................................38
Grandison, Simeon
    Black Patriot soldier..............................76
Grandma Fitzpatrick (Ann Green King Fitzpatrick).......................................126
Jenks, Margaret "Peggy".............................79
Great Boom and Bridge
    between Fort Ticonderoga and Mt. Independence 92, 93
    British warships breaking through.............93
Great Escape, originally Storytown, Storytown, now Great Escape, Queensbury, NY.......117
Great Northern Turnpik, from Cambridge to Granville, NY....................................73
Green Mountain Boys
    and Battle of Bennington.........................97
    and Blacks as......................................76
Green, John
    Village of Mechanicville village president.....134
Green, John Francis, Mechanicville, NY.........133

Greenwich Free Library.............................44
Greenwich, NY, and Frederick Douglass.........45
Griffin, Mark and Joy
    rooftop Santa...................................130
Grinnell, William "Bill"...................119, 120
Hague, New York...................................38
Hague, NY, first named Rochester.................38
Hannay, Eileen
    and Rogers Island Visitor Center...............151
Hannay, Eileen, educator
    and Jane McCrea history...........................50
Harris, Josephine Cardinale
    Con Amore, The Italian History of Fort Edward.........41
Hart's Cafe, Glens Falls
    now Talk of the Town Restaurant................119
Hartford, NY's enlistment center begins, 1862 87
Hartman, Louis, collective memory of Big Boom and Feeder Canal................................118
Harvard Law School
    and Louis F. Hyde..................................3
Hatch, cabinetmaker Sylvanus
    , shop as Hartford, NY, enlistment center.......87
Haviland's Cove Park, Glens Falls, NY.............5
Haynes, Rev. Lemuel.......................74, 75, 76
    and Blacks in the Revolution......................75
    with Ethan Allen at Ticonderoga 1775...........75
Haynes, Rev. Lemuel, Black Partriot
    and pastor, South Granville Congregational Church...75
Haynes, Rev. Lemuel
    pastor, Congregational Church, West Rutland, VT 76
Hazewski, Dan and Jan
    and "Victorian Christmas Past" celebration downtown Glens Falls............................148
Heart, rock group..................................136
Heck family, Loyalists, flee to Canada.............64
Heck, Barbara, Brockville area of Ontario, where Barbara, founds Methodist congregation, first in Canada.......................................64
Henry Forbes Bigelow
    and Louis F. Hyde..................................3
Hill, William....................................120
Perry, Kenneth "Ken".............................98
Perry, Kenneth "Ken".........................72, 73
History of Glens Falls, New York
    Louis F. Hyde......................................3
Hitchcock, Enos, D.D.

and Massachusetts lottery in the Revolution.........53
diary of a Continental Army minister..................144
Hogan, John..119
Hogan, Roger...119
Holden, Dr. A. W. 120
Holden, Dr. A. W., historian
    description of Jessup brothers.......................65
Holden, James A.
    1895 address on civic improvement...............16
    Crandall Library, Holden Collection of Americana
   16
Holman, Ralph
    Haviland's Cove 1st Recreation Supervisor............7
Hometown Memories
    book by Byron Lapham.........................40, 150
Hometown USA
    1944 *Look* magazine series............................39
Hoopes, Maurice
    Glens Falls Hotel Corporation.......................13
Hoopes, Maurice president Glens Falls hospital's
    Board of Directors...4
Hoopes, Polly
    friend Elizabeth Hughes.................................11
Hoosac Tunnel, North Adams
    and Blizzard of 1888.....................................133
Hope, Bob
    and Queensbury Hotel....................................15
Hovey, Ivory, Patriot soldier
    and 1 July 27, 1777 letter re McCrea murder.........96
Howard Hanna Memorial Enlistment Center
    and Hartford Museum.....................................86
    and Civil War..86
Howard Johnson's "Double Bubble" in
    Queensbury...79
Howe, British General William
    and role in Burgoyne's defeat.......................103
Howe, Cato
    Black Patriot Revolutionary War soldier...............75
Howe, Lord George Viscount
    French and Indian War re-enactment 2001.........56
Howe, Lord George Viscount, death at
    Ticonderoga
    and Robert Bearor' re-enactment of, 2001...........56
Hubbard Hall...150
Hubbardton Battlefield State Historic Site...........93
Hudson Falls High School......................................70
    history teachers Matthew Rozell, George Neisz 70
Huffer, Sandy..111

Hughes, Charles Evans
    Gov.NYS; Chief Justice, US Sec. of State; Justice,
    World Court...........................8, 9, 10, 11
Hughes, Charles Evans, 36th NYS Governor.....8
Hughes, Elizabeth
    daughter Charles Evan Hughes.......................11
Hughes, Gov. Charles Evans, reformist actions
   10
Hughes, NYS Gov. Charles Evans.........................8
Hyde Collection
    and Louis F. Hyde..3
Hyde, Charlotte..120
Hyde, Louis...120
Hyde, Louis F.
    President of Crandall Public Library 1931.............4
Hyde, Louis F., maries Charlotte Pruyn.................3
Hyde, Louis Fiske, architectural contributions to
    Glens Falls..3
Indian and Loyalist raids, Burgoyne Campaign
   102
International Paper
    and Henry Gordon Burleigh...........................61
International Paper, South Glens Falls
    and Haviland's Cove...7
Ireland, Irving W.
    and Daggatt House, Boston...............................87
Italian community Fort Edward...........................41
J. J. Newberry's Ticonderoga...............................145
Jane..48, 50, 51, 54
Jessup brothers..25
Jessup brothers, Ebenezer and Edward
    buy Hyde Township, Palmer purchase, Totten
    and Crossfield purchase.................................65
Jessup brothers, Loyalists
    Lake Luzerne, NY, settlers...............................65
Jessup Brothers, Loyalists of Lake Luzerne, NY
   64
Jessup's Royal Rangers
    part of Carlton's 1780 raid of region...............66
Johanson, Saara, wrote letter as 8-year old
    prompting restoration of Saratoga
    Monument...85
Joy Store, South Glens Falls...............................129
Joy Store, South Glens Falls, NY.......................117
Joyce, Pat and LARAC......................................150
Julie Krone, Julie, jockey
    at Saratoga Race Course August 20, 1993.........138
Kalbaugh, Aubrey "Jim".....................................126

Kamyr purchases Queensbury Hotel 1976....... 14

Kelleher, Kathleen, Glens Falls City Chamberlain
    and Zonta Club of Glens Falls.................5

Kin, Michael George................................ 153

King, George
    and Christmas..............................145

King, George & Jane........................16, 33

King, Jane
    and Christmas..............................145
    and Frank Sullivan........................134

King, Jane, and porches.......................142

King, Martha Jane Kalbaugh
    aka Jane King................................131

King, Martha Jane, author's sister............141

King, Martha Jane, sister of author................154

King, Michael "Mike"
    artist, brother of author...................126

King, Michael George...........................134

King, Michael George "Mike".............135, 140

King, Michael George, artist
    Black Swan Image Works....................5

King, Scott Bruce, brother of author............154

King, William F.
    and Fort Ticonderoga........................24

King's Garden, Fort Ticonderoga, reopening..23

Kirby Wilcox's furniture store, Ticonderoga...146

Klotz, Kenneth, Saratoga Springs Mayor 77, 127, 149

Knipes, Sharon and Joe.........................150

Kosciuszko, Thaddeus, Polish engineer
    and Battles of Saratoga....................104

Kyle Minogue, The Locomotion................136

Lake George.......................................6

Lake Sunnyside pavilion........................33

Lake Sunnyside, Queensbury, NY................33

Lansingburgh to Whitehall turnpike.............73

Lantern Inn
    and the Queensbury Hotel..................15

Lapham, Byron "By"............................150

Lapham, Joan.....................................150

LaPointe, John.....................................60

LaPointe, Karl
    and collective memory of Ticonderoga.....118
    and Fort Ticonderoga....................24, 116

LARAC...150

LARAC (Lower Adirondack Regional Arts
    Council)....................................11

Larkin, H. Bertha, Tri-County Blind Assoc

and Zonta Club of Glens Falls...................5

LaSelva, Barbara...................................79

League of the South, Cofederacy and slavery.....43

Learned, Ebenezer................................105

Learned, Ebenezer, General in Continental Army
    in Battles of Saratoga......................104

Lemery, Leo
    and Queensbury Hotel......................15

Lew, Barzilai
    Black Patriot Revolutionary War soldier.......75

Lewis, Katherine Campbell Norton
    and Facts and Traditions concerning the
      Argyleshire Clan Campbell..................50
    descendant of Sarah McNeil...................50

Lexington and Concord
    and Blacks in the Minutemen.................75

Lincoln Avenue, Saratoga Springs..............134

Lincoln, American General Benjamin, wounded
    at Saratoga................................106

Litchfield, Connecticut
    and Gov. Nathaniel Pitcher, Jr..................8

Little Eva, The Locomotion....................136

Loding, Paul, Kingsbury historian...............79

Loding, Paul, Kingsbury Town Historian...........8

logs bound into rafts to float down the Hudson
    River, pre-Revolutionary War................27

Lombardo, Guy
    and the Queensbury Hotel..................15

Long Winter of 1816
    aka Cold Summer of 1816...................47

Long, Colonel Pierse, American
    and Burgoyne at Whitehall, NY...............58

Look Magazine photographs of Glens Falls 1943
    in Crandall Public Library...................40

Loretta Bates
    Deputy Historian, Washington County 59, 108, 119, 120

lottery, Massachusetts, in Revolution............53

Louis F. Hyde.......................................3

Louis Fiske Hyde
    Crandall Public Library.......................3

Lowery, Dennis, Washington County Archivist
   77

Lowery, Washington County Archivist Dennis
   112

Jones, David, David of Kingsbury
    and Jane McCrea's fiance.....................95

Loyalists, aka Tories..............................65

Lucci, Betsy E.
   and Zonta Club of Glens Falls 5
MacFinn's Drugstore
   Saratoga Springs 135
MacFinn's Drugstore, Saratoga Springs 125
MacFinns Drugstore, Saratoga Springs
   destroyed in great fire of 1957 125
Maddox, Anne
   Saratoga Springs 135
Mahoney, Mark, *The Post-Star* editor 2, 117
Major General Friedrich von Riedesel
   Superior of Lieut. Col Friedrich Baum 97
Malecki, Stan, and Robin Wright
   Chapman Historical Museum educators 39
   Chapman Historical Museum's education team 35
Manchester VT, mineral waters 38
Mandolare, John
   Con Amore, The Italian History of Fort Edward 41
Markham, architect Jared C., designed Saratoga
   Monument 85
Marsh, Wallace T., home
   and Queensbury Hotel site 13
Martha Stewart
   and Boston Candy Kitchen 150
Maurice Hoopes
   and Louis F. Hyde 3
Maury Thompson 21, 89, 138, 146
McCarty, R. Paul 25
McCarty, R. Paul, Executive Director of the Old
   Fort House Museum of Fort Edward
   Historical Association 26
McCrea, Jane 50, 59
   and defeat of British General Burgoyne 95
McCrea, Jane, murder July 26, 1777
   and Enos, D. D. Hitchcock's diary 54
McCrea, Jane, murder of 1777 95
McCrea, John, Patriot brother of Jane McCrea 95
McCrea, John, Patriot officer in the Albany
   County Militia 95
McCreery, Benjamin
   Glens Falls Hotel Corporation 13
McDonald, Christine, Crandall Public
   Library's Director 3
McGuire, Kevin, Hubbard Hall 150
McIlvaine, Hilma
   and Queensbury Hotel 15
McKernon, Kendall, interior designer

   and The Queensbury Hotel 15
McNeil, Sarah, captured with Jane McCrea
   first cousin to British General Simon Fraser 95
McPhillips, James
   Glens Falls Hotel Corporation 13
Mechanicville 134
Mechanicville "father of free mail delivery" 134
Mechanicville A&P 140
Mender, Mike
   and *The Post-Star* 2
Merkel and Gelman
   and Haviland's Cove 7
Merrill, Richard C., Crandall Public Library Board
   Chair 3
Methodism in North America
   and Philip Embury and Barbara Heck 64
Metivier, Don 120, 128
Mettawee or Mettowee
   and spelling of river's name 48
   and spelling of river's name 51
Mickey Mouse Club 137
Miller Hill, Queensbury 119
Miller, Irene 37
Milton Berle 79
Mineral waters
   and Ballston Spa, Saratoga Springs, and Whitehall,
   NY 38
Minnick, James "Jim," Jr. 36, 37
Minnick, Rose
   Warren County Court and Probation System 6
   Zonta Club of Glens Falls 6
Minutemen Peter Salem, Cuff Whittemore
   Black Patriot soldiers 76
Minutemen, Revolution
   Black Patriot soldiers in 75
Molly McGuire, a union man 133
Monroe, Kim 119
Morgan, American Colonel Daniel
   in Battles of Saratoga 85, 104, 107
Morrell, Martin 119
Morse, Phil and Sue 149
Mount Belvedere, Italy
   and Bruce Adams 34
Mount Belvedere, Italy, 1945
   and Tenth Mountain Division 34
Mount Defiance 57
   Generals Schuyler and Gates reject fortifying 57
   Sugar Loaf Hill in 1777 91

Mount Independence 57, 58, 90, 91, 92
Mr. DeWitt
    and dance lessons at the Queensbury Hotel........15
Mt. Tambora, Indonesian volcano
    and Cold Summer of 1816...................................48
Munafo, Anna, and Francesco Perdichizzi 111
Munafo, original surname spelling of Munoff111
Munoff, Americanized spelling of Italian Munafo
   111
Munoff, Joseph...111
    Con Amore, The Italian History of Fort Edward 41
Murray, Anne D'Angelico
    Con Amore, The Italian History of Fort Edward 41
Murray, Christine Catone
    Con Amore, The Italian History of Fort Edward 41
Museum of Dance, Saratoga Springs 149
My Bondage and My Freedom....................................46
    by Frederick Douglass....................................46
Namias, June, historian, anthropologist
    and analysis of McCrea captivity.....................50
Nathaniel Pitcher, Nathaniel Jr, NYS Governor
    and Sandy Hill (Hudson Falls), Town of
    Kingsbury...8
Native Americans..80, 90
    and Burgoyne Campaign..................................90
Neilson farm on Bemis Heights
    in the Burgoyne Campaign.............................104
Neisz, George
    History teacher Hudson Falls High School.........70
Nemcek, Gretta
    now Post-Star reporter Gretta Hochsprung.......78,
    100, 144
Nesbitt, Thomas "Tom" 53
New Hampshire Governor Benning
    Wentworth
    and Robert Rogers..80
New Pruyn St, Glens Falls creation by West
    Street cemetery removal.................................115
New York Army National Guard Armory
    Saratoga Springs...56
New York State Governors
    of Glens Falls, Hudson Falls...............................8
New York State Military History Museum and
    Veterans Research Center
    in Saratoga Springs, NY..................................56
Newton, Dr. Ephraim H., , Presbyterian minister,
    Glens Falls 1835...114
Nicholas, Mary Ann Choppy

Con Amore, The Italian History of Fort Edward...........41
North Country Arts Center
    now North Country Arts.................................147
Northern Campaign, Revolutionary War...........98
now Double H Hole In the Woods R
    formerly Hidden Valley Dude Ranch...............120
number 7 building, International Paper mill
    Ticonderoga 117
NY State workers' compensation law, nation's
    first
    and Charles Evans Hughes.................................11
NYS Railroad Commissioner I. V. Baker, Jr.
    Burleigh, Henry Gordon, battle with.................62
Old Fort House Museum
    and Jean Wing Davis.......................................26
    first Washington County, NY courthouse 71
    home and courthouse of Justice Patrick Smyth..71
    tavern of Adiel Sherwood...............................71
OMA's Pizza...36, 37
OMA's Pizza building
    and history of...37
Orson Richards, the 'Lumber King of the Hudson
    by William Lee Richards.................................29
Panic 1873-78
    and Orson Richards' demise.............................30
paper straws..77
Paramount Theater, Glens Falls.......................117
Pataki, Governor George 7, 9, 47, 56, 57, 137
Pearl Harbor's 60th anniversary..........................68
Pee-wee's Playhouse..79
Pell, Mr. and Mrs. John
    and Fort Ticonderoga, King's Garden...............24
Pell, Stephen and Sarah
    and Fort Ticonderoga, King's Garden...............24
Peltz, Charles...129
Peltz, Charles, Glens Falls Symphony 151
Perham, Asa (also sp. Purham and Pearham)
    Black Patriot soldier.......................................76
Peter's Diner, South Street, Glens Falls.............151
phrase "wasn't worth the powder to blow him to
    Whitehall."
    and Jack Wiberg...49
Pickle Hill Road, Queensbury, NY 32
Pink Sheet, Saratoga Race Course....................139
Pitcher, Gov. Nathaniel Jr.
    and Burgoyne's invasion 1777...........................8
Platt, Charles Adams, architect
    designs 1931 Crandall Library............................4

Pleasant Valley Infirmary
    formerly Washington County Poorhouse..........100
Poor, Enoch..104
Poor, Enoch,
    Brigadier General in Continental Army, Battles of
        Saratoga..104
pop-beads...79
Porter, Mort, Gardener
    Fort Ticonderoga, King's Garden 24
Portraits of Poverty
    and Washington County Poorhouse....................100
Youker, Darrin...81
Prince Taylor, Ticonderoga pioneer settler
    Black Patriot...76
Pruyn sisters, Mary Pruyn Hoopes, Charlotte
    Pruyn Hyde, and Nell Pruyn Cunningham. 4
Quaker Road
    originally " the by-pass"....................................19
Queensbury Hotel..................................12, 14
    and personal memories....................................154
    Grand opening...14
Queensbury Hotel adds 56 rooms in 1929........14
Queensbury Hotel history.................................14
Rayno, Paul..120
Regan, Robert, Glens Falls Mayor.......77, 127, 149
Regan, Robert, Mayor City of Glens Falls 78
Relihan family, Eagle Bridge..........................133
Relihan, Catherine...133
Relihan, Mary Elizabeth................................133
Rev. Billy J. Clark....................*See* Clark, James C.
Rialto in Glens Falls
    and Schine 14
Richards, William "Bill"....................................50
Richards, William Lee..............................27, 119
Richards, William Lee, author
    "Orson Richards, the "Lumber King of the
        Hudson"..29
Richardson, Loyalist Thomas
    home protected during Revolution by friend
        James Watson, Patriot..............................67
    shares sawmill with friends Daniel Parkes and
        James Watson, Patriots.............................67
Richardson, Thomas, Kingsbury Loyalist..........67
Ricotta, Paulette, General Manager
    and the Queensbury Hotel................................15
Ridge Street firehouse, Glens Falls, original.........37
Ridley, Sidney
    last doorman at the Queensbury.......................15

Riedesel..92, 93, 104
Riedesel, Philip von
    in Battles of Saratoga.....................................104
Robert Rogers, history by John R. Cuneo..........80
Robin Wright and Stan Malecki
    Chapman Historical Museum's education team35
Robinson, Walter
    and Haviland's Cove...7
Rockwell Hotel, Glens Falls
    and Queensbury Hotel.....................................13
Rockwell House, Glens Falls................................5
Rogers Island Visitors Center....................80, 151
Rogers Island Visitors Center, Fort Edward, NY
   31
Rogers Island, Fort Edward.............................38
    and naming of...38
Rogers Rangers...................................38, 80, 81
    and Rogers Island, Fort Edward......................80
Rogers Rangers and Rogers Island
    and origin of the US Special Operations Forces, the
        "Special Ops"...80
Rogers Rangers in Fort Edward.........................81
Rogers, Teri Podnorszki *See* Ulrich, Teri
    Podnorszki
Rogers' "Standing Orders"
    first military manual..81
    written by Robert Rogers in Fort Edward..........81
rooftop Santa
    and Mark and Joy Griffin.............................130
Rooney, Andy
    column on Brooks Brothers.............................124
Roosevelt, Eleanor
    and the Queensbury Hotel...............................15
Roosevelt, President Franklin D.
    and Charles Evans Hughes...............................11
Rosoff, Robert and barb...................................127
Rosoff, Robert, Glens Falls Symphony.............151
Rote-Rosen family, West Rutland, VT..............110
Rote-Rosen, Morris..120
    and Granville, NY..109
Rote-Rosen, Morris, Albany Business College
   110
Rote-Rosen, Morris, and Mariampole, Lithuania
   109
Rote-Rosen, Morris, Granville Village Clerk
    (1924-1974)...109
Rote-Rosen, Morris, in U. S. Base Army Hospital
    No. 33 in England & France.........................110

Rote-Rosen, Morris, son of Avraham and Haia
    Reizel (Mevzos)..................110
Round Pond
    orig. name of Lake Sunnyside, Queensbury, NY.
   33
Rozell, Greta, collective memory of Storytown
   117
Rozell, Matthew "Matt"
    History teacher Hudson Falls High School..........70
Russert, Michael
    New York State Military Museum..................56
    on Commission on NYS Battle Flags..................56
    on return of captured Confederate battle flags....56
Saara..................68
Sagamore Hotel, Bolton Landing..................38
Al Cormier, William "Al"
    aids with restoration of Black burials in Salem's
        Evergreen Cemetery..................81
Salem, Peter
    Black Patriot Revolutionary War soldier..................75
    Black Patriot soldier..................76
Salem's Revolutionary War Cemetery..................82
Samuel Pruyn
    and Louis F. Hyde..................3
Samuel Yellin, famed Philadelphia iron artisan
    First Presbyterian Church of Glens Falls..................4
Sanborn Insurance maps..................36
Sandman, Scott, Division of Military and Naval
    Affairs
    and the NY State Military History Museum..................57
Sans Coick, now North Hoosick..................97
Sarah McNeil
    and descendant, Katherine Campbell Norton
        Lewis..................50
Saratoga County..................2
Saratoga Monument Association..................85
Saratoga Monument reopened by National Park
    Service 2002..................85
Saratoga Monument, cornerstone laid 1877......85
Saratoga Monument, Victory, NY..................84
Saratoga National Historical Park54, 57, 85, 104,
    106, 107
Saratoga Race Course..................138
Saratoga Springs..................37
Saratoga Springs, mineral waters..................38
Saratoga Springs, NY
    and Gov. Charles Evans Hughes gambling
        reforms..................10

Saunas in Shushan..................153
Schine purchase of Queensbury Hotel, 1956....14
Schuyler, American General Philip
    forced out by General Gates..................102
Schuyler, General Philip, Fort Ticonderoga 1777
    and Enos, D. D. Hitchcock's diary..................54
Schuyler's summer home burned by Burgoyne
   106
Scripter, Judy..................119
Seagle Colony..................129
Searleman, Sand and Marty..................127
Sears, Katherine B.
    Little Theater Group of the Glens Falls Operetta
        Club..................6
Sears, Katherine B., Dean of Girls of the Glens
    Falls Academy
    and Zonta Club of Glens Falls..................6
See Farrell's Hotelll..................
Selleck farm, Hubbardton
    and St. Clair's retreat..................92
Sembrich, The..................129
Shaeffer Beer..................79
Shanahan, Glenna
    1944 *Look* magazine "Hometown USA"..................39
Shangraw's Pharmacy, Glens Falls..................117
sharpshooter Timothy Murphy
    and death of Simon Fraser, 2nd Battle of Saratoga
   106
Sheffold, Heinz, General Mgr
    the Queensbury Hotel..................15
She-Ra, He-Man and Skeletor..................79
Sherman, Ruth H., Travel Bureau
    and Zonta Club of Glens Falls..................5
Sherwood, Justus, Loyalist troops
    St. Clair drives from Castle Town, VT..................92
Sherwood, Justus, Vermont Loyalist..................64
    originally Green Mountain Boy..................66
Sherwood's Loyalist troops
    St. Clair drives from Castle Town..................92
Shirley, Massachusetts Governor William
    and Robert Rogers..................80
Shushan, NY, communal sauna in..................120
Shushan, NY, Finns, Norwegians and Swedes
   120
Skene, Philip
    role in Battle of Bennington..................97
    with Burgoyne Campaign..................97
Skene, Philip,

ship The Katherine, Arnold refits into USN
  Liberty..58
Skenesborough (now Whitehall), NY
  Burgoyne attacks July 6, 1777........................58
Skenesborough (Now Whitehall), NY
  and Burgoyne Campaign 1777752, 53, 54, 55, 58,
  83, 92, 93, 94
Skidmore College "house mother" Spring Street
  House
  Ann Green King Fitzpatrick..........................126
Skiing industry 1945
  and effect on Queensbury Hotel......................14
Smalley, Frank M.
  Glens Falls Hotel Corporation........................13
Smallpox vaccination, 1777
  and Enos, D. D. Hitchcock,..............................53
Smith, Ben
  Assistant District Attorney for Warren County,
  NY..70
Smith, Colleen
  and Ben Smith..70
Smith, Dan .....*See also* Colleen Smith & Ben Smith
Smith, Daniel "Dan"
  Civil War re-enactor 2001................................56
Smith, Governor Alfred E.
  visits A. B. Colvin in Glens Falls......................9
Smith, Mary Casini..111
  Con Amore, The Italian History of Fort Edward 41
Smith, Phillip..119
Smith-Stewart, Barb...119
Smyth, Dr. George
  brother of Patrick, first Justice of Charlotte County
 67
Sodom, Town of Johnsburg...................................32
Soul Train..79
South Granville Congregational Church
  Rev. Lemuel Haynes, pastor.............................75
Special Operations Forces, the "Special Ops"
  and Rogers Island, Fort Edward.......................80
Spier Falls hydroelectric dam................................32
Spier Falls Road..33
Spier, William E.
  Spier Falls hydroelectric dam...........................33
Spier, William E., former Glens Falls homesite...33
Spring House, Skidmore College, Saratoga
  Springs
  my Grandmother a House Mother...................126
St. Clair, American General Arthur

retreats from Fort Ticonderoga and Mt.
  Independence..91, 92
St. Clair, Major General Arthur
  at Fort Ticonderoga 1777..................................58
St. Jacques, Joyce
  and Washington County Fair Farmer's Museum
 59
St. Leger, Barry, General
  and Oriskany, Battle of....................................102
St. Paul's Church, Hudson Falls...........................116
Stark, General John
  and Battle of Bennington...................................97
stereopticon "French postcard" images.............140
Stewart, L. Lloyd, trace's roots in Salem's
  Evergreen Cemetery...81
Stiegerwald brothers
  Saratoga Springs...134
Stillwater, NY..140
  in Burgoyne Campaign....................................104
Stock Market Crash 1929
  and effect on Queensbury Hotel.......................14
Stoddard, Gregory...119
Stoddard, Seneca Ray...20
Stone, historian William L.
  and Saratoga Monument Association...............85
Stonequist, Martha, Saratoga Springs City
  Historian...116
  collective memory of Van Raalte clothing factory
  on Excelsior Ave..119
Stonequist, Martha, Spa Saratoga Springs City
  Historian...150
Storytown, now Great Escape, Queensbury, NY
 117
Perdichizzi, Francesco...111
Stroscio Carmen, grandson Francesco
  Perdichizzi..111
Sugar Loaf Hill
  now Mount Defiance...91
Sullivan, Frank, humorist.....................................134
Sullivan, Kate
  Frank Sullivan's sister......................................135
Taft, President William Howard
  appoints Charles Evans Hughes to Supreme
  Court 1910...11
Tait, George
  Glens Falls Hotel Corporation.........................13
Tait, George, president

Imperial Wallpaper and Chemical *See* Queensbury Hotel and Glens Falls Chamber of Commerce

Talk of the Town Restaurant, Glens Falls
formerly Hart's Cafe..................119

Talkington, Hebron Town Supervisor Kenneth (Ret. SGM)..................80

Ted Weems' "Heartaches"..................137

Tenbroek, American Brigadier General Abraham
and Battles of Saratoga..................105

Tenth Mountain Division, US Army
and Bruce Adams..................34

Teriele, Teddy, Gardener
Fort Ticonderoga, King's Garden..................24

Terp, Gail, author..................5

Tessier, Lou..................128

The Glens Falls Club, men's social club
and Charles Evans Hughes..................11

The Granville Sentinel
and Morris Rote-Rosen's weekly column..........109

The Granville Sentinel, "Main Street" column by Morris Rote-Rosen..................109

The Locomotion, song..................135

The Post-Star 3, 4, 5, 6, 2, 5, 14, 21, 34, 54, 55, 67, 69, 78, 80, 82, 89, 116, 149, 152, 156, 157

The Post-Star's Don Coyote
and author's rebuttal..................21

The Queensbury Hotel..........*See* Queensbury Hotel

The Sexagenary – Or Reminiscences of the American Revolution
Becker, John P., author..................48

The Whitehall Times, Henry Gordon Burleigh obituary, August 23, 1900..................60

Thierolf, Aunt Kinks and Uncle Frank
Cornelia and Frank Thierolf..................140

Thierolf, Cornelia "Kinks"..................143

Thomas, William, Warren County Board of Supervisors Chair..................79

Thompson, Maury..................21, 89, 138, 151

Thompson, Nancy
and Maury Thompson..................146

Thompson, Town of Greenwich
home of Gov. John A. Dix..................8

Thurber, James
and Frank Sullivan..................134

Thurman, John
Colonial settler in Charlotte County, NY..................65

Ticonderoga parties on Christmas Eve, Christmas Day, Christmas night..................146

Ticonderoga Pulp and Paper Company
and Henry Gordon Burleigh..................61

Ticonderoga, King family's move to..................154

Tingley, Ken, Managing Editor of *The Post-Star*..................5, 2

Tingley, Ken, *Post-Star* publisher..................77

Tommy Berrigan
Saratoga Springs..................134

Tories, aka Loyalists..................65

Train, first to Fort Edward and to Glens Falls...38

Trainor, Mary..................119

Trask, Katrina..................120
and Yaddo..................150

Trello, Tony..................119

Tri-County Blind Assoc
and H. Bertha Larkin..................5

Tri-County United Way
orig. Community Chest of Glens Falls..................13

Tripp, Donald "Don"..................48, 51

Tripp, Donald "Don" and wife Mary..................49

Tru-Ade..................79

Turley, Leo, Manager, Queensbury Hotel..........15

Turning Point of The Revolution..................102, 103
and Battles of Saratoga, 1777..................102

Tuttle, Charles H.
and Governor's Day 1933..................9

Ulrich Teri Podnorszki..................117

Ulrich, Teri Podnorszki..................116

United States Hotel, Saratoga Springs..................126

US Army's Tenth Mountain Division..................34

US Navy birthplace, Whitehall (Skenesborough)..................58

Van Raalte clothing factory, Excelsior Ave, Saratoga Springs..................119

Van Rensselaers
Saratoga Springs..................134

Village of Glens Falls..................9, 11, 114

Vintrom, Nicholas (aka Nicholas Vixtrom)
Black Patriot soldier..................76

Wagner Act of 1937
Chief Justice Hughes' support of..................12

Wallace T. Marsh home
and Queensbury Hotel site..................13

War of 1812..................47

Warner's Green Mountain Boys
and Battle of Bennington..................97

Warren County Court and Probation System
    and Minnick, Rose 6
Warrensburg Masonic lodge
    Benjamin P. Burhans & Peletiah Richards,
        cofounders 21
Washington County Courthouse, former, Salem,
    NY 22
Washington County Fair..59
Washington County Historian's Department 109
Washington County Poorhouse, founding 100,
    See Pleasant Valley Infirmary
Washington County, NY
    renamed from Charlotte County 1784 71
Washington County, NY, courthouse
    battle over placement of................................71
Washington County's 123rd Regiment
    Company E
        comprised of men from Towns of Hebron and
            Hartford..87
Washington County's 123rd Regiment, formed
    1862..87
Washington, American General George
    and Battles of Saratoga................................103
Washington, George................................32, 74
    observation on the lack of volunteers and
        desertions..74
Washinton County, NY, second court location
    hotel of Mary Dean, in Sandy Hill................72
Waters, Mrs. Elizabeth
    Haviland's Cove 1st Matron................................7
Weidner, Timothy................................25
Wentworth, New Hampshire Governor
    Benning
        and Robert Rogers................................80
West Street, Glens Falls
    renamed section of Luzerne Road................115
West Street, now Broad Street, Glens Falls......115
West Virginia Pulp and Paper Company,
    Mechanicville
        aka Westvaco................................133
West, Egbert W.
    Glens Falls Hotel Corporation................13
West, Egbert W., president
    Glens Falls Chamber of Commerce board.........12
    Glens Falls Insurance Co. *See* also Glens Falls
        Chamber of Commerce
West, Elmer
    Spier Falls hydroelectric dam................................32

West, Elmer J., president
    Adirondack Power and Light Corporation............7
Westminister Hall in Great Britain's Houses of
    Parliament
        basis for St. Mary's Academy................................4
White Barrel, Luzerne Road, Queensbury
    reputed house of prostitution................................120
White Captives
    Gender and Ethnicity on The American Frontier by June
        Namias..50
White Creek, NY..133
White, Benjy, Hubbard Hall................................150
Whitehall
    and phrase "not worth the powder to blow it to
        Whitehall."..52
Whitehall (then Skenesborough), NY
    Burgoyne attacks July 6, 1777................................58
Whitehall Lumber Company
    and Henry Gordon Burleigh................................61
Whitehall, birthplace of US Navy................................58
Whitehall, mineral waters................................38
Whitehall, New York
    only naval battle of General John Burgoyne's
        Campaign..57
Whitehall, NY, birthplace of the U.S. Navy........55
Whitney, Mary Lou, Saratoga Springs
    philanthropist................................149
Whittemore, Cuff
    Black Patriot Revolutionary War soldier..............75
    seizes Burgoyne's horse at Saratoga................76
Wiberg, Jack and Ann................................78
Wiberg, Jack, of Glens Falls, collective memory
   119
Wiberg, John "Jack"........48, 52, 119, 120, 148, 151
Wiberg, John "Jack"................................16
Wickes, Roger, Washington County Attorney.24
Wiley, Fred W.
    Glens Falls Hotel Corporation................................13
Wilkinson, American Deputy Adjutant General
    James
        in Battles of Saratoga................................105
William Randolph Hearst
    and Charles Evans Hughes, 1906 NYS
        gubernatorial campaign................................10
Williams, Frank V. (Francesco Vincenzo
    Guglielmini)
        Con Amore, The Italian History of Fort Edward............41
Williams, General John

and Charlotte County Militia................................71
Williams, Sherman, and NYS Dept. of Education
....55
Wilmarth, Martin Luther
    and Wilmarth's furniture making company.......117
    Glens Falls Chamber of Commerce board.........12
Wilmarth's house on Glen St., Glens Falls........117
Wilson, President Woodrow
    Charles Evans Hughes runs against........................11
Wilson, Richard, author
    and *Deaths at the Washington County Poorhouse*........100
Wilson, Titus
    Black Patriot soldier..76
Wing, Abraham II, dies in prison 1815................25
Wing, Abraham II, son of Abraham
    black sheep of Wing family................................25
Wing, Abraham III, lumber baron...........................20
Wing, Calista, mother of Jean Wing Davis.........25
Wing, Polly, Tory burning raid of 1780................25
Wing's Tavern
    and Jessup brothers' bar tab.............................65
Women's Rights Convention
    and Frederick Douglass..46
Wood, Charles R., Great Escape and Storytown
....31
Wood, Charley, Glens Falls philanthropist.......149
Wood, Stan..79

Woody Herman at Queensbury Hotel.................14
Woolworth's, Glens Falls
    now home of Charles R. Wood Theater.............130
World Awareness Children's Museum.................114
World Trade Center
    9/11 attack on...28
Wright, Robin and Stan Malecki
    Chapman Historical Museum educators...............39
    Chapman Historical Museum's education team35
Wright, Wayne, Glens Falls City Historian.......116
WW II wartime restrictions
    and effect on Queensbury Hotel.........................14
Yaddo..129
Yeskoo, Dona...79
YMCA
    and Haviland's Cove..7
Zollinger, Dan, cover designer
    Con Amore...42
Zonta Club of Glens Falls...6
    first officers and Directors.................................5
    founding meeting..5
    origin..4
Zonta International
    founding...5
Zonta members' professions, 1924
    Zonta Club of Glens Falls...................................5

ENDNOTES

---

[i] It has always been such a pleasure working with Bob Condon, City Editor of *The Post-Star*. His certainly has a challenging job and profession in these years of shrinking newspaper budgets and shrinking newspapers. He's a stickler for detail, has a wry sense of humor, and has been unfailingly gracious whenever I have called to ask for help. Thanks, Bob!

[ii] Ken Tingley retired as Managing Editor in this year, 2020. Congratulations to him on a long and illustrious career.

[iii] Will Doolittle is *The Post-Star*'s Project Editor. Among his many journalism awards, and perhaps the most notable and poignant, was one he shared with his wife, Bella, for their 2019 series of podcasts, The Alzheimer's Chronicles. Will and Bella were awarded second-place for Journalistic Innovation in the 85th National Headliner Awards. Will has also written courageously and openly in *The Post-Star* about Bella's younger onset Alzheimer's.

[iv] David "Dave" Blow was a journalist and editor for *The Post-Star* for 15 years and has been a 15-year Professor of Media and Communication at Castleton University, VT. He still freelances for *The Post-Star*.

[v] Fred Daley a journalist and editor at *The Post-Star*. He went on to become Editor of the Hill Country Observer, the independent newspaper of eastern New York, southwestern Vermont and the Berkshires. He has been Editor for two decades.

[vi] Michael "Mike" Mender was a journalist and editor at *The Post-Star*. For many years now, he has served as the Assistant to the Mayor of the City of Glens Falls, NY.

[vii] Mark C. Mahoney is Editorial Page Editor at The Daily Gazette. He was winner of the 2009 Pulitzer Prize for editorial writing while working at The Post-Star.

[viii] Richard C. Merrill (1935-2009). "Dick Merrill," as he always introduced himself, defined the word "extraordinary." A quiet, self-effacing man, he was an engineer with GE. Dick led the team that found the biodegradable substitute for PCBs. That would be a major achievement in anyone's life. However, Dick was a also a historian, author, antique collector and restorer, and was passionately interested in educational institutions, be they libraries, museums, or colleges. He was an incredibly bright man who was loved by many people. It was the good fortune of Sara and me to have met Dick and his wife Mary when I was Director of the Chapman Historical Museum. Dick was President of the Board in the late 1970s and early 1980s. The second was 2007-2010 when Dick and his wife, Mary, were Board members of the SUNY Adirondack Foundation, of which I was Executive Director. Dick died in 2009, a great loss for his family and friends. He left behind a legacy of community enrichment, a love of history, personal integrity, and love for his family.

[ix] Specifically, newsprint.

[x] I incorrectly called the "Unitarian Universalist Church" the "Unitarian Fellowship." I shall always lovingly remember it as the place where Sara and I were married. The

Unitarian Universalist Church later moved to 21 Weeks Rd, Queensbury, NY. The Hoopes House is now part of the Hyde Collection.

xi Formally named St. Mary's-St. Alphonsus Regional Catholic School, on 10-12 Church St., Glens Falls, NY.

xii I had the privilege of knowing Walter Robinson and his wife Lorna, a volunteer at the Chapman Historical Museum, when I was first there in 1975.

xiii The "Call" in Call Hardware, is made up of the surname first initials of its co-owners, Chapman, Adamson, Looker, and Luck. It was located on the first floor of the old YMCA building, home of today's SPoT Coffee on 221 Glen St., Glens Falls. Fred Chapman was the second husband of Juliet Goodman Chapman whose home is part of the Chapman Historical Museum.

xiv Elmer J. West was also a co-partner in the creation of the Spier Falls Dam. In the 1920s, West drove the move to build the Conklingville Dam, creating the Great Sacandaga Lake. The controversial project is the subject of the excellent video documentary, "Harnessing Nature: Building the Sacandaga," by Pepe Productions of Glens Falls (http://www.pepeproductions.com/).

xv The Glens Falls Elks Lodge #81, now located on Cronin Road, Queensbury.

xvi I'm indebted to Maury Thompson's "Ed Moore buys The Queensbury Hotel" published in *The Post-Star* on March 29, 2016.

xvii This is misleading. Continental Insurance Co. had bought the Glens Falls Insurance Co. in 1968. It erected a 10-story white marble building in 1971 (333 Glen Street). Then it demolished the third and last headquarters of the old Glens Falls Insurance Co. on the NE corner of Glen and Bay Streets, at Monument Square, in 1976.

xviii Finch Pruyn & Co. was sold in 2007. It was the last of the huge, locally grown and owned industries to be sold.

xix Christine A Mozal went on to open two of her own restaurants. The first was on South Street, Glens Falls. She opened the second, The Docksider Restaurant on Glen Lake, in 1999.

xx Evergreen Bank, which bought out First National Bank of Glens Falls, was itself absorbed by TD Bank. The only operating vestige of Evergreen Bank/First National Bank of Glens Falls in the City of Glens Falls is that same parking lot and drive-in bank to the west of the Queensbury. None of the fanciful wishes I had for that empty space have come true. The last home office building of First National Bank of Glens Falls, the white marble edifice on 251 Glen Street, stands empty as of this writing.

xxi Barry Mann recorded the 1961 hit he had co-written with Gerry Goffin.

xxii Author and historian Maury Thompson was a reporter and Business Editor at *The Post-Star* from 1996 to his retirement in 2017. Maury is now a freelance writer and documentary filmmaker on the history of politics and labor organizing. In 2021, Maury will release "My Native Air: Charles Evans Hughes and the Adirondacks," a documentary done with Snarky Aardvark Films.

xxiii Roger R. P. Dechame, was the husband of Stephanie Sarah Pell Dechame, a granddaughter of Stephen H.P. Pell and Sarah G.T. Pell, who reconstructed Fort Ticonderoga in 1909. Roger and Stephanie married in France in 1945, where she was serving as a nurse in the medical corps formed by Dr. General Le Dantec at the liberation of the French mainland, 1943 to 1945. Roger was a member of the French Navy. Roger died in 1994, Stepahinie in 2012.

xxiv Karl J. LaPointe (1910-2003) ran the Log House Restaurant at Fort Ticonderoga. I worked for him in the summers of 1963-65, along with his sons George and Cy. [See also in *Over My Shoulder 2*, the column titled "Residents recall dedication of Crown Point Bridge."]

xxv History of Warren County, with illustrations and Biographical Sketches of Some of its Prominent Man and Pioneers. Edited by H. P. Smith. D. Mason & Co., Syracuse, NY. 1885.

xxvi Richards, William Lee, *Orson Richards, the "Lumber King of the Hudson."* Queensbury, NY. 2001.

xxvii Once before I'd written about Mr. Clark's success in getting me to read. He offered the class a chance to buy paperback books through a program. My first choice were a collection of WW II columnist Ernie Pyle's articles. Mr. Clarke asked if I planned to read the whole book. Oh, yes, I said. He replied that I had to promise, otherwise he'd have to help me select, which would have been so embarrassing. I read it cover to cover and discoveredthe joys of reading everything I could. Also, I developed a lifelong passion for 20th century European history. [See also in *Over My Shoulder*, the column titled "School daze."]

xxviii Niagara Mohawk Power Corporation, acquired in 2000 by National Grid.

xxix I first met my friend Stan Malecki the 1970s, when I first became Director of the Chapman. He brought his Jackson Heights School elementary grade students to the museum, and I would visit his classes at the school.

xxx Originally Erlanger's Men's & Boy's, Erlanger's Fashions, a women's clothing store, founded in the 1950s by Lester Erlanger. Lester Elsa Erlanger moved from Montreal to Glens Falls in the mid-1950s. They had two children, David J. and Carol. David assumed ownership of Erlanger's at his father's death and expanded into Saratoga Springs and Rutland, Vermont.

xxxi Holden, Dr. Austin W., *The History of the Town of Queensbury, New York.* Joel Munsell. Albany, NY (1874).

xxxii I had mistakenly written "Ivy" not Irene Miller. It was corrected in the next column.

xxxiii Honorable John DeLong Austin Jr. (May 31, 1935—June 17, 2019). The accomplishments of John D. Austin would make a good book. A Warren County Family Court and County Court Judge, John had also served as Queensbury Town Supervisor and Warren County historian, among his many "hats." I first met him in his role as a Founder and Trustee of the Chapman Historical Museum of the Glens Falls-Queensbury Historical Association in Glens Falls. John was a descendant of the DeLong family, whose home served as the organization's first headquarters and museum. An amazing historian and genealogist, John kept a running record of his finds, which his children have thankfully preserved for posterity.

xxxiv James Henry Minnick Jr. (June 6, 1939 – August 25, 2019). Son of James H. Minnick Sr.

xxxv James H. Minnick Sr., son of Rose Minnick. (See history the Zonta Club of Glens Falls in this volume.

xxxvi In this instance, I have added a name to the column itself, as I wrongly omitted Patty Bethel , cofounder and co-owner with Ed Bethel at that time. The owners now are Ed, Patty and Adrian Bethel.

xxxvii This is one of many rants—aka diatribes—I wrote on New York State not appointing a State Historian. The gap went from the mid-1990s to 2007.

xxxviii Among Jerry Cimo's many credits is that he created the nickname "Flying Forts" for the Fort Edward basketball team. He said the idea came from the B-17 Flying Fortress bombers of WW II.

xxxix Joseph Munoff (1934-2013). Joe taught biology at Joe taught biology for 38 years at South Glens Falls High School. He was a passionate ornithologist and was a licensed cooperator in the U.S. Fish and Wildlife Service banding program. Joe proofed the Con Amore, an exacting task he did so well.

xl Mary Casini Smith (1928-2017). Mary was the co-chair and love of our committee. A retiree from Farmer's Home Administration where worked 30 years, Mary kept us on track in our tasks. She was the perfect organizer and boss.

xli Frank V. Williams (Francesco Vincenzo Guglielmini) died in 2007. His name is typical for many Italian families who came to the US and had their names mangled or translated, in his case the latter. Frank V. Williams is a translation of Francesco Vincenzo Guglielmini.

xlii Charley Reese (1937-2013) was a nationally syndicated columnist. Reese called himself a "conservative." I believed him a reactionary, especially regarding the Confederacy. He glorified the Confederacy. under the cloak of "states' rights." (See also Over My Shoulder 2, "Reese, Rebel flag boosters have skewed view of history.")

xliii Becker, John P. *The Sexagenary – Or Reminiscences of the American Revolution*. Albany, NY: J. Munsell, 78 State Street. 1866

xliv With apologies to George Gershwin and Ira Gershwin.

xlv Namias, June. *White Captives: Gender and Ethnicity on The American Frontier*. University of North Carolina Press. Chapel Hill, North Carolina. 1993.

xlvi I first met Eileen Hannay when she was Educator at the Old Fort House Museum in Fort Edward. In 2001, when I was president of the volunteer board governing the Rogers Island Visitor Center, Eileen was hired as Director and the Center thrived under her decade of leadership. Eileen is a great historian, intelligent, personable and with a wonderful sense of humor. I was and am delighted to call my friend.

xlvii The Old Fort House is now the principal structure of The Old Fort House Museum in Fort Edward. Built in 1772, it was originally the home of Charlotte County Justice Patrick Smyth, and it served as the county's first courthouse. Its name derives from its ownership by the Fort family in the 19th century.

xlviii As I used the word "Indian" instead of "Native American" several times in the article, I have left it as printed.

xlix Holden. A. W. *A History of the Town of Queensbury of the State of New York*. Albany, NY. Joel Munsell. 1874.

---

[l] Skenesborough was named for Philip Skene, who became a loyalist in the Revolution and fought alongside Burgoyne. Why the name Whitehall was chosen to replace Skenesborough is not known.

[li] I've known Tom Nesbitt since the mid-1970s when I first came to work at the Chapman Historical Museum. A historian and Revolutionary War reenactor, Tom shares my passion for that period, although he is far better versed in it than I.

[lii] The boot sculpture is generally known as the Boot Monument, located in Saratoga National Historical Park, Stillwater, NY. It memorializes the leg wound Major General Benedict Arnold received during his valiant action at the second Battle of Saratoga. The monument does not name Arnold.

[liii] Whitehall, NY, Philadelphia, PA, and Beverly, MA were all in a dead heat for that distinction, but in 1960 the US Navy stopped trying to decide which held the honor.

[liv] In 1881, under the leadership of Dr. Sherman Williams, then Village of Glens Falls established a formal education system based on the NY State model adopted several years before. Williams later went on to an influential career at the NY State Department of Education.

[lv] The Smith family, parents Dan and Colleen, and sons Ben and Chris, were all Civil War Reenactors. Our family first met theirs when this book's editor, Julia Cutshall-King, became a Civil War reenactor. Julia later changed to French and Indian Warr and Revolutionary War reenacting, as it gave her the opportunity to play her bagpipes.

[lvi] Michael Russert is an author, historian, and editor who focuses upon American Civil War history. Mike is a member of The Company of Military Historians, helped found the NY State Military Museum, has published more than 300 book reviews, and served as coordinator of the New York State Veteran Oral History Program.

[lvii] Ketchum, Richard M. *Saratoga: Turning Point of America's Revolutionary War.*
It was my distinct pleasure to have met Richard Ketchum t a book signing in Vermont. He even graciously looked at a manuscript I was writing at the time.

[lviii] Colonel Pierse (also spelled "Pierce") Long of New Hampshire.

[lix] Anne Clothier went on to take her BA in history from SUNY Oneonta in 2005 and her MA in Museum Studies Cooperstown Graduate Program in 2007. Since 2011 he has been the Director of Education at Brookside Museum, home of the Saratoga County Historical Society in Ballston Spa, NY. Her many interests include women's history, medical history, textiles, the history of photography, and reenacting. I'm confident in saying Anne's passion for history must have started with her mother, Rachel A. Clothier, whom I've known many years. Rachel is the Corinth Town Historian, Curator of the town's museum, and a published author.

[lx] I've known John LaPointe since the mid-1960s, when my family first came to Ticonderoga, John's birthplace. I was grateful to John for this information on Burleigh, which he gave it to me while I was serving as Washington County Historian (1998-2003). John was Town of Putnam Supervisor for 32 years (1987-2019), as well as the Washington County Board of Supervisors Budget Officer for 10 years. My County Historian's budget was always under John's eagle eye.

lxi Hadden, Lieut. James M. *Hadden's journal and orderly books : a journal kept in Canada and upon Burgoyne's campaign in 1776 and 1777*. Albany: J. Munsell's Sons, 1884.

lxii Watts, Gavin. *The Burning of the Valleys - Fall 1780*. Dundurn, Toronto. 1997. Watts books provide an excellent counterpoint to US histories of the Revolution.

lxiii Coldham, Peter Wilson. American Loyalist Claims;. abstracted from the Public Record Office, Audit Office series 13, bundles 1-35 & 37. Washington, D.C. National Genealogical Society. 1980.

lxiv Matthew Rozell is an award-winning history teacher, author, speaker and blogger on World War II and the Holocaust. I first came to know him when we served on the Board of the Rogers Island Visitors Center in Fort Edward. There is not room enough here to describe the wonderful work he has done as a high school teacher, and in his own history books on local veterans of WW II. In addition, he has been rightly honored and awarded for his ongoing efforts to keep the Holocaust remembered and understood, so it will never be repeated.

lxv Johnson, Crisfield. *History of Washington Co., New York*. Everts & Ensign, Philadelphia. 1778

lxvi Bennett, Jr., Lerone. *Before The Mayflower: A History of Black America 1619-1964: The Classic Account of the Struggles and Triumphs of Black Americans*. Penguin Books. 1993.

lxvii Among the indispensable books on Haynes, the reader should start with Sketches of the Life and Character of the Rev. Lemuel Haynes, A . M , by Timothy Mather Cooley, D D . It was published in 1837.

lxviii Williams, Colonel John. *The Battle of Hubbardton: The American Rebels Stem the Tide.* [Montpelier]: Vermont Division for Historic Preservation, 1988. Col. Williams was very generous in spending time in speaking with me on my own book about the Burgoyne Campaign. He also sent me a copy of his book, a valuable contribution to Revolutionary War history.

lxix Now Gretta Hochsprung, a reporter and columnist for *The Post-Star*. I so enjoy Gretta's human-interest articles and stories about regional history.

lxx Also gone now are Palm Pilots.

lxxi Dobert's Dairy began as an independent dairy on 68 3rd St, Glens Falls, NY in 1931. For decades Dobert's produced and delivered milk and milk products under its own label. It ceased doing that in 2013 and today sells only other manufacturers' goods. One item for which Dobert's was locally famed was its Cranberry Sherbet, using a recipe of Nettie Patterson of Glens Falls. For a fine history on ice cream in Glens Falls, see Maury Thompson's "Back in The Day: We All Scream for Ice Cream" (Glens Falls Living blog, July 22, 2019).

lxxii Paul Loding (1949-2016) was Historian for the Town of Kingsbury and the Village of Hudson Falls from 1990 to 2016. His book Kingsbury and Hudson Falls was published in 2001. He was an avid re-enactor as Lieutenant Colonel of the 53rd Regiment of foot in North America.

lxxiii William "Al" Cormier. A Webster, MA, native, Al moved with his family to Salem NY in 1965 to be Assistant Superintendent of Schools. He retired in 1992 as its Superintendent. He served as Town of Salem Historian from 1983-2019 and Village

Historian from 1983 to 2017, the year of the Village's dissolution. In that time, he did herculean work as historian, preservationist, and advocate for the history of Salem, especially its role in the American Revolution. He is currently Deputy Historian for his successor, Judy Flagg.

lxxiv See also, "More data needed on minorities" August 24, 2002.

lxxv The Charles R. Wood Theater, 207 Glens Street, Glens Falls, NY. Over the last 18 years, this theater has brought a new vitality to downtown Glens Falls and is among those "sparks" in downtown's regrowth. Live theatre is and will always be, part of any thriving city's cultural heartbeat.

lxxvi Saara Johanson was at the rededication of the Saratoga Monument October 10, 2005. The monument, which was across the street from her house, was closed for safety concerns in 1989. I 1993, Saara wrote then-Village of Victory Mayor Bruce Cornell to ask why she could not go into the monument. Cornell gave the letter to U.S. Sen. Daniel Patrick Moynihan and U.S. Rep. Gerald Solomon. Solomon secured the needed funding, but sadly died in 2000, before the reopening.

lxxvii Sylvester, Nathaniel B. *History of Saratoga County, New York, with illustrations biographical sketches of some of its prominent men and pioneers.* 1878.

lxxviii John P. Crouch was Grand Master of the Most Worshipful Grand Lodge of Free and Accepted Masons of New York State.

lxxix Brayton, Isabella and John B. Norton, comp. Story of Hartford: A History. 1929. Isabella Brayton was Hartford Town Historian. She was succeeded by daughter, Sylvia Brayton Van Anden. Milton (Mike) Armstrong succeeded Sylvia. Though I did not meet Isabella Brayton, I am privileged to have known Sylvia and to know Mike.

lxxx Freiherr Friedrich Adolf Riedesel Freiherr zu Eisenbach. The use of "von" in his name is incorrect. He was a Baron.

lxxxi Col. Pierse Long brought his Regiment from New Castle, New Hampshire.

lxxxii At the time of the Battle of Fort Anne, the name "Anne" was the correct spelling. The Township had been named for Anne, Queen of Great Britain. Later the name was shortened to Fort Ann.

lxxxiii Somewhere in the late 18th or early 19th century, the murder of Jane McCrea came to be called the "Massacre of Jane McCrea." A massacre is the slaughter of many people. I theorize that because Jane McCrea's murder was among the many individual and multiple killings of civilians during Burgoyne's Campaign, her death symbolically became the death of all, and so was referred to as the 'Massacre of Jane McCrea.

lxxxiv I had originally and mistakenly written "Leominster, New Jersey."

lxxxv British born William Duer moved to Fort Miller, NY, at the urging of Gen. Philip Schuyler. He became a Patriot;;, was a Provincial Congress member in 1775; helped draft the original New York Constitution in 1776; was a member of the 1st New York State Legislature in 1777-78; member of the Continental Congress in 1778 and 1779; and served on finance committees and the Board of War during the Revolution. Postwar, he was in the New York General Assembly in 1786. In 1789, Alexander Hamilton, Schuyler's son-in-law, became first Secretary of the Treasury. Duer was appointed first Assistant Secretary. Through both ill-advised and illegal financial schemes, Duer went bankrupt in the Panic of 1792. He died in debtor's prison.

[lxxxvi] Kenneth Perry is a historian and author who lives in Washington County. I've been privileged to know Ken since my days as Washington County Historian (1998-2003). Ken has recently published a book, *People of Lowly Life: Early Persons of African American Heritage in Washington County, N. Y.* This important work chronicles the African American population in Washington County from the late 1700s to the 1940s. It is dense with family histories and rigorously done scholarly research.

[lxxxvii] Richard Wilson of South Glens Falls, NY, died Nov. 19, 2007 at age 91. A veteran of WW II, Dick was a wise man who always greeted everyone with a smile. His research is a testament to him.

[lxxxviii] Wilson, Richard. *Deaths at the Washington County Poorhouse.* 2002. Washington County, NY, publisher.

[lxxxix] Then called Saratoga.

[xc] The site of the two Battles of Saratoga, now Saratoga National Historical Park, is in the Town of Stillwater, NY.

[xci] John Neilson, who fought on the Patriot side, farmed on Bemis Heights before and after the Battles of Saratoga, as the guided tour of Saratoga National Historical Park will tell you. Neilson's restored farmhouse is there today. One of the earliest proponents for saving the Battlefields was Neilson's grandson, whose 1844 book was among the first to advocate for their preservation. That would take many decades.

[xcii] Now Fish Creek.

[xciii] Loretta Bates, Washington County Deputy Historian . I met my longtime friend Loretta in 1998, when I became Washington County Historian. Loretta had been a volunteer in the Historian's Office since 1990. So, this marks her thirtieth anniversary of continuous service to that office and to the County. She graduated to a paid position in 2006 when the Washington County Clerk Deborah Behan was officially designated as Clerk/Historian. In 2008, under Washington County Clerk Dona Crandall, Loretta was given the title Deputy Historian, a post she holds to this day. In my five years as Washington County Historian, I relied heavily on Loretta's immense knowledge of county history and genealogy. She was a joy to work with and we disrupted many hard-working researchers with our uproarious laughter. Loretta is a published historian. She researched the records of the Washington, NY, Poorhouse records and published *Those Called Paupers* (2013). She also published *Memories of Early Sandy Hill* (2017) from records of Orson Richards.

[xciv] American Legion Post 323 Granville, NY.

[xcv] *Bridging the Years.* Glens Falls-Queensbury Historical Association, publisher. 1977.

[xcvi] Now Oakland Avenue, Glens Falls. Oakland Avenue technically runs through to Shermantown Road, but a section was sold to Finch Paper. Oakland Avenue now curves northward to join Warren Street, roughly opposite of the intersection of Oak Street and Warren.

[xcvii] In 1969, the YMCA, under Director Ray Bennett, moved into a new building, the current one on the north end of Crandall Park. By 1977, the old YMCA building was

facing an uncertain future, when the Godnick family of Rutland, VT bought the building. John Snyder, who had been a live-in custodian of the old YMCA downtown (see *Over My Shoulder 2*, "Remember the old "Y"?"), told me that there were many boxes of old records in the attic. I was then the director of the Chapman Historical Museum and told Chapman Trustee Dick Merrill about the records. With Dick leading other volunteers, we all went up into the old YMCA's attic and literally shoveled books and other records off the floor. Among the saved records were the original hand-written minutes of the Glens Falls YMCA.

[xcviii] Christopher Anderson was the last Glens Falls Cemetery Superintendent. The position was eliminated in the 2014 city budget and the duties merged in the Public Works Department.

[xcix] Dr. Orel Friedman (1913-2014) was born in Glens Falls and must be counted as one of its finest native sons. An ENT physician, Dr. Friedman was intelligent, kind, loving and wise, and he had great sense of humor.

[c] Kevin A Ankeny is Professor of Radio/TV Broadcasting and Technology at SUNY Adirondack in Queensbury, NY. Kevin came to SUNY Adirondack in 1998 and immediately befriended my wife, Sara, whose classes were next to his. His wife, Sherry, works at Skidmore college. Kevin and Sherry are western Pennsylvania's gift to our region.

[ci] Historian and author Teri Podnorszki Rogers is Executive Director of the Warren County Historical Society. I first met Teri when she was high school student Teri Podnorszki, who came to volunteer at the Chapman Historical Museum, where I was Director. I was delighted to see her early interest grow into a lifelong passion for and profession in the history field.

[cii] Price Chopper Supermarket is no longer on Cooper Street in Glens Falls. Its former building still stands. Price Chopper, which the Golub family began as "the Central Market" in Schenectady is now going through another rebranding as Market 32.

[ciii] Wayne Wright has been Glens Falls City Historian since 2000. He is also a published author. I've known him and admired his love for Glens Falls history for several decades. (See John Coleman's "Give Me 5: Glens Falls City Historian/clerk Wayne Wright" article in *The Post-Star*'s March 31, 2010 edition for good background on Wayne. It does need a sequel!)

[civ] Martha Stonequist was appointed Saratoga Springs City Historian in 2002. She is also a published author.

[cv] Dr. Marilyn Van Dyke was Queensbury Town Historian from 1991 to 2016. A cofounder of the Warren County Historical Society, she has championed our region's history. There is not appropriate space here to discuss breadth of the work Marilyn has done to promote and preserve our heritage.

[cvi] Farrell's Hotel, North Creek, was owned and operated by Francis and Helen Farrell. It was a North Creek landmark for decades. Their son, Brian Farrell, and I met when students at Fordham College and have been friends ever since.

[cvii] Burgey's Cave, Hague. The Cave, as everyone knew it, was in the cellar of the Beachside, which burned and was razed in 1991. According to Warren County 200

Bicentennial Celebration (http://warrenny200.org/towns/hague/places-100.php) it was first Garfield's Hotel, which burned in 1863. It was succeeded by The Phoenix, which S. R. Stoddard photographed and wrote about. It was lastly The Beachside.

cviii Saratoga Springs was renowned in the mid-20th century for the having the greatest number of unsolved fires, especially arsons, in the United States. My friend Robert Dillon, whose father had been legal counsel for the old Glens Falls Insurance Company, said his father dreaded having to underwrite property there. Between 1930 and 1970s, the arsons were incredible. Sadly, one man lost his life in 1957. Saratoga Springs Public Library's has a database of all the fires in the city's history. One, the Piping Rock arson, is the basis of my novel.

cix It was 1949.

cx In 1987, Kaydeross Park on Saratoga Lake was sold for development. It appeared the famed 1910 carousel and its 28 horses would be lost at auction. Then DPW Commissioner, Thomas McTygue, led a group of volunteers to raise the money to keep it in Saratoga Springs. The carousel, hand carved around 1900-10 by Marcus Illions, was placed in storage. For the next 14 year, a battle raged over whether to put it in Congress Park, Saratoga Springs. By 2002, the pro-Congress Park faction won and it has been there ever since. The carousel has been fully restored.

cxi Nickname for Skidmore College students.

cxii The descriptive phrase was first used in the 1950s by Fort Edward attorney Robert Bascom.

cxiii As of this year, Jane would 102. She is missed as much now as she was in 2002, perhaps more.

cxiv Catherine Relihan lived to her 99th year in the house where she was born. A strong, independent and loving woman, Catherine (my first cousin three times removed) was a schoolteacher. Born in 1913, she learned to drive at age 13. On her last day alive, she drove her car to Cambridge for servicing. Returning home, she had her regular afternoon company and peacefully died. She would have turned 100 on October 31st.

cxv John and Mary moved to Mechanicville, where they raised a large family.

cxvi John Green's daughter, Ann (my father's mother) went to work at the mill as a girl. My mother's father, Aubrey Vincent Kalbaugh, also worked there, as did my mother, Jane Kalbaugh King, and my Aunt Carolyn Kalbaugh Aldrich.

cxvii That is in my house.

cxviii Sallet was another spelling for salad.

cxix Maury came to know my parents when his wife Nancy worked in Burleigh's Pharmacy with my father. I feel I have a special link with Maury because of it.

cxx This later purchased by Joseph Regan, who had been a copartner in Regan Denny Stafford Funeral Home in Queensbury, NY.

cxxi Oh, what a mistake I made here. Our dear friends Chris Scoville and Debra Vales kept their surnames after their marriage. I performed an appropriate *mea culpa* for calling Debra "Debra Scoville" that in the column for December 28, 2002.

cxxii Sara Cutshall (her name when we first met) was the first Director of North Country Arts Center (NCAC) now NorthCountryARTS. In 1976, she led the NCAC Board to move the organization from Warrensburg, where it began in 1971, to Glens Falls, where it is today. Sara served as Director while simultaneously serving on committees dedicated to the arts and tourism, and on boards of several different organizations. Among the latter were the Board of the Lower Adirondack Regional Arts Council (LARAC) and Board of the Glens Falls Farmers Market, of which she was a cofounder.

cxxiii Now SUNY Adirondack, formally Adirondack Community College.

cxxiv Dan and Jan Hazewski had opened their amazing Country Fare store on Glen Street in downtown Glens Falls in 1981. In a recent phone call, Jan reminisced with me about those times, when she, Dan, and a whole organization of people struggled to rejuvenate downtown. They recruited me (and my wife, Sara), when I was Director of the Chapman Historical Museum. For the Victorian Christmas Past, the downtown was decorated by the City of Glens Falls, which also held its first ever tree lighting. Merchants stayed open for an evening and there were horse-drawn carriage rides. Joan Aronson directed a reading of Dicken's Christmas Carol at Christ Church Methodist on Bay Street for which over 1,100 attended. The Chapman Historical Museum was decorated as it could have been in Victorian times and that night over 900 people came through.

cxxv This was my apology to Debra Vales.

cxxvi The Town of Fort Edward Supervisor Merilyn Pulver and others staged an enormous reenactment of the Battles of Saratoga on her farm in Fort Edward. There were hundreds of re-enactors, who made the event spectacular. The event's being held in Fort Edward irked Stillwater's Town Supervisor Hall, but all was later forgiven. Merilyn Pulver loved Fort Edward and worked hard for it. She was great at recruiting volunteers and I ended volunteering for six years on the board of Rogers Island Visitors Center. Merilyn died August 13, 2020, too soon for all the life and love she had in her.

cxxvii As it was, Byron "By" Lapham (1930-2019) left it at two volumes. He had collected over 200 stories of Glens Falls life from the 1920s to 1960s for the two books, *Hometown Memories* volumes 1-2. By was an incredible man— warm, witty, intelligent, and with a wry sense that must have served him well in his teaching career. By is survived by his wife Joan, the perfect match for all his qualities; and their three sons and grandchildren.

cxxviii It is finally closer to coming out of the hopper.

cxxix John "Jack" Wiberg (1927-2002), a beloved friend. Born in Brooklyn, NY, Jack first saw this region as a boy visiting Camden Valley in Shushan, which he loved dearly. Jack later moved to Glens Falls, married and raised a family. He was a private contractor who also served, among other things, as a Commissioner on the City of Glens Falls Water Board.

cxxx Edna Cutshall (1908-1991). How I lucky I was to have a mother-in-law whom I could love as a mother. Born Edna Johnson in Indiana, she and her husband Harland Cutshall (1907-1969), also an Indiana native, settled in Glens Falls in 1934. They established Cutshall Dry Cleaners on Warren Street, Glens Falls. Edna and Harland worked as a team to build a highly successful business and to raise four children.